IMAGES
of America

# LAKE ELSINORE

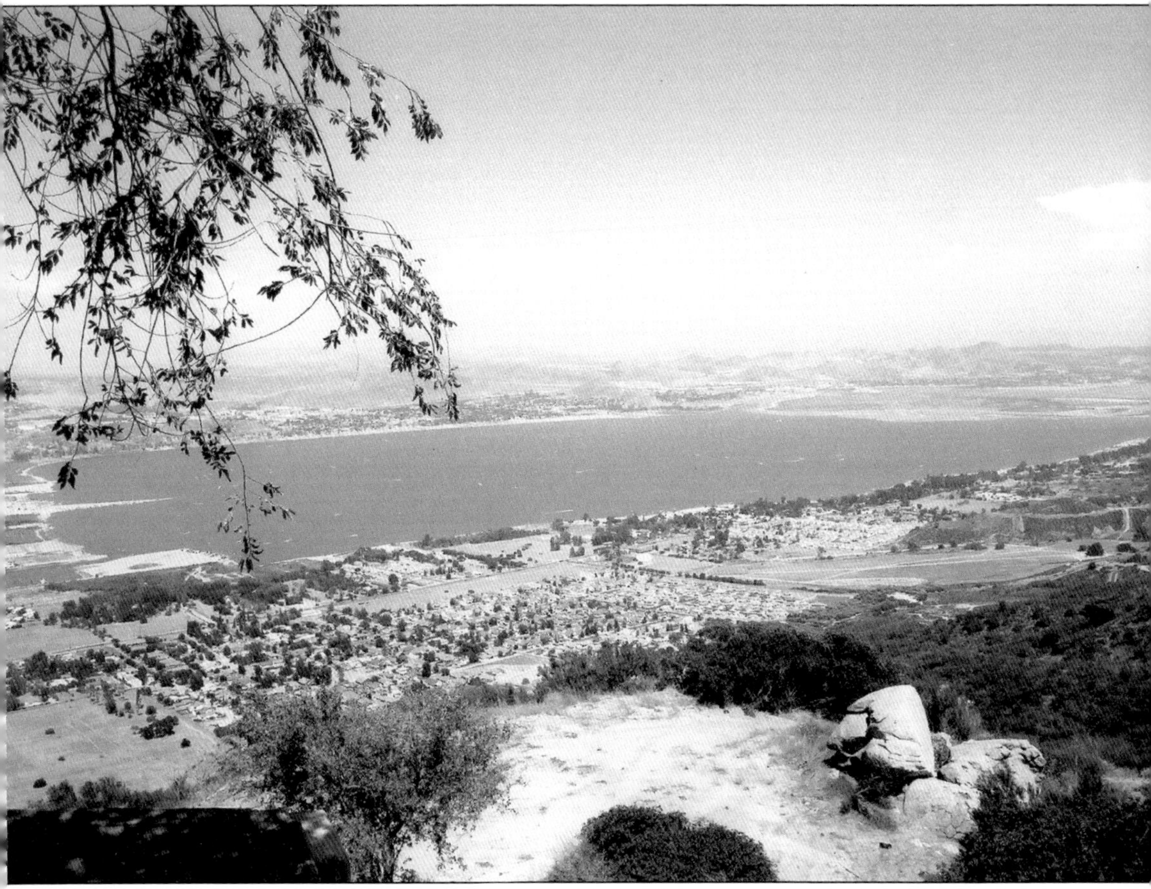

This photograph of the enduringly beautiful Lake Elsinore was taken from high in the Ortega Mountains in July 2004. (Courtesy Edythe J. Greene.)

**ON THE COVER:** Early-20th-century bathers enjoy Lake Elsinore. (Courtesy Chad Mora.)

IMAGES
*of America*

# LAKE ELSINORE

Edythe J. Greene, Elizabeth Hepler, and Mary Louise Rowden

ARCADIA
PUBLISHING

ISBN 978-0-7385-3066-6

Published by Arcadia Publishing
Charleston, South Carolina

Printed in the United States of America

Library of Congress Catalog Card Number: 2005930095

For all general information contact Arcadia Publishing at:
Telephone 843-853-2070
Fax 843-853-0044
E-mail sales@arcadiapublishing.com
For customer service and orders:
Toll-Free 1-888-313-2665

Visit us on the Internet at www.arcadiapublishing.com

*This book is dedicated to my late husband, Joseph A. Greene, a great artist who gave me the ability and vision to see beauty in every walk of life.*

# Contents

ACKNOWLEDGMENTS

The information in this book was gathered from many sources, individuals, and organizations. Much of the information contained herein was based on the books *Lake Elsinore Valley* by Tom Hudson and *Happy 100th Birthday, Lake Elsinore* by Roger and Dolores Mayhall, as well as *A Glimpse of the Elsinore Valley*, a resource handbook for the Elsinore Union School District. The authors also consulted reference materials in the possession of the Lake Elsinore Library, Lake Elsinore Historical Society, City of Lake Elsinore, the Lake Elsinore Valley Chamber of Commerce, Lake Elsinore Woman's Club, and the Longtimers Club.

Thanks also to our families for their forbearance and their valuable assistance. We would like to thank the people of Lake Elsinore for being so warm and friendly in welcoming us to their community. Some opened their hearts and showed us their dreams, which were realized when they settled in Lake Elsinore. We thank all of the individuals who were so helpful, from city officials and business owners to the water deliveryman, who not only gave us directions, but led us to one of our destinations.

Most of the historical photographs were obtained through the Lake Elsinore Library and made available to us by Emily Gerstbacher, the branch manager. Additional photographs were obtained from Jeanie Corral, Timothy Kimble, Chad Mora, Joe Ortega, Pauline Rodriguez, Betty Burke, and Main Street Mercantile. The drawings were done by Brian Jahn and Joe Dwaileebe.

We wish to thank George Lunsford for his computer expertise and diligent efforts in preparing the manuscript for publication. Without his hard work, this book might not have ever made it to the publishers. Thanks should also go to John and Darlene Outhuijse, Sonya Mattheis of Pioneer Lumber Company, Michelle Capodanno of Tom's Farms, and Janet Simonsen of the International Church of the Foursquare Gospel.

We didn't realize that what was started in 1998 when Alice Jackson suggested that two of the authors exhibit their photographs entitled "A Day in the Life of Lake Elsinore" in Chuckles Java Junction, that the exhibit would go any further. But here, seven years later, this book is the culmination. Many thanks to Alice and Frank Jackson.

# INTRODUCTION

For centuries, the Luiseno Indians called Lake Elsinore and its environs home, before the arrival of the Spanish and other explorers into the California region. One such explorer was Franklin Heald. In 1888, he founded the City of Lake Elsinore, the first city in what was to become Riverside County. Heald's dream began in 1880, when he sighted a lake from the summit of Mount Wilson and culminated eight years later with the founding of the community of Lake Elsinore.

The dreams have continued to this day, as people have gravitated to Lake Elsinore and made their dreams realities by building and inhabiting a Moorish castle with catacombs and gold doorknobs, or a Ponderosa-style ranch house, or a cabin-style home on nearby man-made Lake Whitney. They come to Elsinore for the skydiving, Glen Ivy Spa, Tom's Farms, Glen Eden Sun Club, or to operate a family business, such as a local hardware store that has lasted 100 years. Within a stone's throw of Lake Elsinore, the largest gold nugget ever discovered in California was unearthed. Over time, many events have helped to shape the community into what we see today, including the building of the railroad, the wars, and the Great Depression.

The 3,000-acre Lake Elsinore, one of Southern California's largest lakes, is a natural jewel set in the beautiful Elsinore valley next to the impressive Ortega Mountains and the Cleveland National Forest. Once this area was a playground for the rich and famous, including many Hollywood celebrities and United States presidents, as well as people from other states and countries who have either visited or moved here. Some came to soak in the healing waters of the hot sulfur mineral springs. The lake itself offers such sports as boating, fishing, water and jet skiing, and windsurfing. The area is also well-known for its thermal winds, making it ideal for skydiving, hang gliding, and for sailplanes.

Midway between two of California's largest cities, Los Angeles and San Diego, Lake Elsinore is an hour's drive from Pacific Ocean beaches. It's situated in southwestern Riverside County on the edge of Cleveland National Forest. Grown into a modern and up-to-date city in every way, Lake Elsinore registers an average daily temperature of 78.5 degrees, with blue skies and clean air.

# One

# EARLY SETTLERS

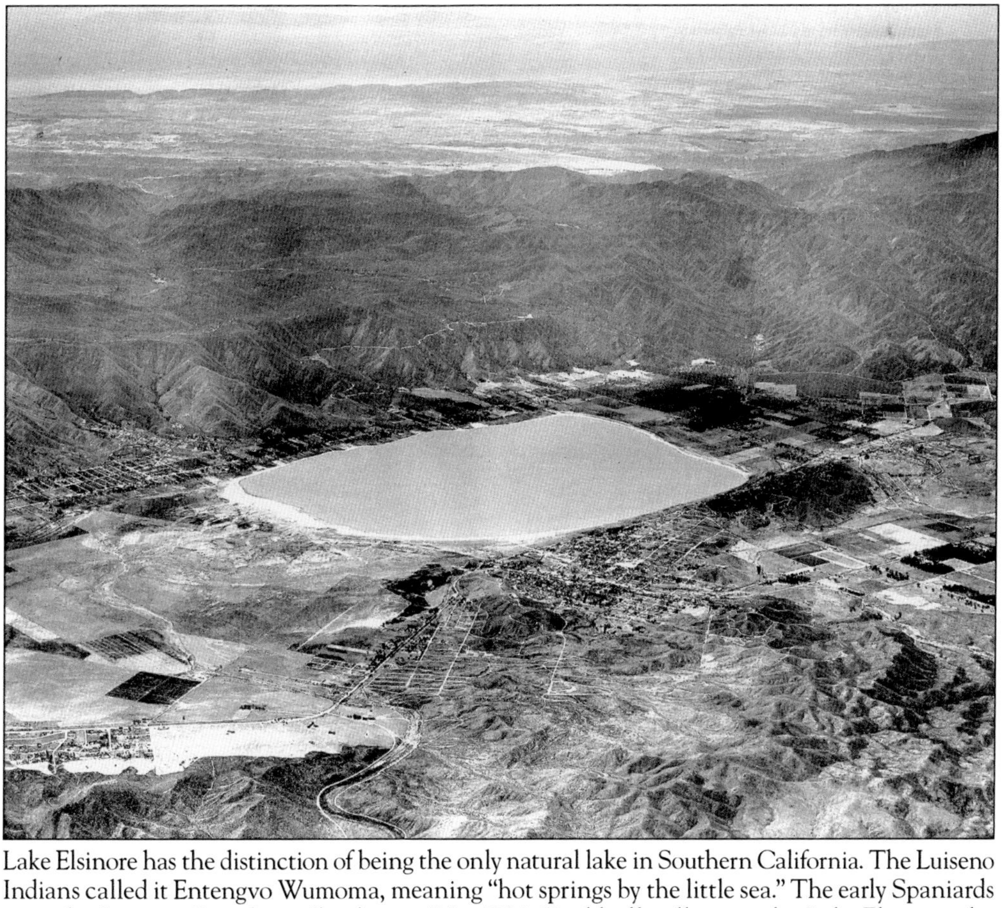

Lake Elsinore has the distinction of being the only natural lake in Southern California. The Luiseno Indians called it Entengvo Wumoma, meaning "hot springs by the little sea." The early Spaniards named it Laguna Grande, or "big lagoon." In 1884, Heald officially named it Lake Elsinore, the name of the castle in William Shakespeare's *Hamlet*. (Courtesy Dr. Timothy Kimble, D.C.)

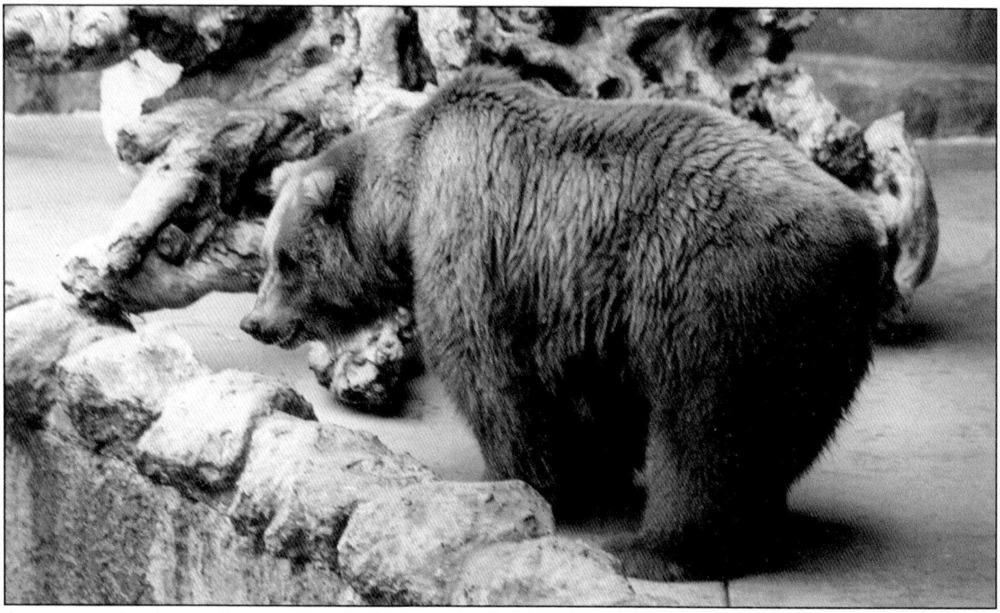

Bears were held in high regard in the Luiseno culture. The peace-loving Luiseno Indians created a world of plenty that lasted for hundreds of years. Their ancestors found a peaceful way of dealing with the changes brought about by the repeated incursions into their homelands. (Courtesy Edythe J. Greene.)

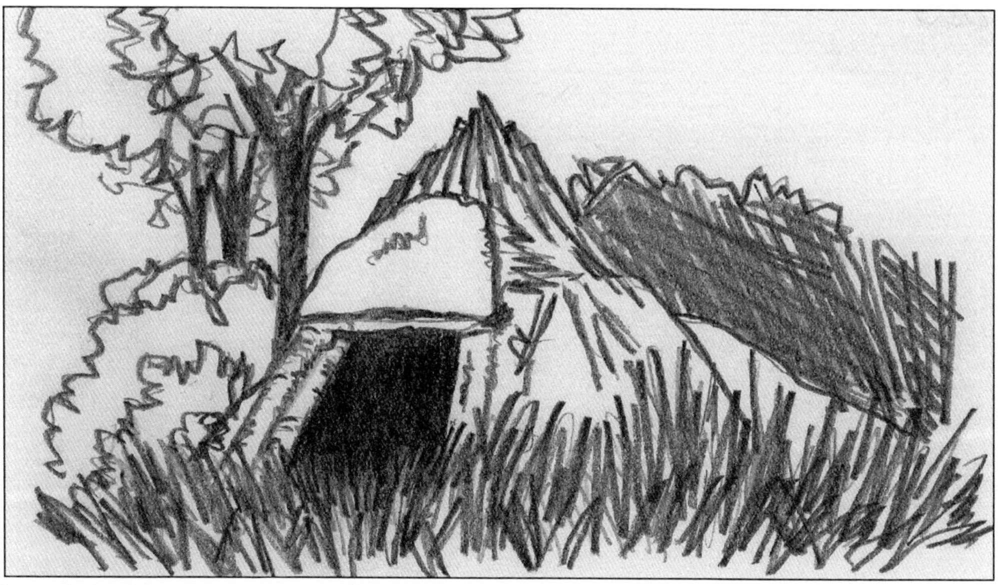

Long before Europeans came to what is now California, Native Americans enjoyed the blend of warm and cool waters flowing naturally from Coldwater Canyon. What we now know as Glen Ivy Hot Springs Spa was to them a sacred site and the only man-made structures were dome-shaped mud saunas built around the artesian hot springs. This area was home to the tribe the Spaniards later called Lusienos, who named the valley "Temescal." This was an Aztec word meaning "sweat lodge," a reference to the adobe saunas the Native Americans constructed. Tradition held that conflict was not allowed at a hot springs; it was a deeply safe and peaceful place. (Courtesy Joe Dwaileebe.)

The Luiseno Indians roamed widely through what is now Riverside, Orange, and San Diego Counties. Pictured here is Ghala, a Luiseno Indian in full dress. (Courtesy Edythe J. Greene.)

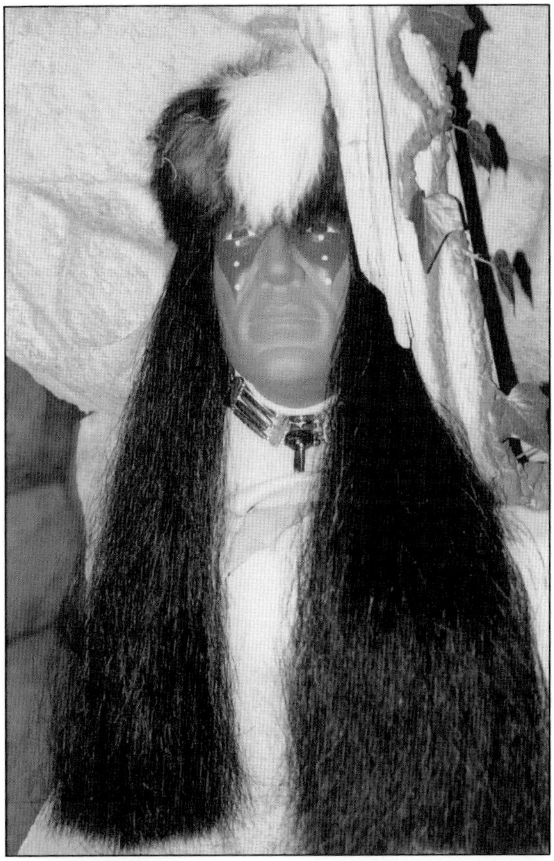

Grinding corn and acorns for food took many hours of labor for the American Indian women. Here we see the many holes in the rocks that resulted from their strenuous grinding work. (Courtesy Edythe J. Greene.)

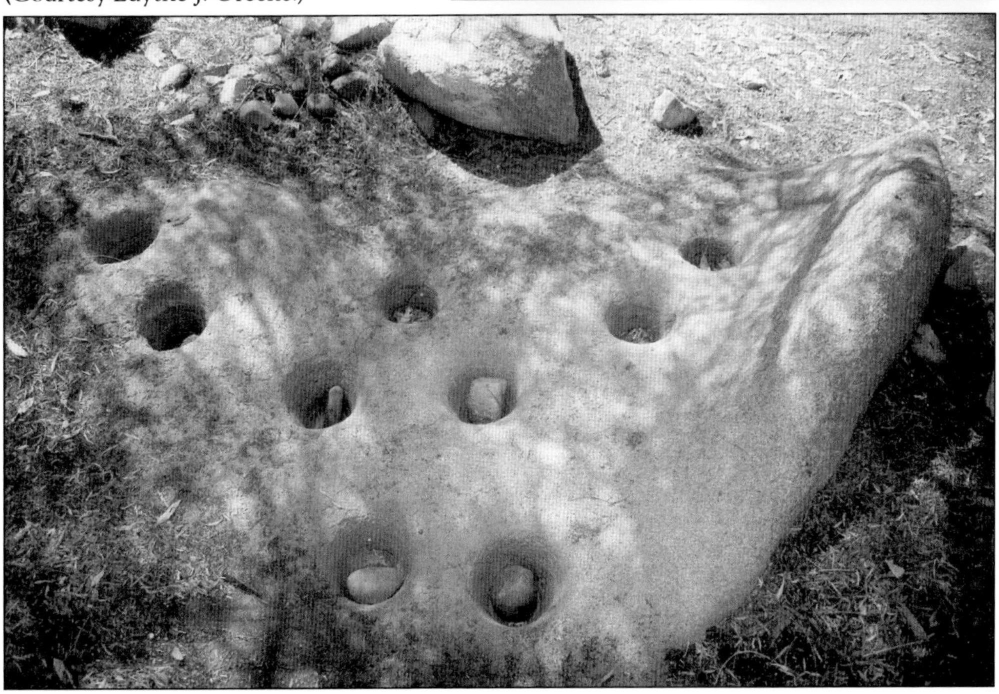

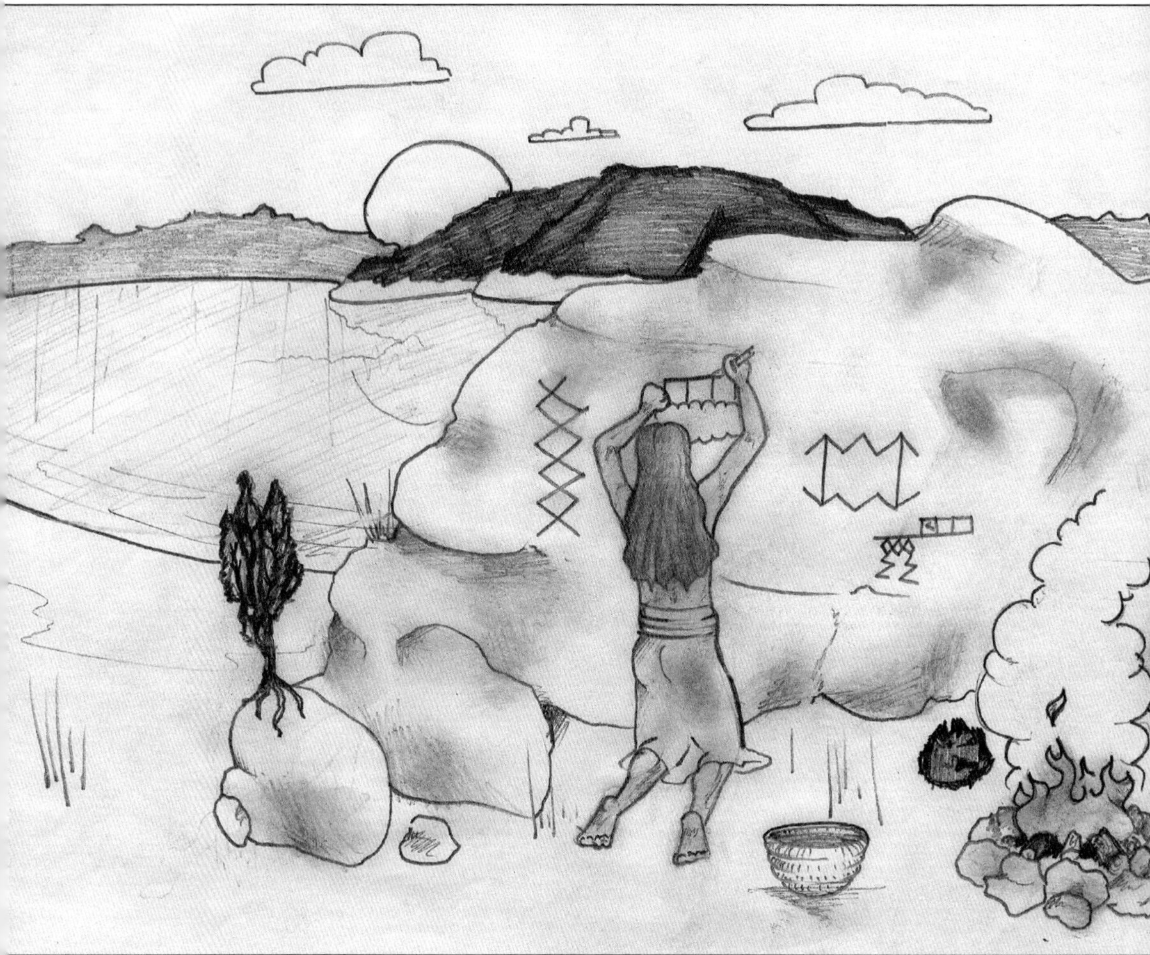

A Luiseno Indian maiden gathered clay and colored rock to celebrate her new life as a woman. All day she toiled, grinding the clay and rocks into the colors prescribed by Wiyot, the Father in heaven. She traces the sacred designs into boulders above the village. (Courtesy Brian C. Jahn.)

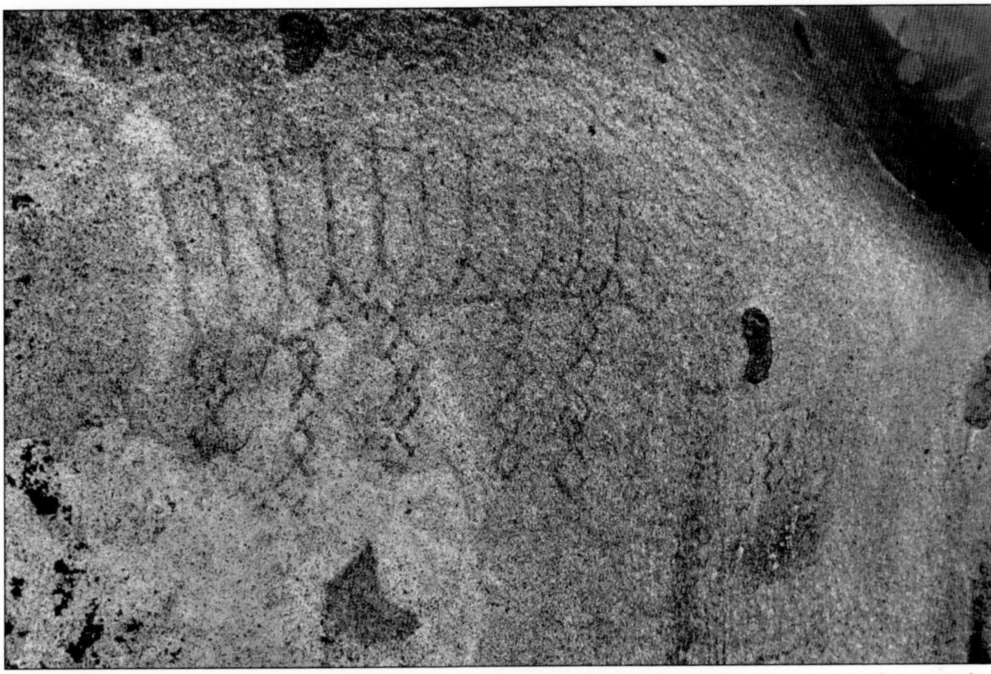

Still visible, high above the lake in the Ortega Mountains, are the rocks where an Indian maiden made her sacred designs centuries ago. (Courtesy Edythe J. Greene.)

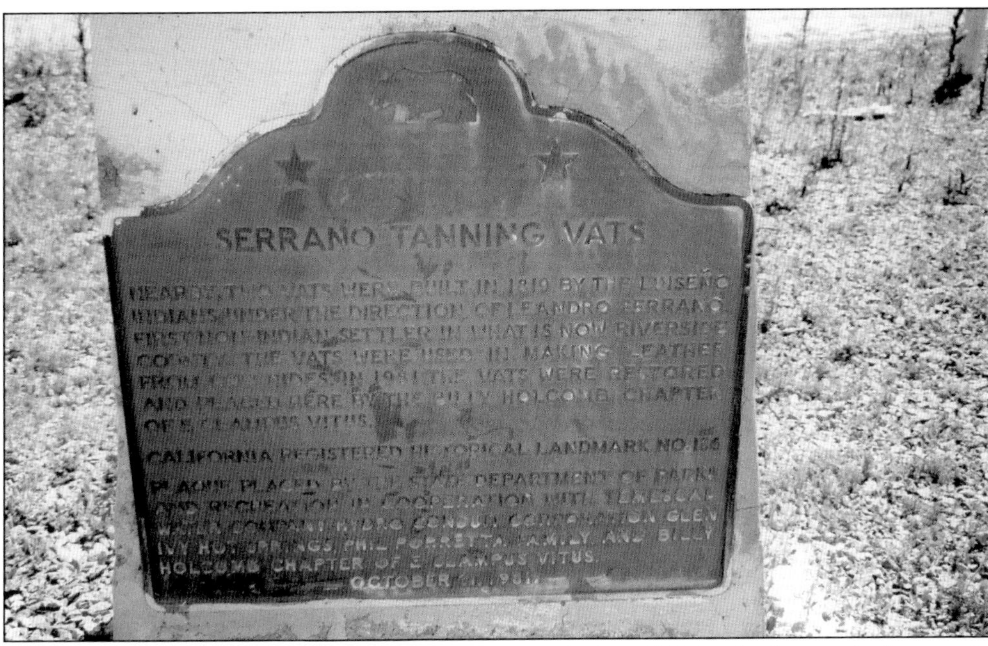


This marker tells the story of two nearby tanning vats built in 1891 by the Luiseno Indians under the direction of the first non–Native American settler, Leandro Serrano. The vats were used by the Luisenos to make leather from cowhides. The marker was placed here by the State Department of Parks and Recreation, and is a California Registered Historical Landmark. (Courtesy Louise Rowden.)

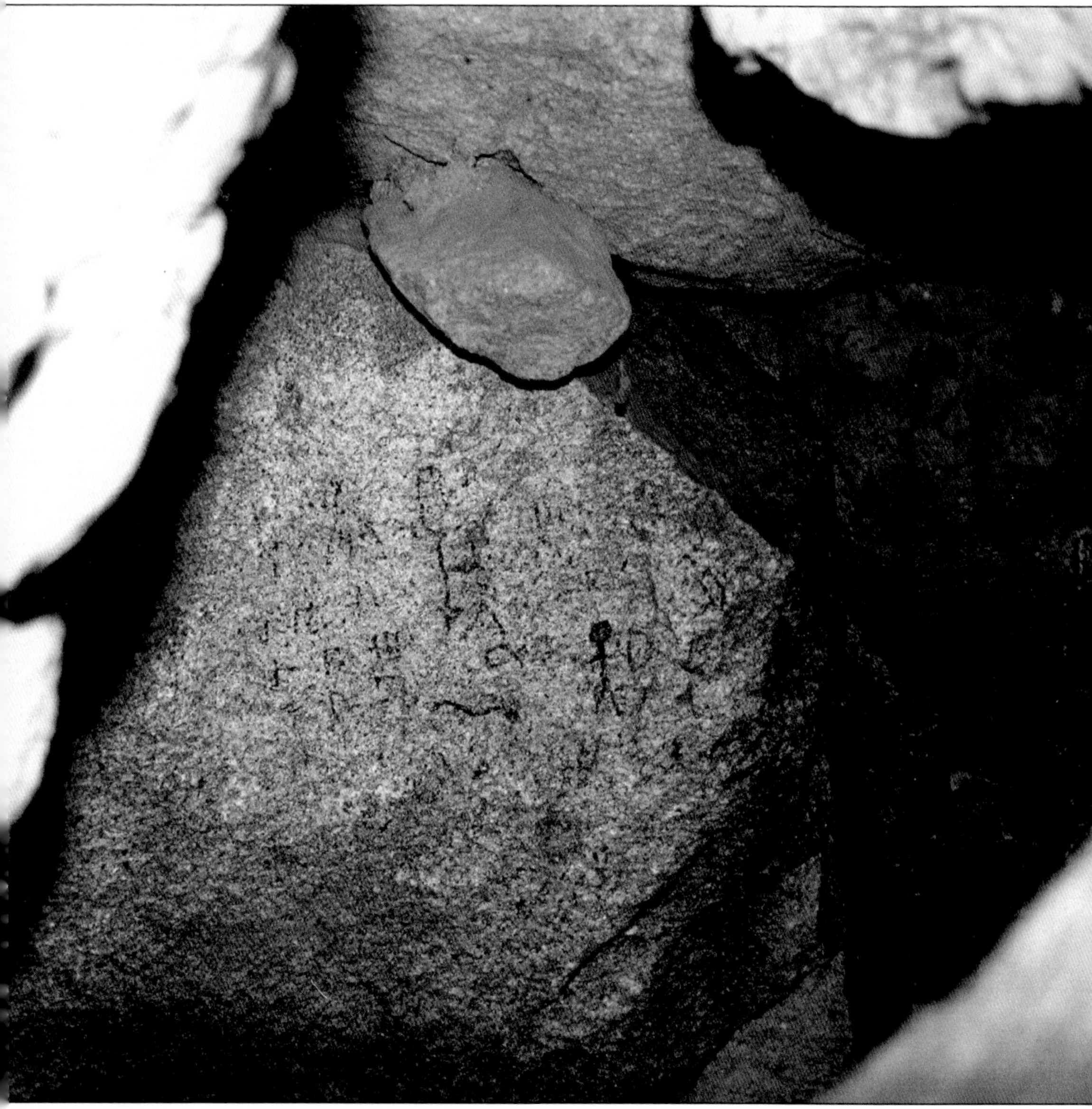

The American Indian pictographs on the rocks seen here can be found inside a cave in Lake Elsinore. Shown are a snake, fish, and other drawings. (Courtesy John Outhuijse.)

# *Two*

# Lake Elsinore Founders

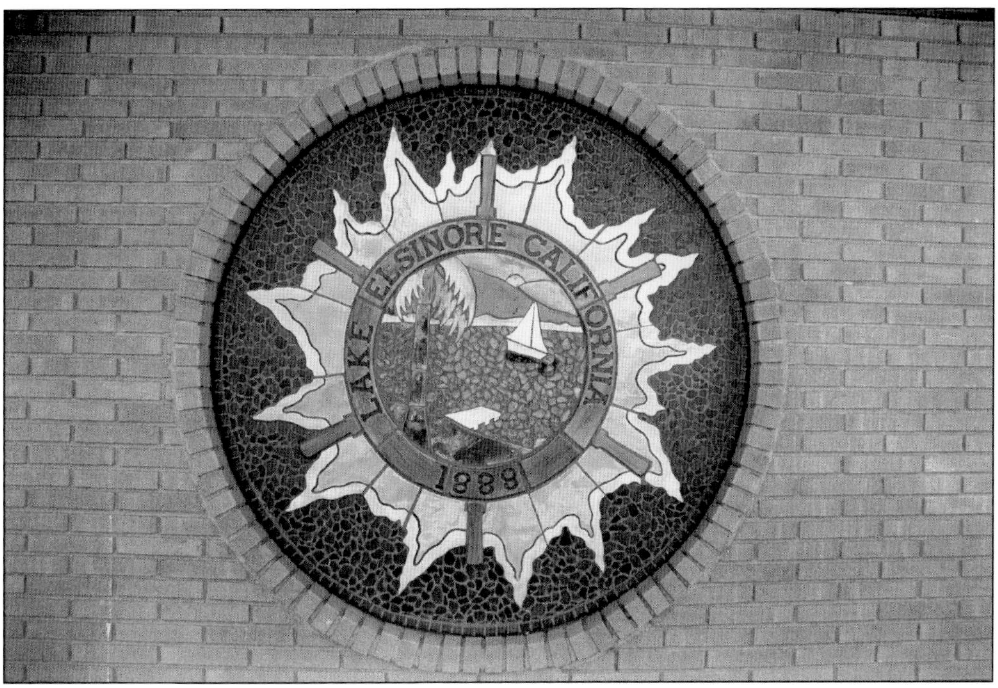


Elsinore, as symbolized here, was incorporated as a city in 1888 and is the oldest city in Riverside County. At that time, the city had a weekly newspaper, two banks, two hotels, and two bathhouses as well as a water system, schoolhouse, three churches, and a railroad connection. (Courtesy Edythe J. Greene.)

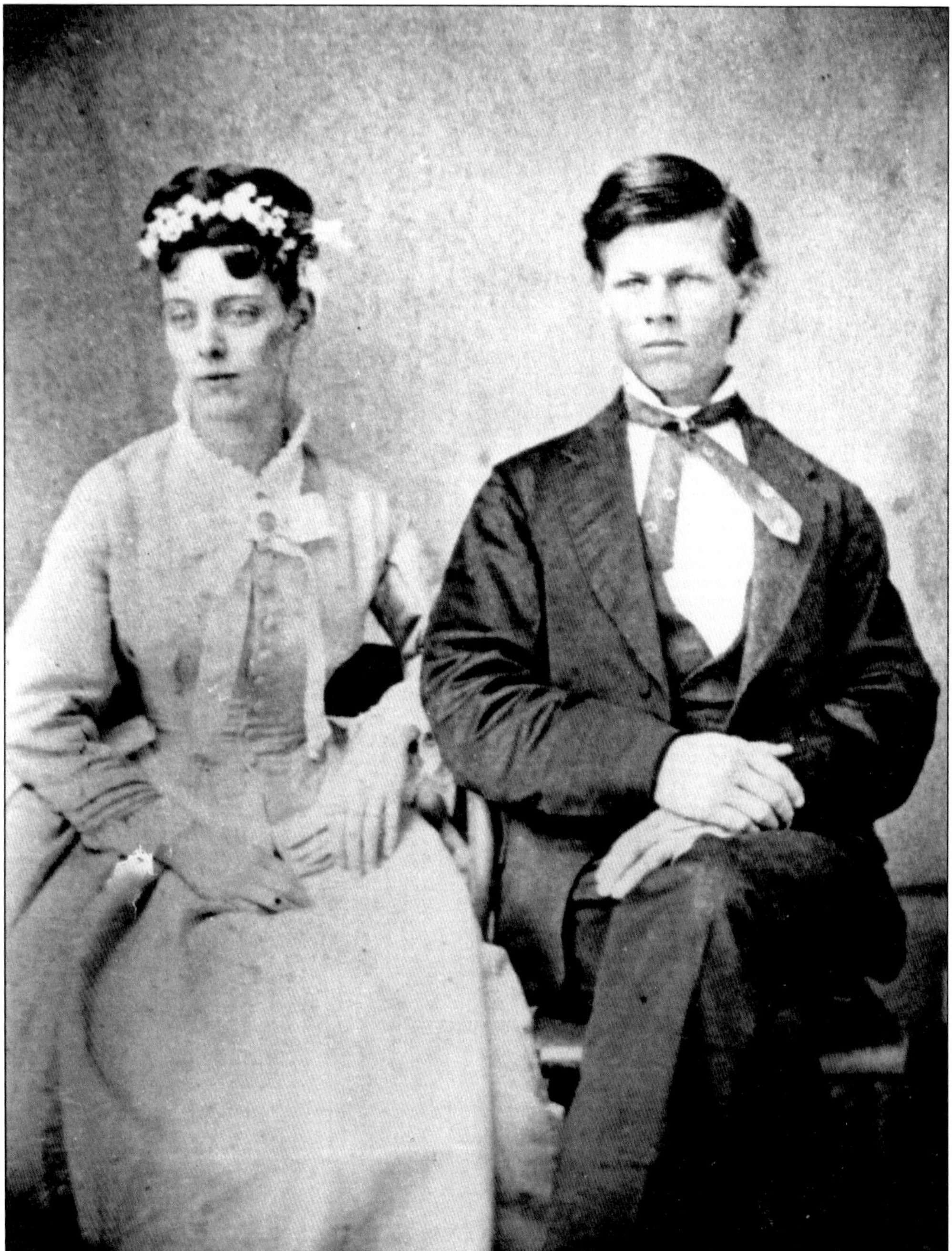

In 1880, Franklin Heald, shown here with his wife, Anne, sighted the lake from the summit of Mount Wilson. In 1883, he purchased the property and established the town of Elsinore. In December of 1932, he passed away and was put to rest in the town he founded. Mr. Heald was always known as an optimist. (Courtesy Riverside County Library System.)

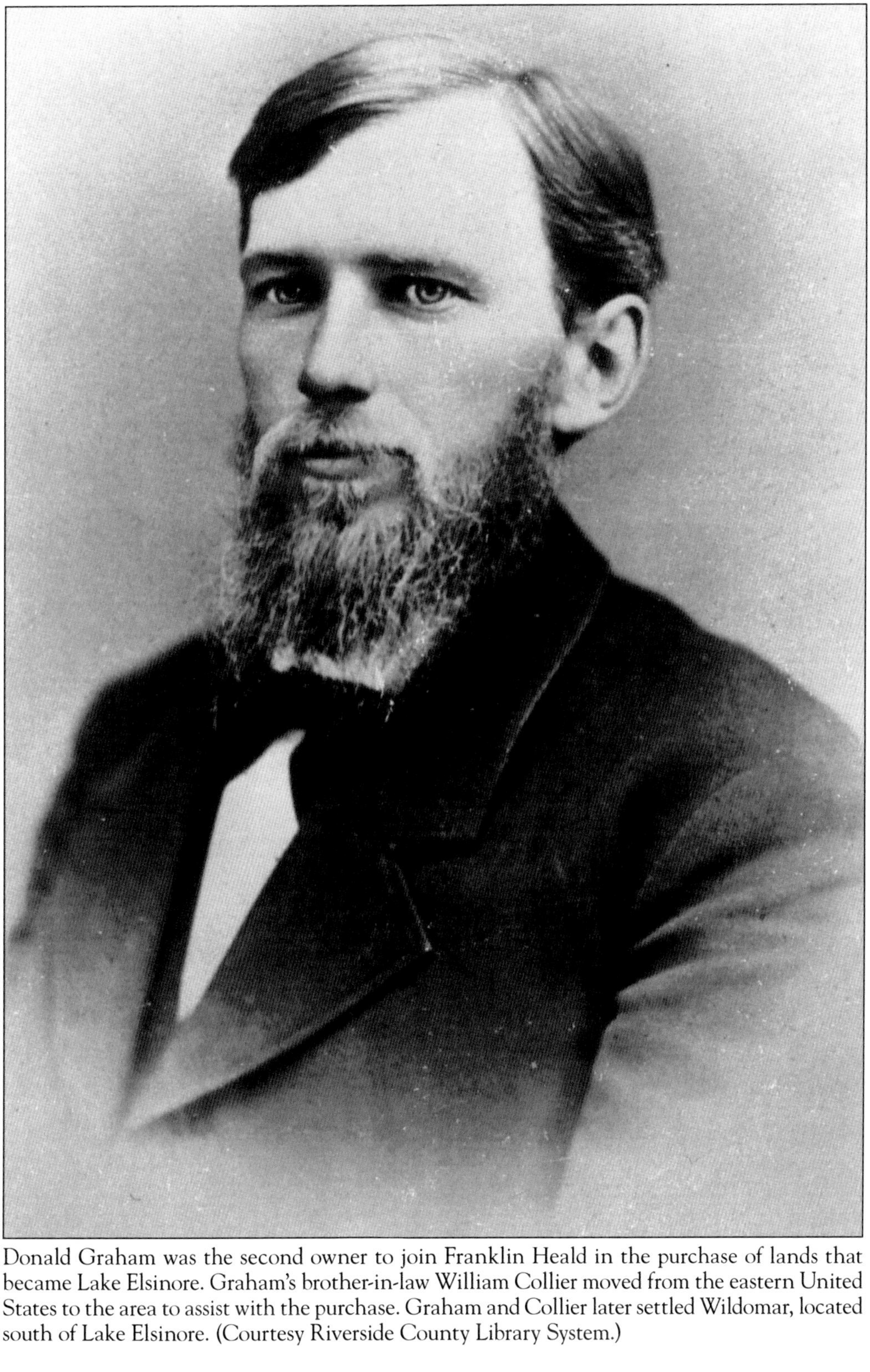

Donald Graham was the second owner to join Franklin Heald in the purchase of lands that became Lake Elsinore. Graham's brother-in-law William Collier moved from the eastern United States to the area to assist with the purchase. Graham and Collier later settled Wildomar, located south of Lake Elsinore. (Courtesy Riverside County Library System.)

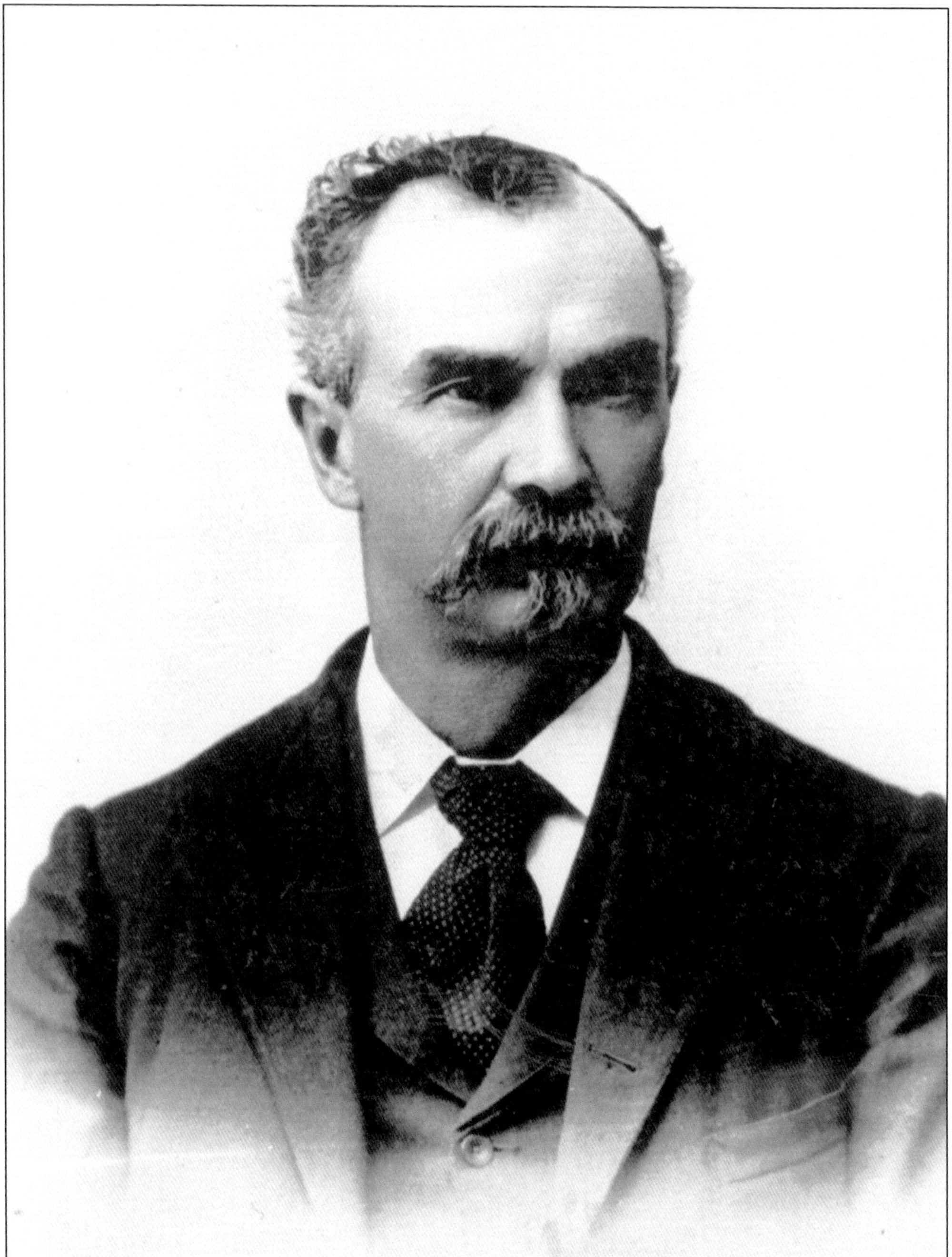

William Collier was the third owner in the 12,832-acre purchase that became Elsinore. He was president of the Bank of Elsinore in 1887. That bank later merged with the Exchange Bank. The settlement of Wildomar, six miles south of Elsinore, was started by William Collier, his sister Margaret, and his brother-in-law Donald Graham. (Courtesy Riverside County Library System.)

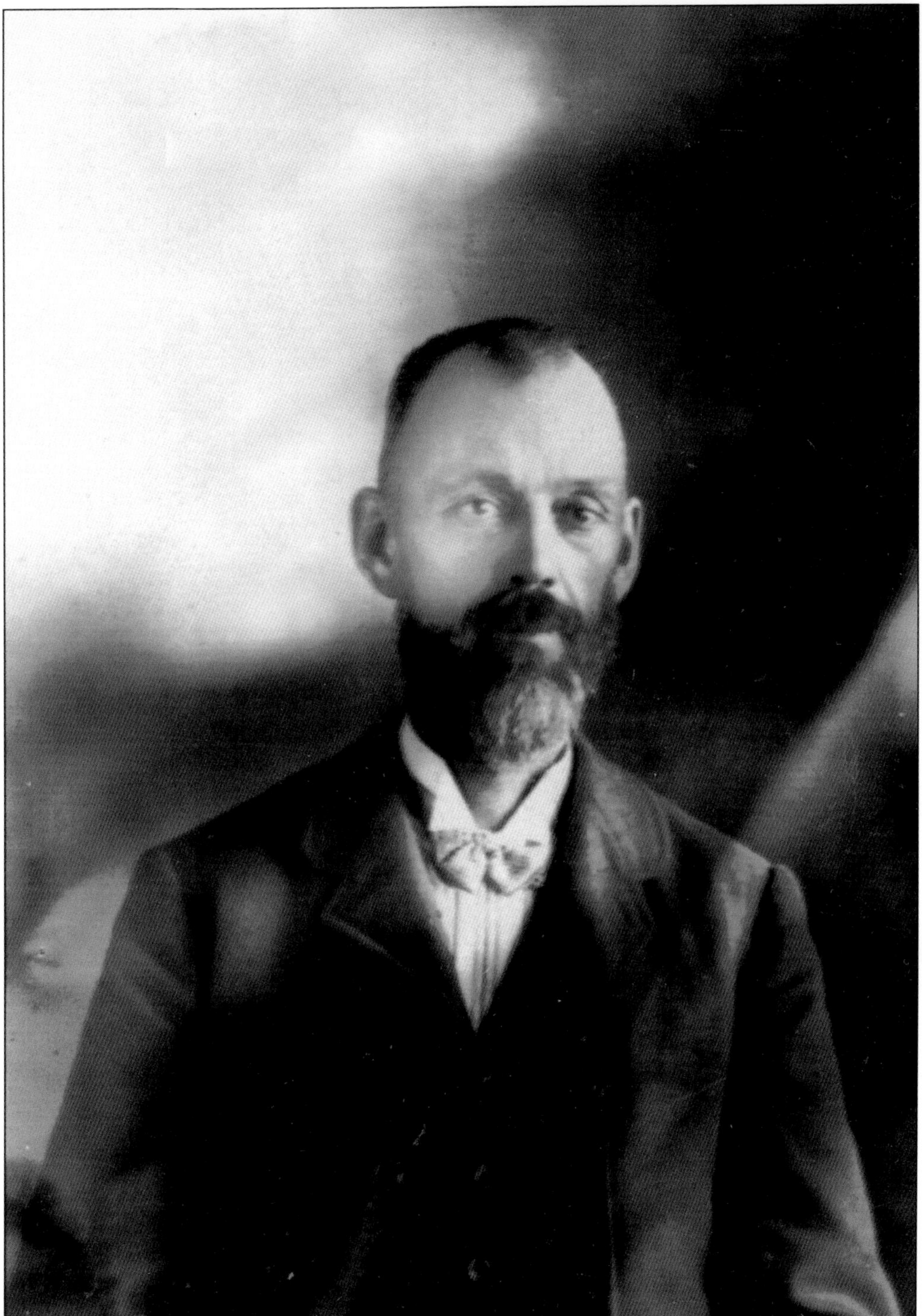

C. S. Merrifield was the builder of the Lakedale Hotel. In the early 20th century, he also ran C. S. Merrifield Building Supplies. He later served as the superintendent of the Elsinore Cemetery, a post he held until his death in 1934. (Courtesy Riverside County Library System.)

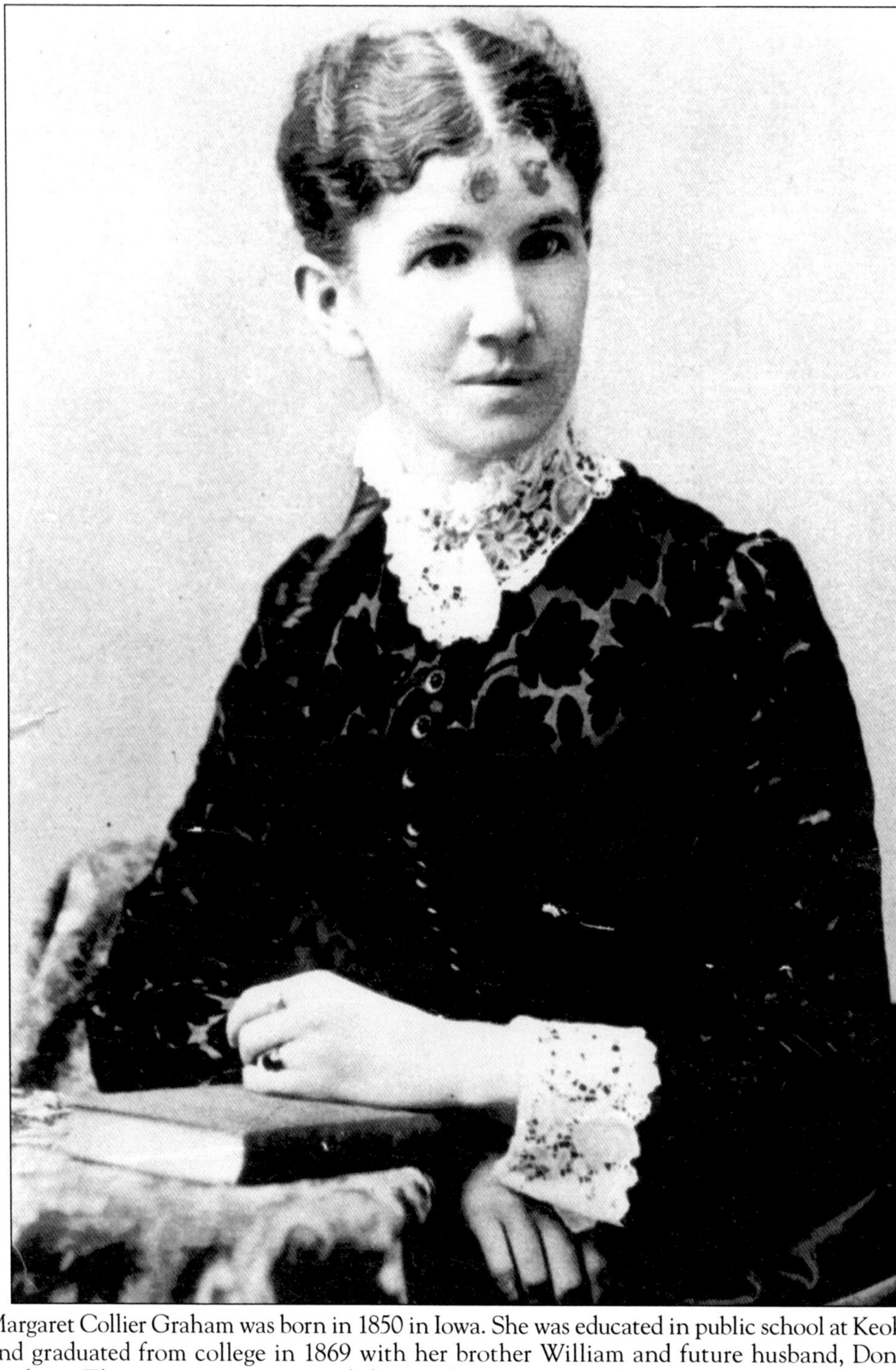

Margaret Collier Graham was born in 1850 in Iowa. She was educated in public school at Keokuk and graduated from college in 1869 with her brother William and future husband, Donald Graham. This was quite an accomplishment for a woman in those days. She was very active in Elsinore and Wildomar and changed the name of Rancho Laguna to Elsinore in 1888. As a writer, her short stories appeared in *Atlantic Monthly* and *Harper's Weekly*. (Courtesy Riverside County Library System.)

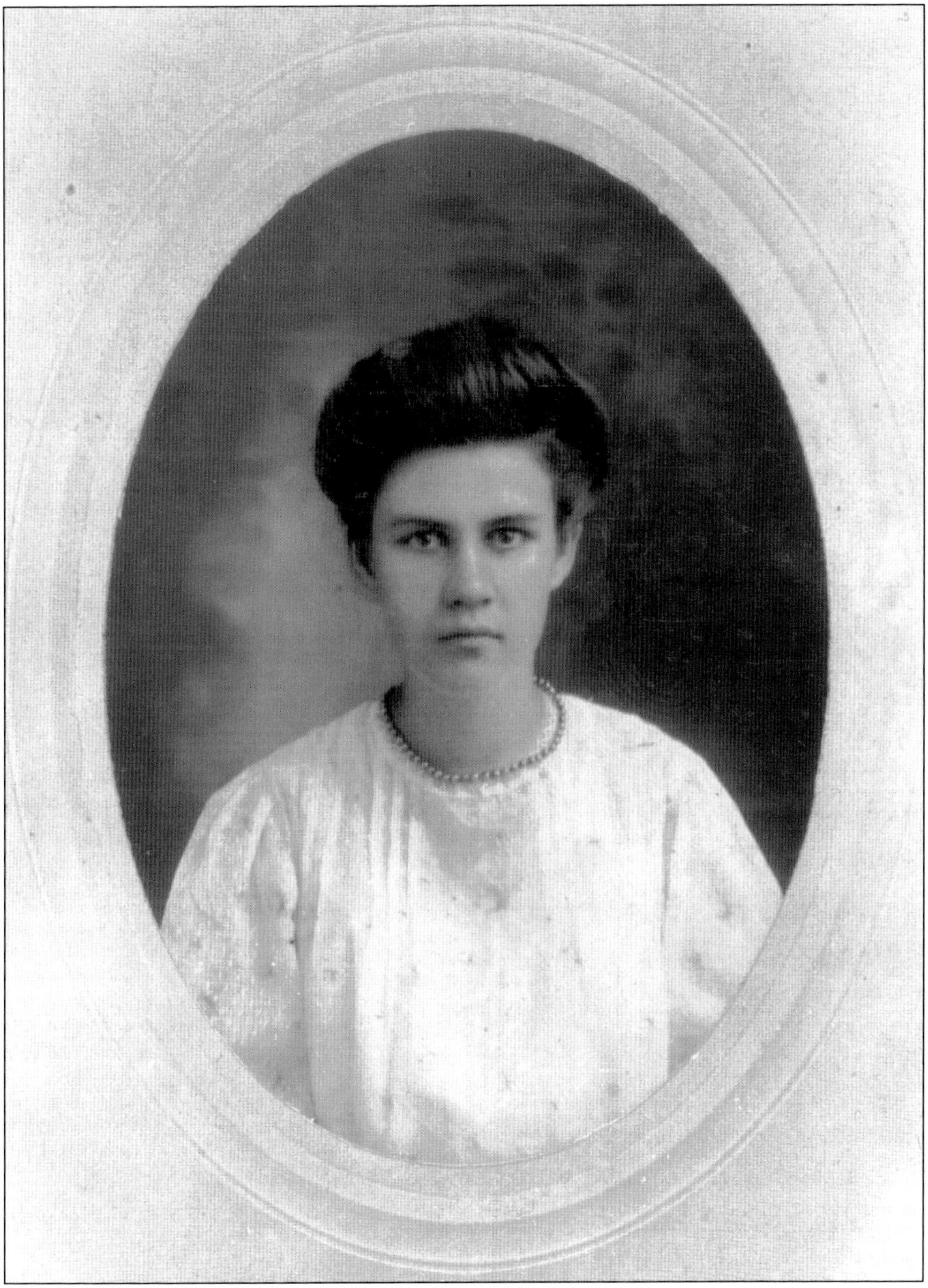

In 1908, Altha Merrifield opened the first library in a corner of her father, C. S. Merrifield's, hardware store on Main Street. Later the store burned to the ground and the library was relocated to city hall. Altha was librarian from 1908 to 1923 and again from 1938 to 1986. (Courtesy Riverside County Library System)

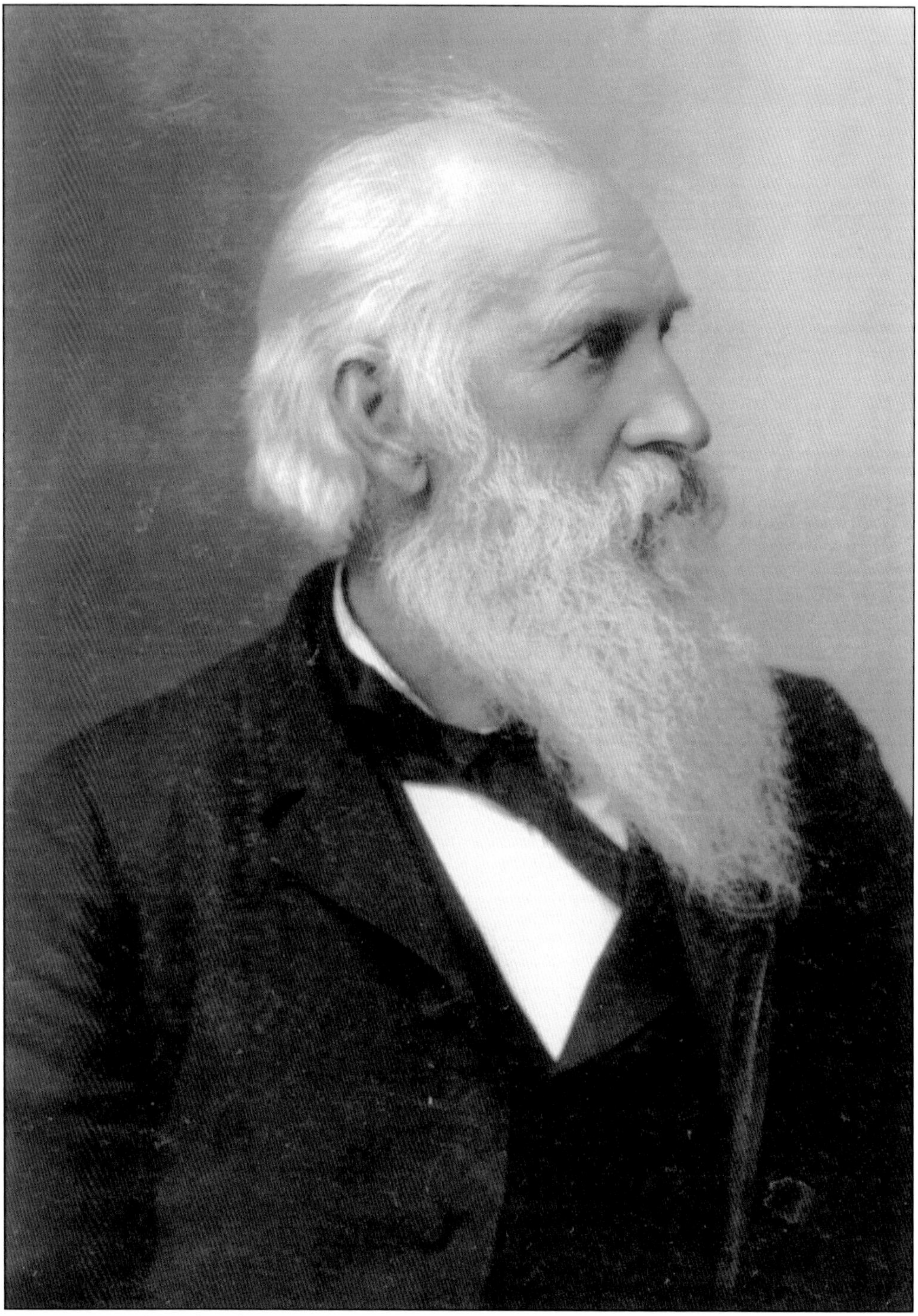

Capt. Leonard Buckingham Peck was a leading citizen of Elsinore, and the man for whom Peck Street is named. His house was the fourth home built in Elsinore. Some of the writings of L. B. Peck are included in the 1812 edition of *History of Riverside County*. (Courtesy Riverside County Library System.)

# *Three*

# Town of Lake Elsinore

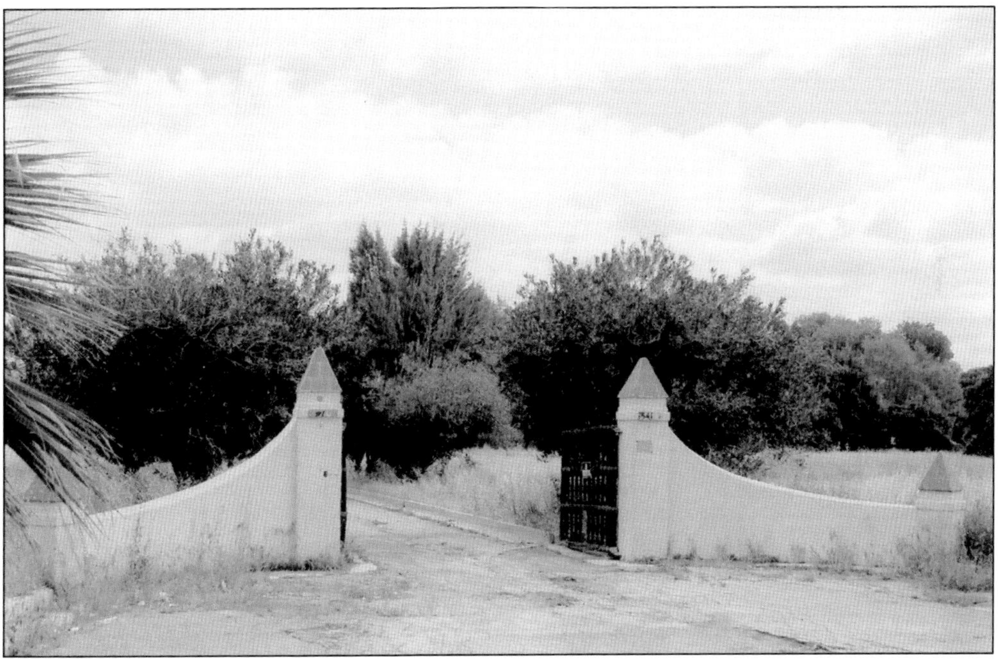

The Machado adobe house was one of the relay stops for the Butterfield Overland Stage Line from 1858 to 1861. The pleasant station in the shade of the cottonwood trees was a welcome sight to road-battered passengers. The travelers were weary immigrants, soldiers, army deserters, and adventurers. The house was also the home of the famous "hanging tree," where many outlaws met their fate. (Courtesy Edythe J. Greene.)

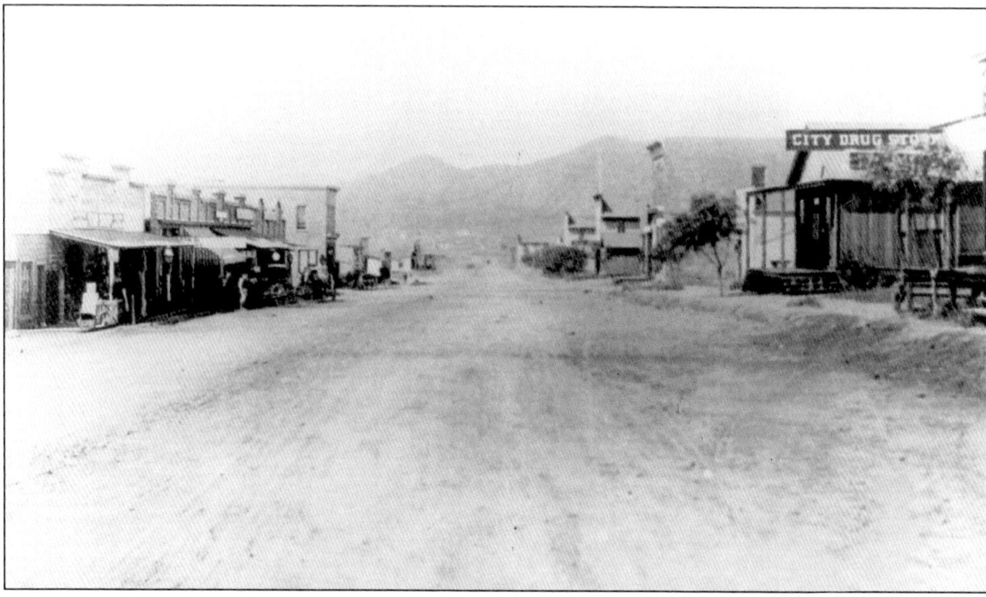

Imagine Triburcio Vasquez and his terrifying gang riding into the sleepy town of Elsinore during the horse and buggy days of the 1880s. Vasquez was one of the most vicious outlaw leaders in history, but was looked upon as a "Robin Hood of the West." He was a frequent visitor here but eluded capture for 20 years. (Courtesy Jeanie Corral.)

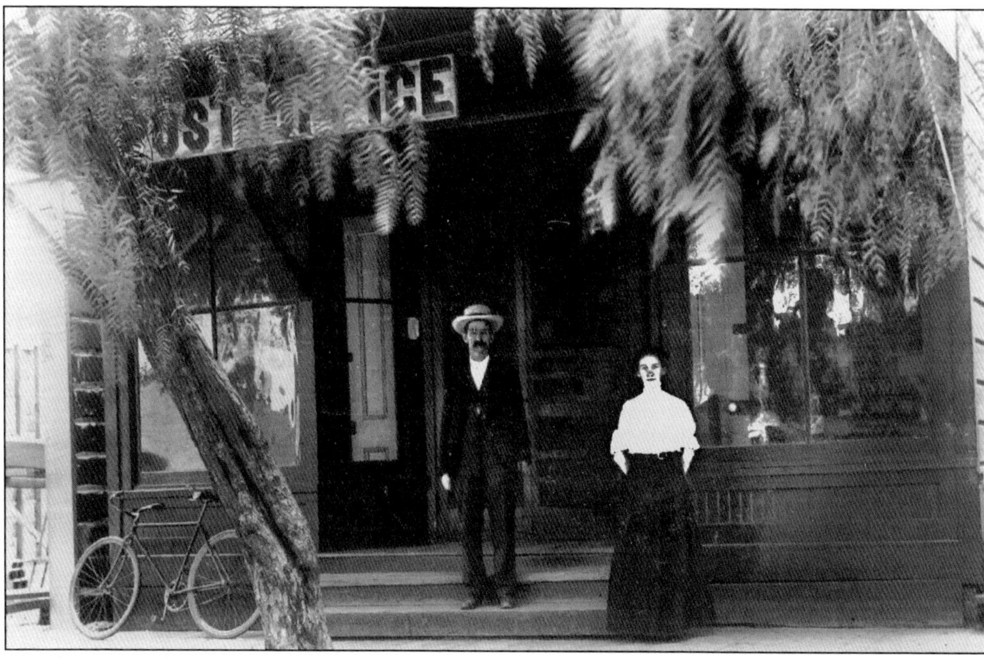

The first post office in Lake Elsinore opened in 1884 on Main Street, between Peck and Graham Streets. The postmaster at that time was Dave Townsend. Before then, the people of Lake Elsinore received their mail from a box nailed to a willow tree. Then, after moving a few times, a new post office building was constructed on East Graham in 1932. In 1969, the *Valley Tribune* moved into this building, while the post office moved to its present location at Graham and Poe Streets. (Courtesy Riverside County Library System.)

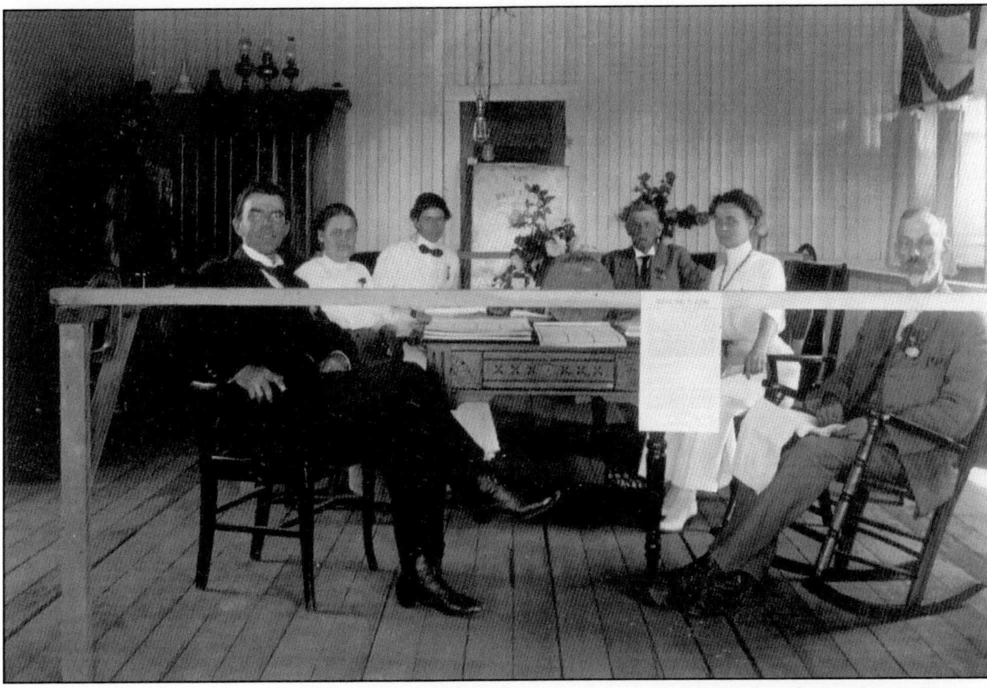

In this 1912 picture in the old Elsinore City Hall, the first election board is seen here after a women's suffrage meeting. Pictured, from left to right, are Green, Emma Graham, Lorena Willsey, James Schanck, Beatrice Clark, and C. S. Merrifield. (Courtesy Riverside County Library System.)

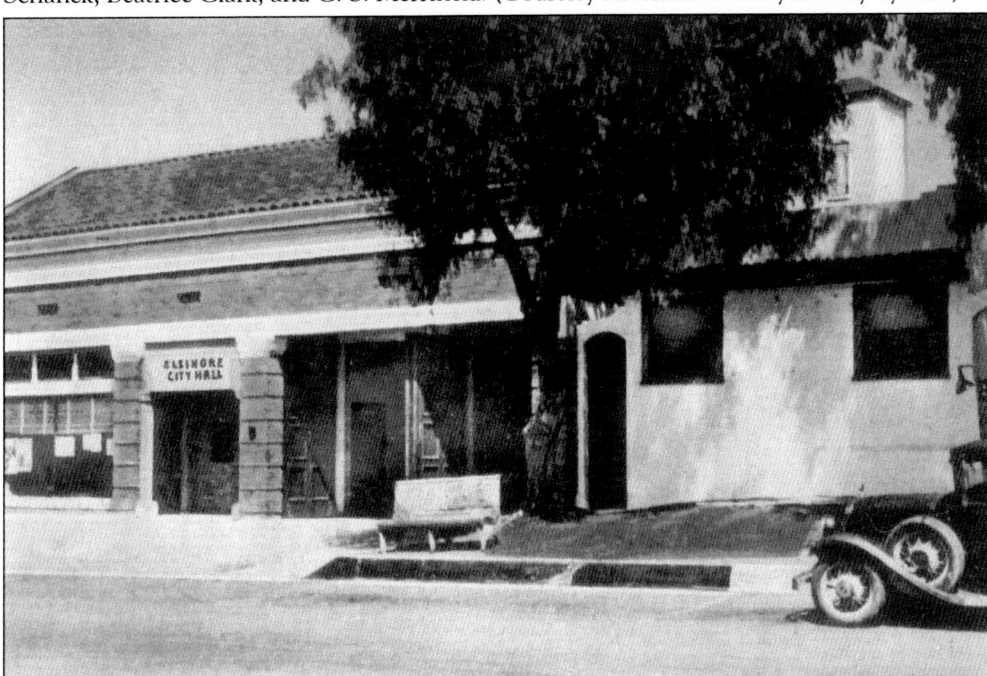


Elsinore City Hall was built in 1934 on South Main Street at a cost of $15,000. A parade down Main Street and a barbeque celebrated the dedication on July 7 of that year. The city administration offices are still located here. (Courtesy Riverside County Library System.)

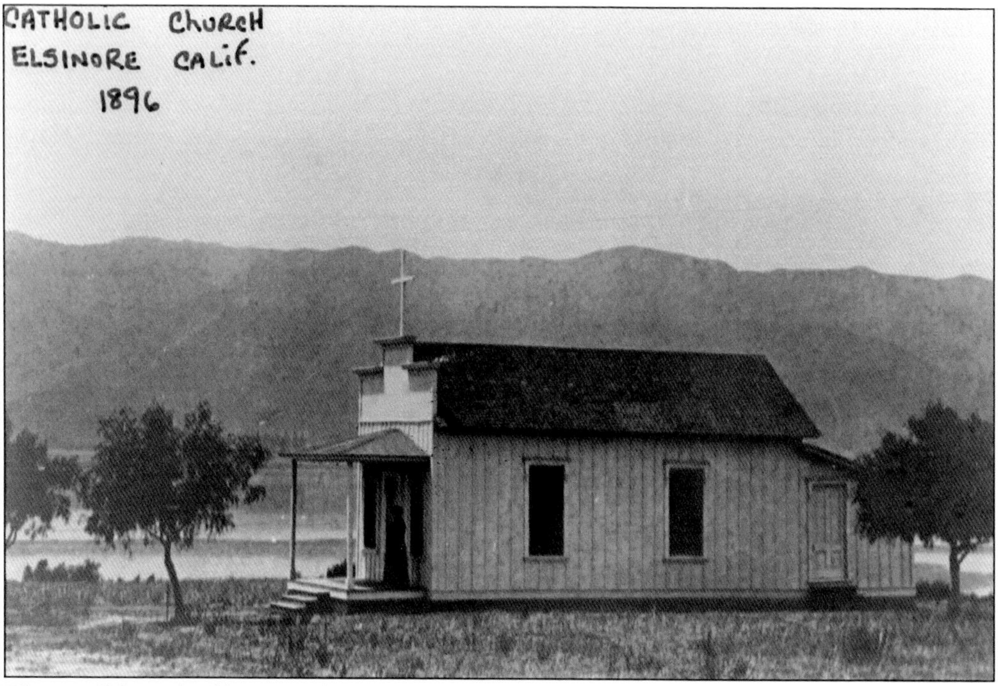


This small frame building was the original St. Francis of Rome Catholic Church on South Spring Street. It was built in 1885 by William and Francis Hampton and was named St. Francis, in honor of Mrs. Hampton's patron saint. (Courtesy Dr. Timothy Kimble, D.C.)

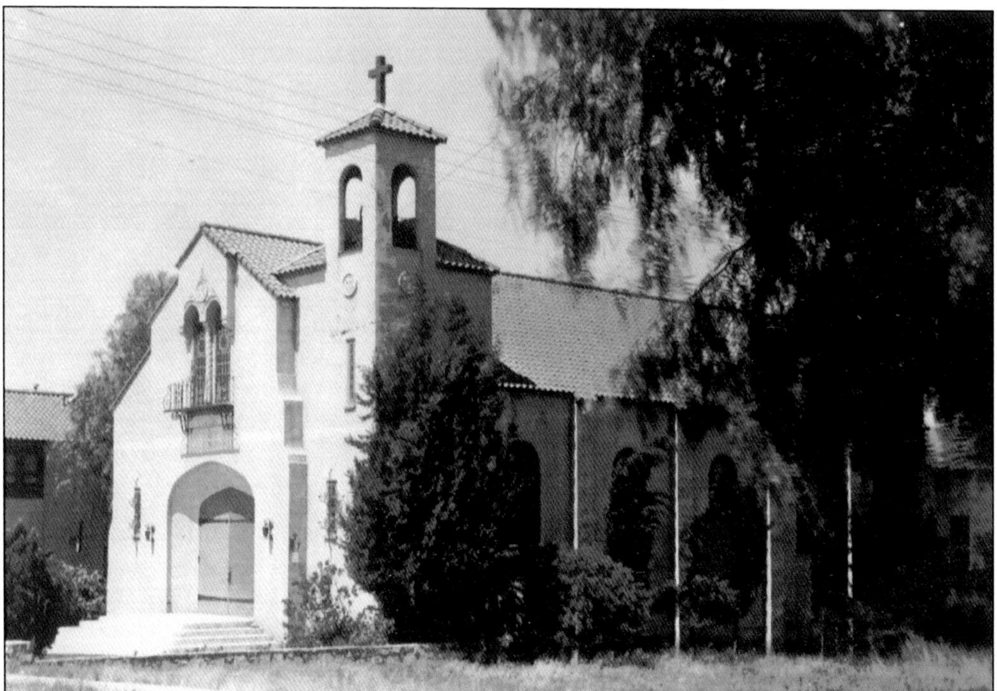

Pictured here is the present St. Francis of Rome Church located on Lowell Street. Father Burri was the church's first resident priest. (Courtesy Riverside County Library System.)

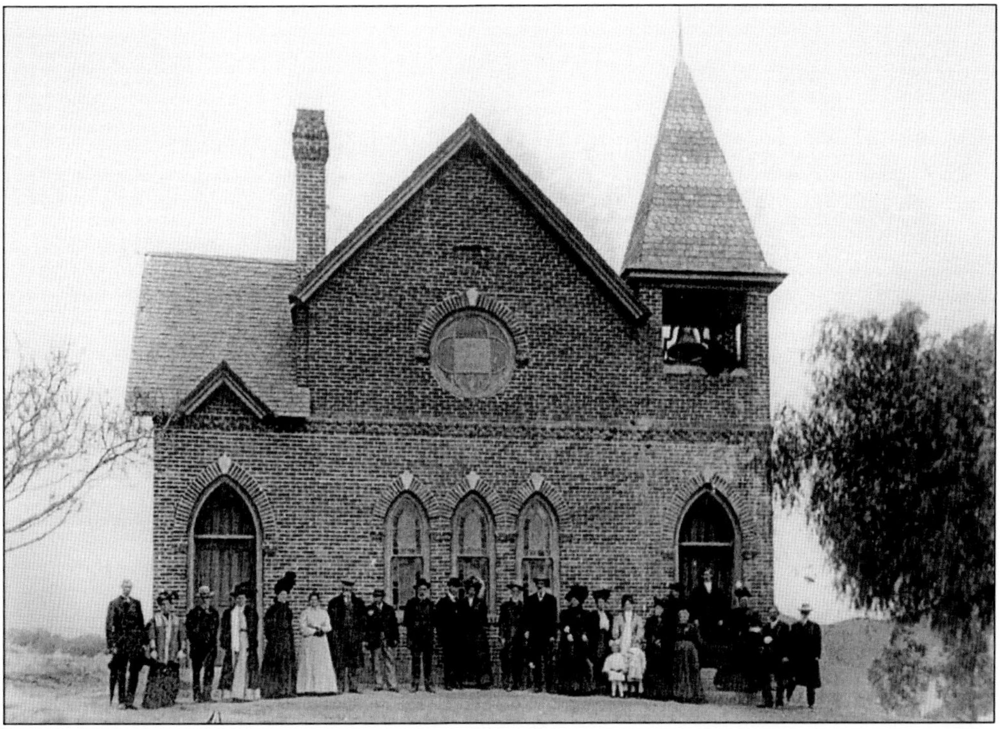

The first church chartered in Elsinore was the Methodist Episcopal church on the corner of Heald and Poe Streets in 1884. The Reverend J. W. Rice was its pastor. Unfortunately, it was destroyed in a wind storm in September 1888. After being rebuilt of stone and brick, it later was occupied by the First Christian Church. (Courtesy Riverside County Library System.)

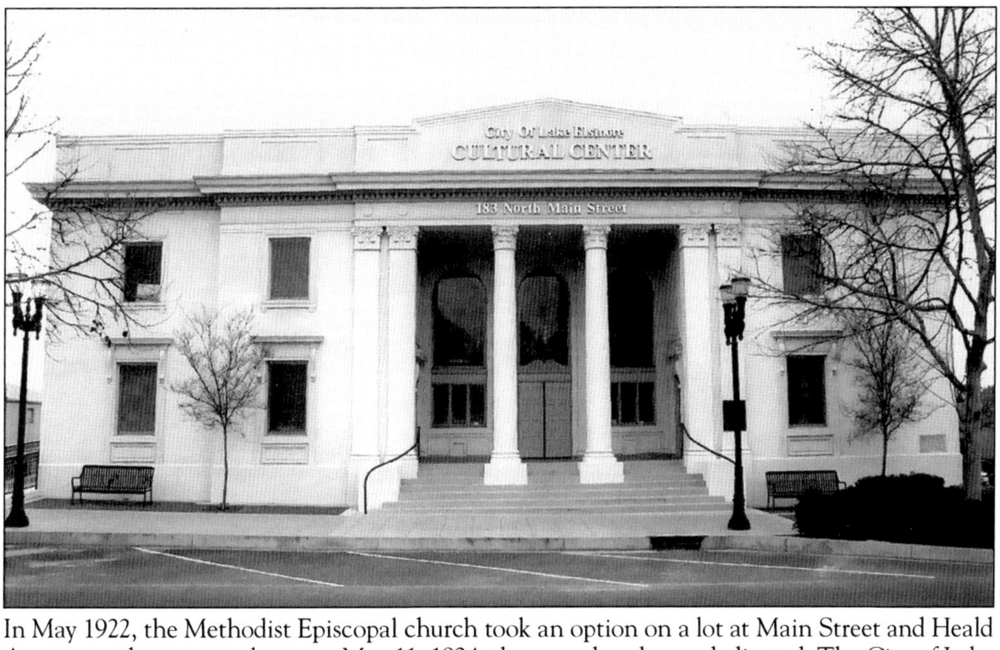


In May 1922, the Methodist Episcopal church took an option on a lot at Main Street and Heald Avenue, and, two years later, on May 11, 1924, the new church was dedicated. The City of Lake Elsinore Cultural Center now occupies the building. (Courtesy Edythe J. Greene.)

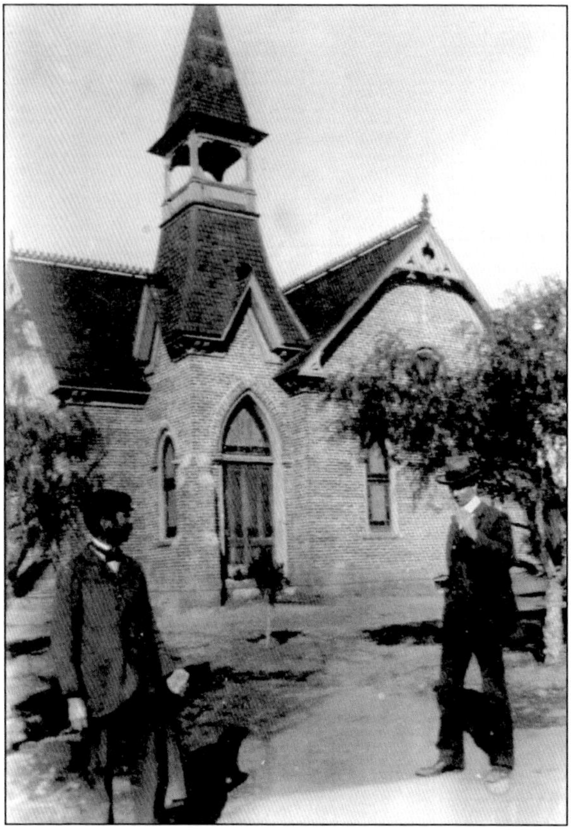

The Presbyterian church was organized in March 1886 in the schoolhouse at Grand and Macy Streets. In 1889, the sanctuary was built at 601 West Graham Avenue, and the house of worship officially was dedicated on May 26 of that year. It's the oldest-standing church in Elsinore. (Courtesy Riverside County Library System.)

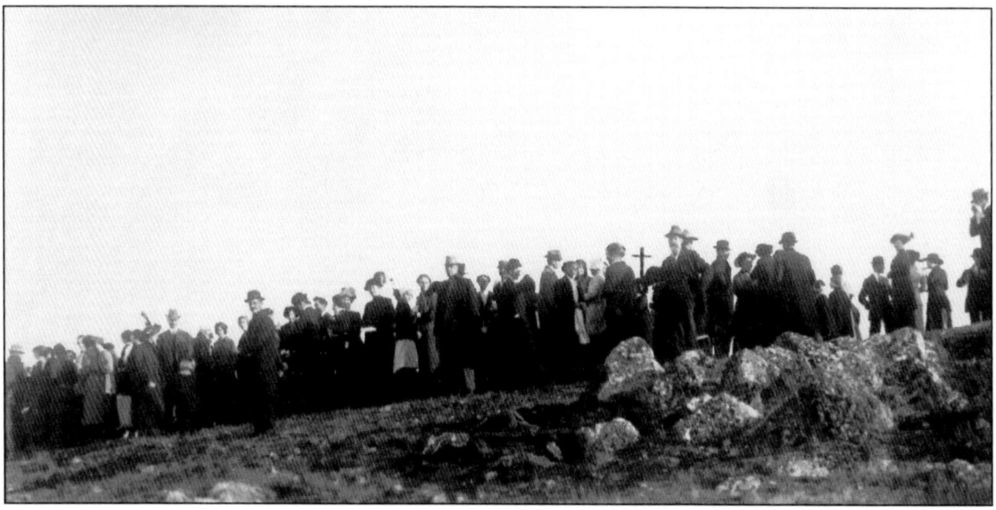

The first Easter sunrise service on Flagstaff Hill was held on April 12, 1914. The property had been deeded to the city in 1908 by W. E. Hampton, and in 1911 Hampton Road was built, leading up to the small park at the top of Flagstaff Hill. The hill is also known as Mount Hampton. On a clear day from the top of the hill, one can view Mount Baldy in the San Gabriel Mountains to the northeast; to the north, Old Grayback (Mount San Gorgonio) in the San Bernardino Mountains; and the San Jacinto Mountains to the northeast. (Courtesy Riverside County Library System.)

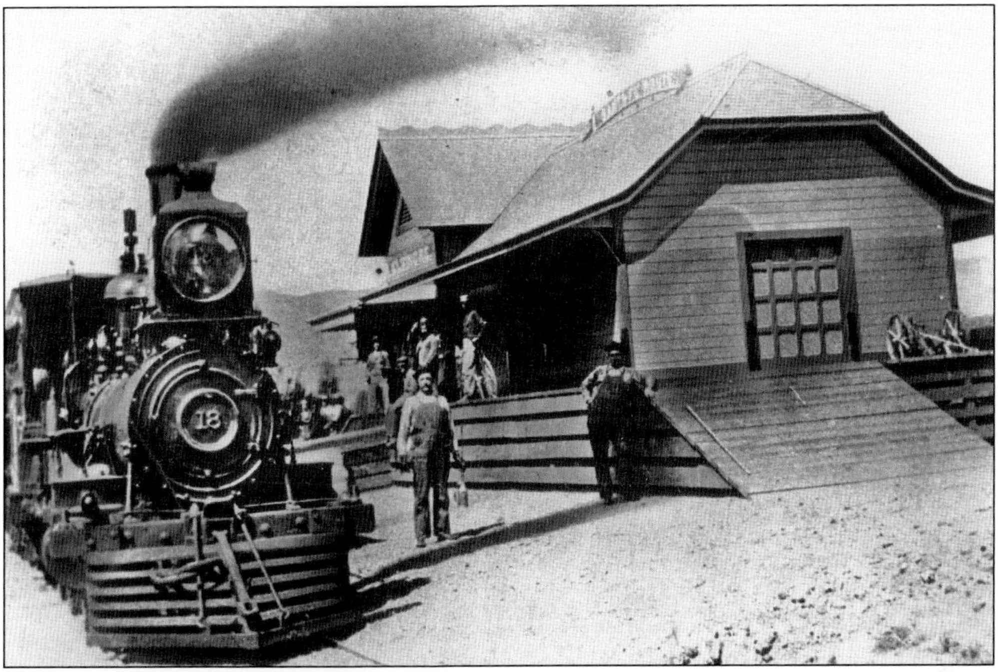

The Elsinore train station was first built by the California Southern Railway Company in 1882 on Lakeshore Drive. In 1896, the Santa Fe Railroad took over the line, moving the depot to the corner of Spring and Graham Streets, where it stands today. At that time, service was extended to Alberhill Coal and Clay Mines. Pictured here on March 31, 1899, is old No. 10 pulling into the Elsinore Station. (Courtesy Riverside County Library System.)

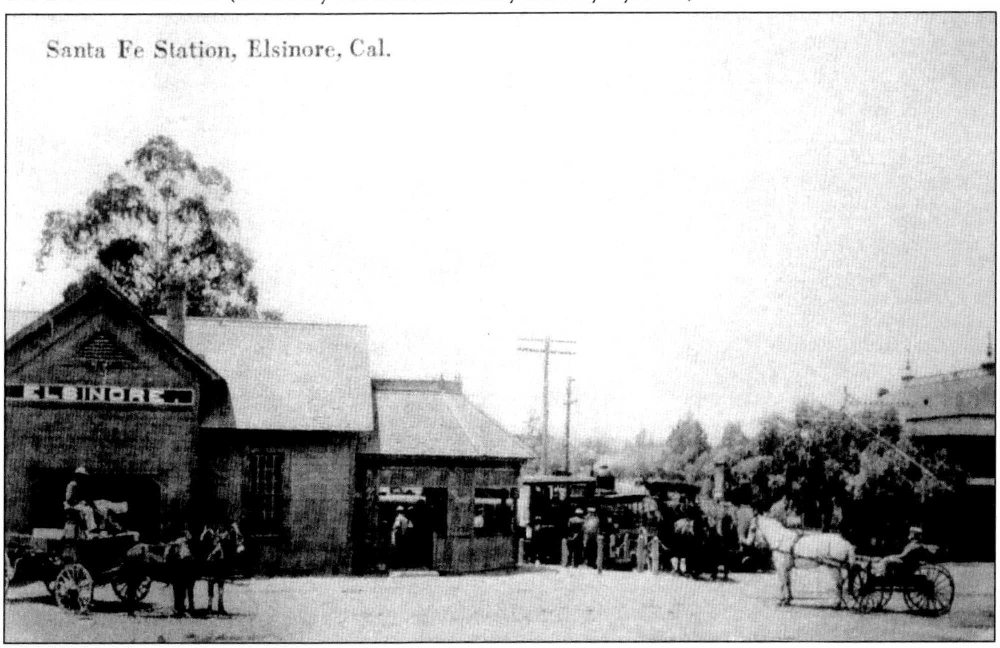


The railroad era proved to be a wonderful time for the people of Lake Elsinore. Shipping could be done, new people arrived, and traveling was made much easier. (Courtesy Lake Elsinore Historical Society.)

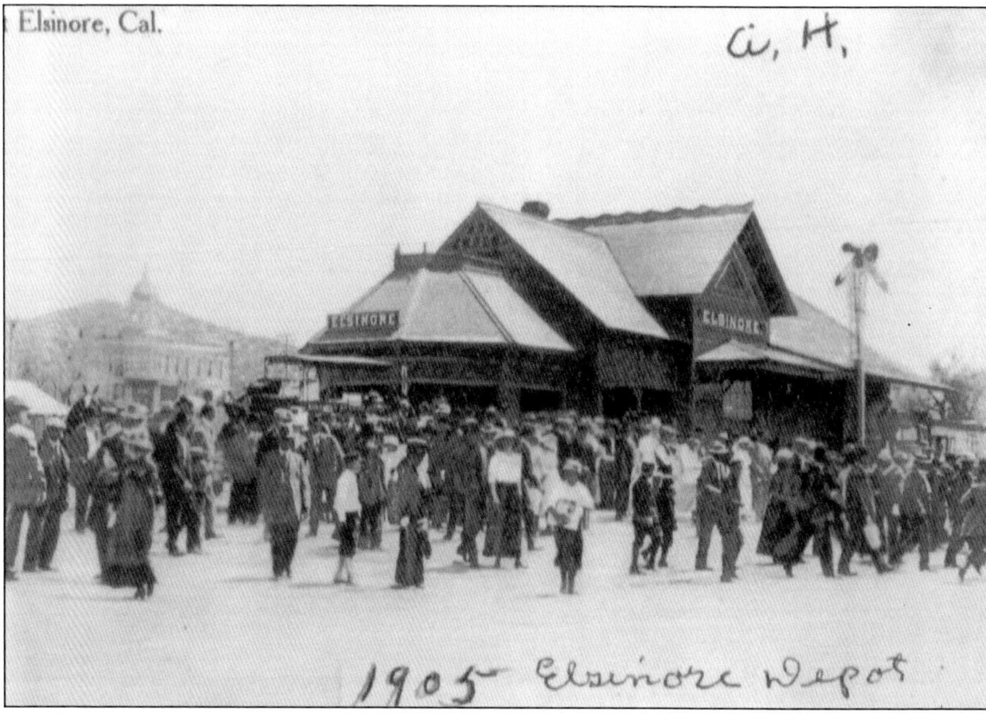


The Elsinore train depot had more to offer than depots in neighboring towns. For example, it contained a comfortable summer waiting room with large bay windows. The freight platform, measuring 32 feet by 46 feet, was painted apple green with an olive green trim. This is the busy depot in 1905, nine years after it was built. (Courtesy Riverside County Library System.)

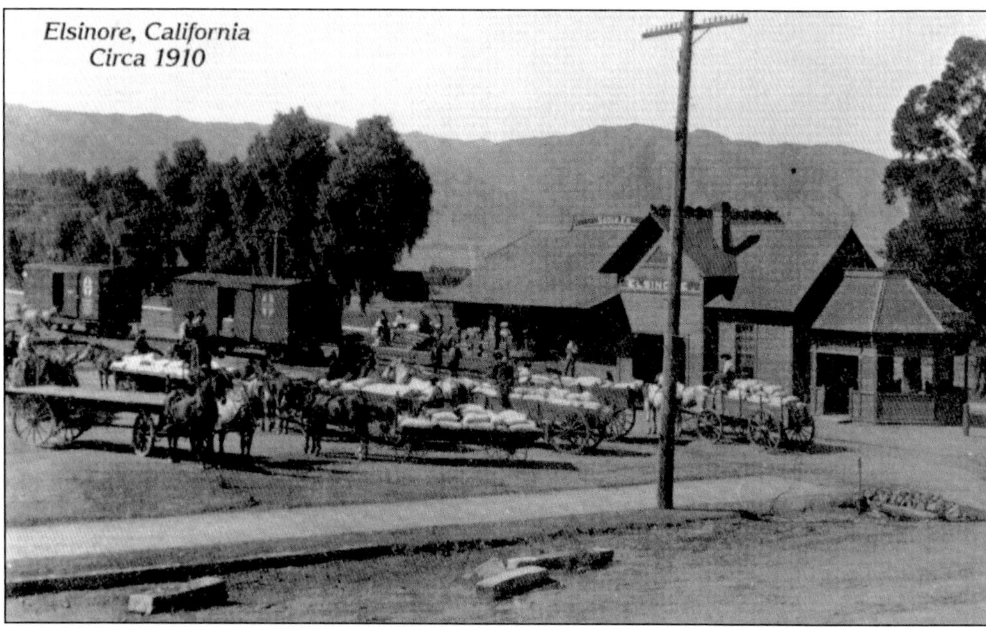


For 60 years, dried apricots were an important crop in the Lake Elsinore area. It was a busy time at the train depot when the crops were ready to be shipped. (Courtesy Dr. Timothy Kimble, D.C.)

These relics are all that is left of the old railroad trains and tracks that used to keep Elsinore bustling. They can be seen on the side of the old Elsinore depot at 132 West Graham Avenue, now the site of the Lake Elsinore Chamber of Commerce. (Courtesy Louise Rowden.)

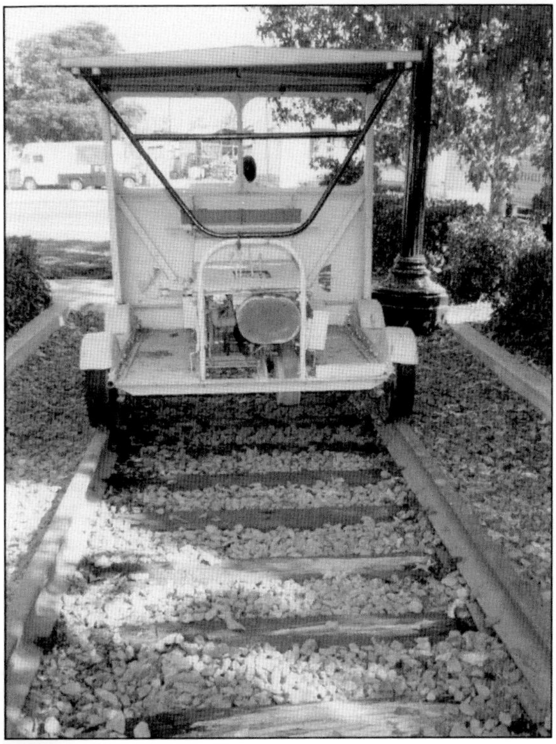

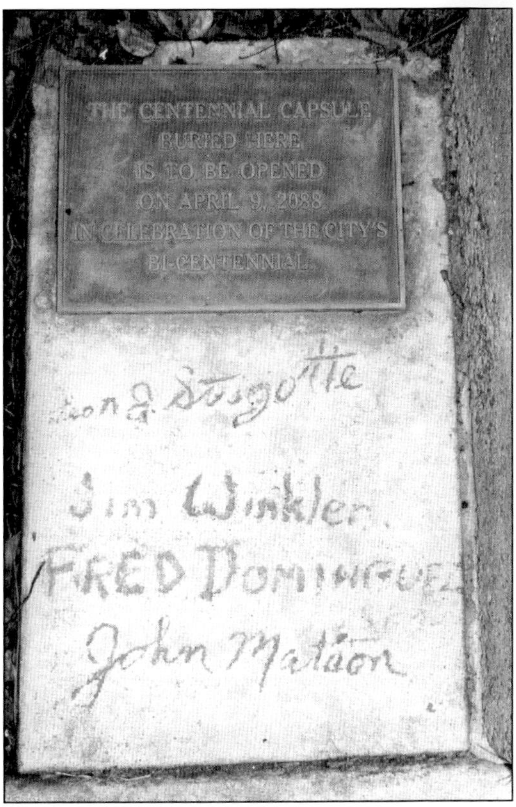


In honor of the City of Lake Elsinore's centennial celebration on April 9, 1988, a time capsule was buried at the railroad station at 132 West Graham Avenue, now the site of the chamber of commerce. In the capsule are letters from the mayor and the city council, historical records, a city map, brochures, a city directory, newspaper articles relating to the centennial celebration, and Tom Hudson's book, *Lake Elsinore Valley*. The capsule is scheduled to be opened at the bicentennial celebration on April 9, 2088. Pictured are signatures of some of the people involved in the 1988 centennial celebration. (Courtesy Edythe J. Greene.)

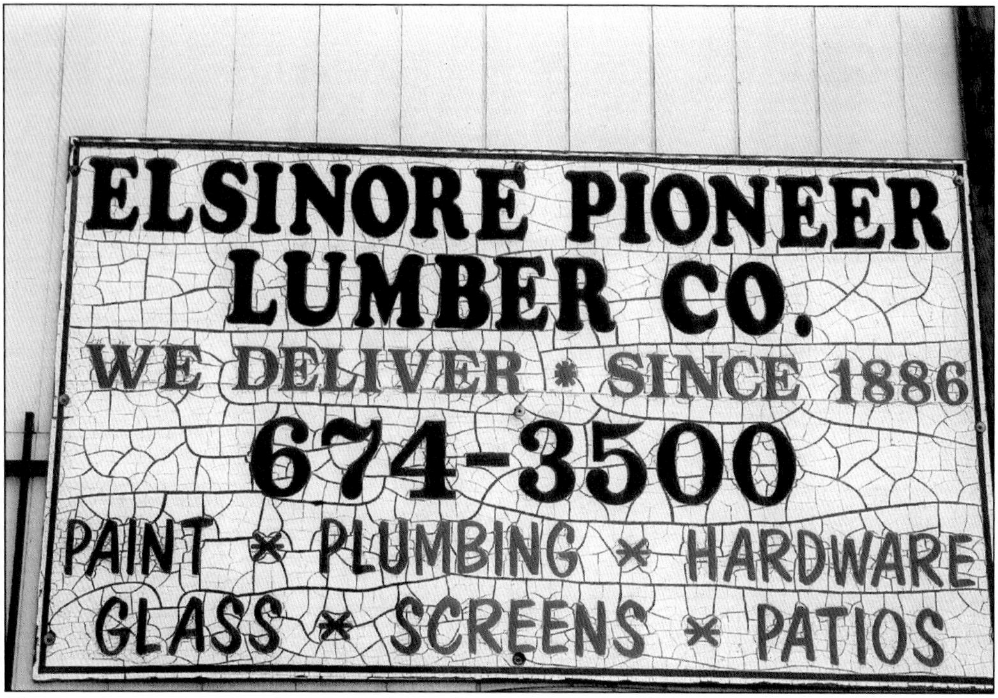


Elsinore Pioneer Lumber Company, located at 127 West Graham Avenue, is the oldest active business in Elsinore and has been serving the community since 1886. The business had five previous owners before Fred Smith became manager in 1924. The Fred Smith family purchased it in 1934. (Courtesy Edythe J. Greene.)

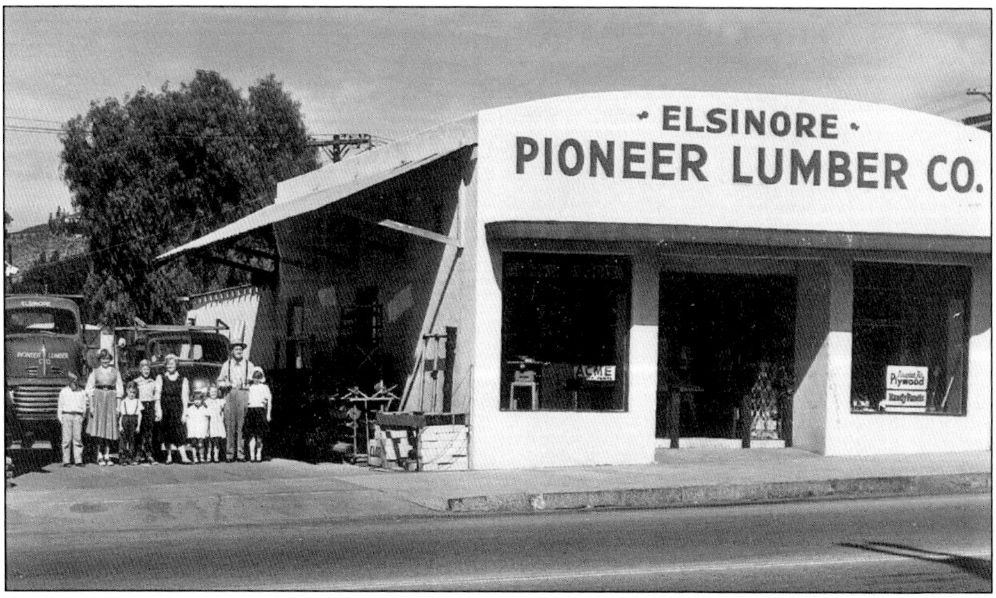


Fred Smith is shown with eight grandchildren standing by the Pioneer Lumber Company. Pictured, from left to right, are James F. Basiger, Jacquetta Wilson, Sterling Smith, Herbert Holtan, Sharon Basiger, Lark Smith, Mary Kay Basiger, Fred H. Smith, and Sony Holtan. (Courtesy Mildred Basiger.)

Times have changed, and although the Elsinore Pioneer Lumber has kept up with the times, it also respects the traditions of the old times. Still for sale as this book went to print is the lumber company's time-honored outhouse, a photograph of which was published in a book, *The Rainbow's End,* by the International Library of Photography. (Courtesy Louise Rowden.)

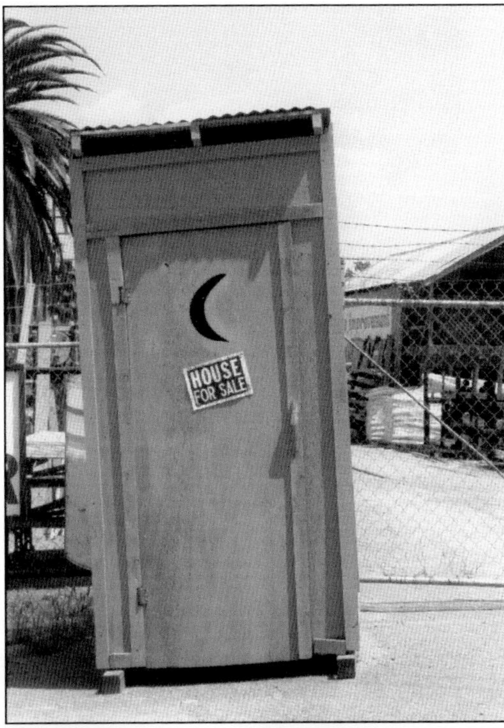


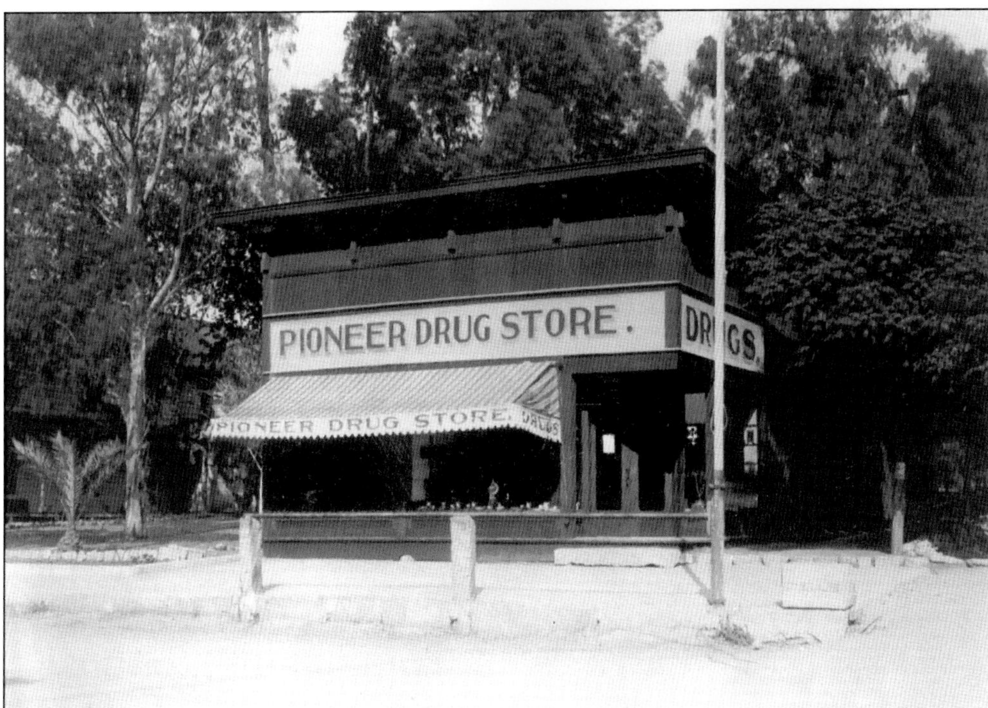


Dr. Thomas E. Ellis, Lake Elsinore's first doctor, bought the Elsinore Hotel and the building where he opened the Pioneer Drug Store, pictured here at Peck and Main Streets in 1890. Chuckles Java Junction later occupied the same site. (Courtesy Riverside County Library System.)

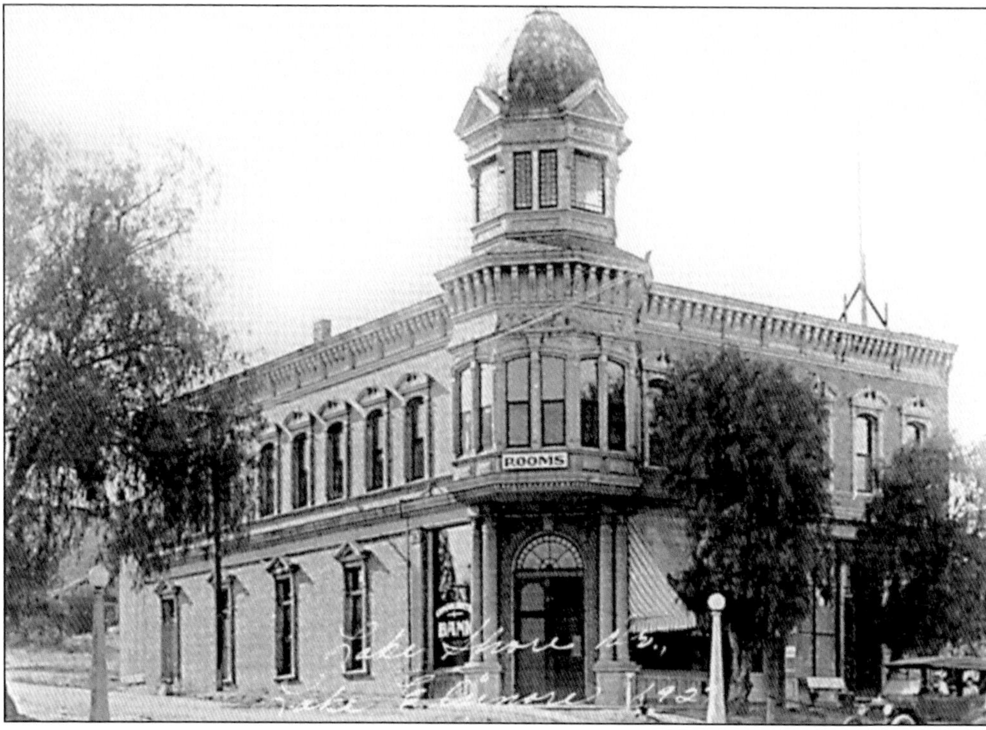


In 1887, the Exchange Bank of Lake Elsinore was founded with Franklin H. Heald as president. It is located on the corner of Prospect and Main Streets, and most of the original building still stands. This 1927 photograph depicts how the bank looked. The Exchange Bank of Elsinore and Bank of Elsinore consolidated in 1890 and assumed the name Consolidated Bank of Elsinore. In 1916, the Consolidated Bank building became the new Ambassador Hotel.

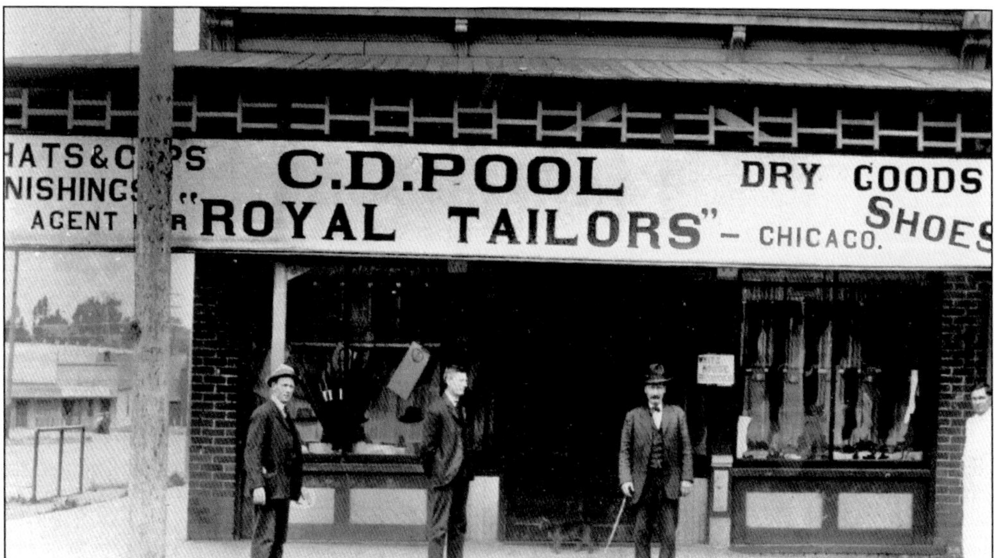


The corner of Main and Graham Streets in Lake Elsinore was a very popular location. C. D. Pool Royal Tailors occupied this store on the lower level of the Stewart Building. Herbelin Dry Goods later occupied this same site. (Courtesy the Riverside County Library System.)

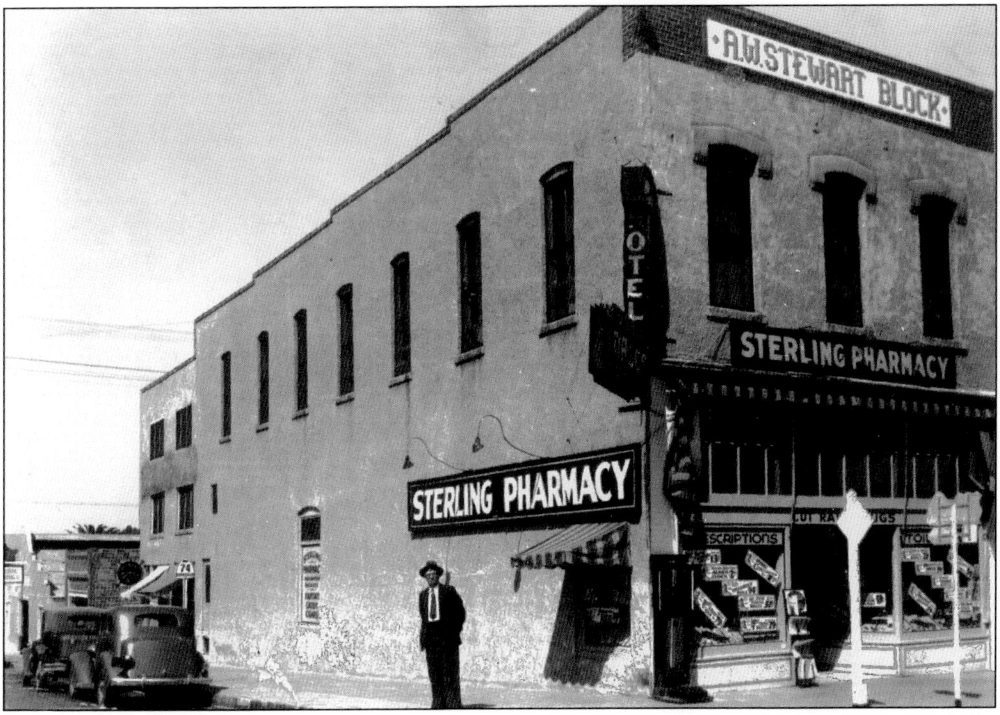


The Sterling Pharmacy operated in the Stewart Building at Graham and Main Streets in Lake Elsinore in the early 20th century. Later Gediman Park was at this location, and today we find the Guadalajara restaurant on this same corner. (Courtesy Riverside County Library System.)

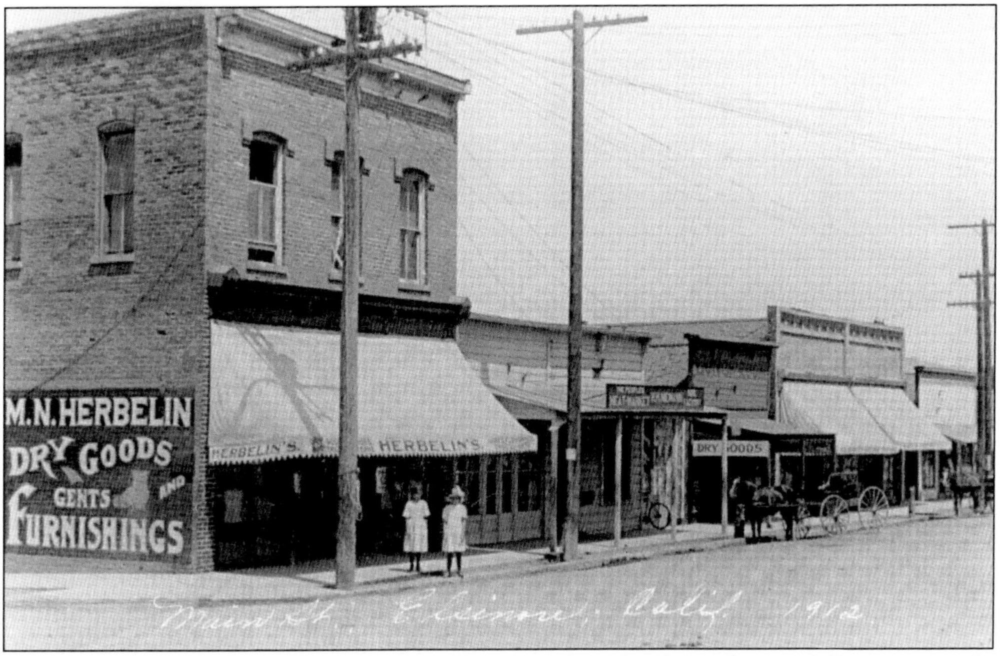


The Stewart Building on the corner of Main and Graham has housed many different stores. In 1912, Herbelin Dry Goods was located here. The building, however, was demolished in the 1970s and became the site of Gediman Park.

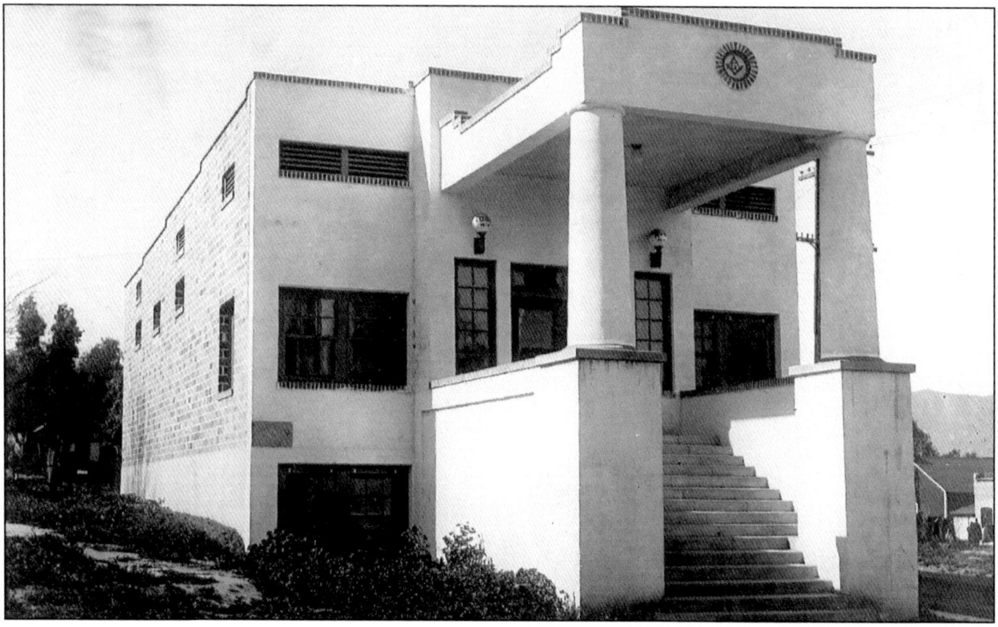

The Lake Elsinore Masons held their first recorded meeting on April 15, 1887, at the Elsinore Post Office. William Erskin Sloan was the freemasons' first master. The charter was granted for Lake Elsinore in September 1888 by the Grand Lodge No. 3259 of Riverside, California. The Masons had this temple built in 1922 on East Graham Street for $25,000. It was dedicated on May 17, 1923. H. Donald Young is now the master of this Lodge No. 289. (Courtesy Masonic Lodge No. 289.)

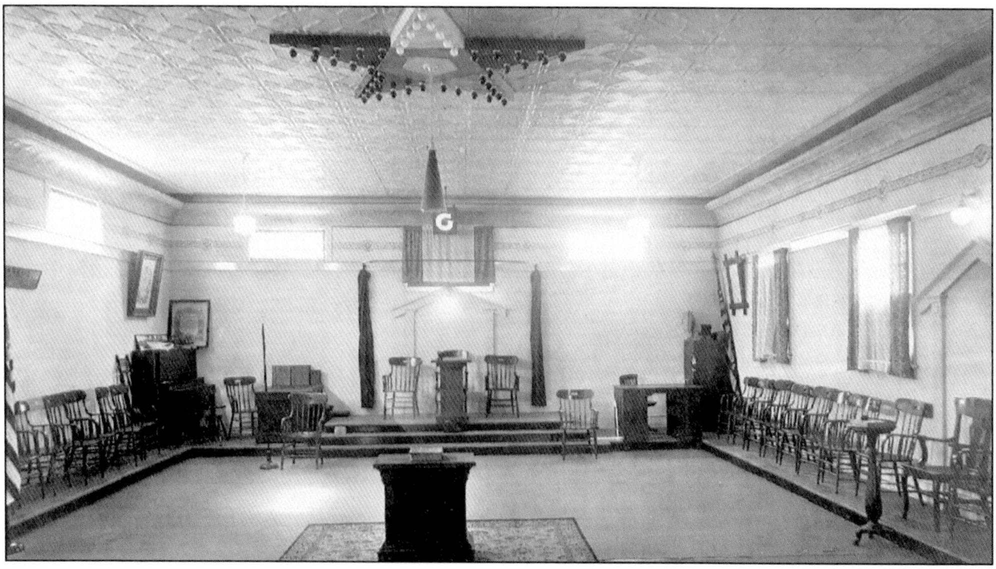

The Masons are the world's oldest fraternal organization. The meetings are held here at the Masonic Hall and are open to the public. The Masons believe in the Holy Bible but welcome people of all faiths. Their goal is to make good men better. Their promise is to keep one's word. They support hospitals, public schools, and scholarship programs. The cornerstones of public schools are laid by the Masons. In 2003, they participated in five local cornerstone ceremonies. (Courtesy Masonic Lodge No. 289.)

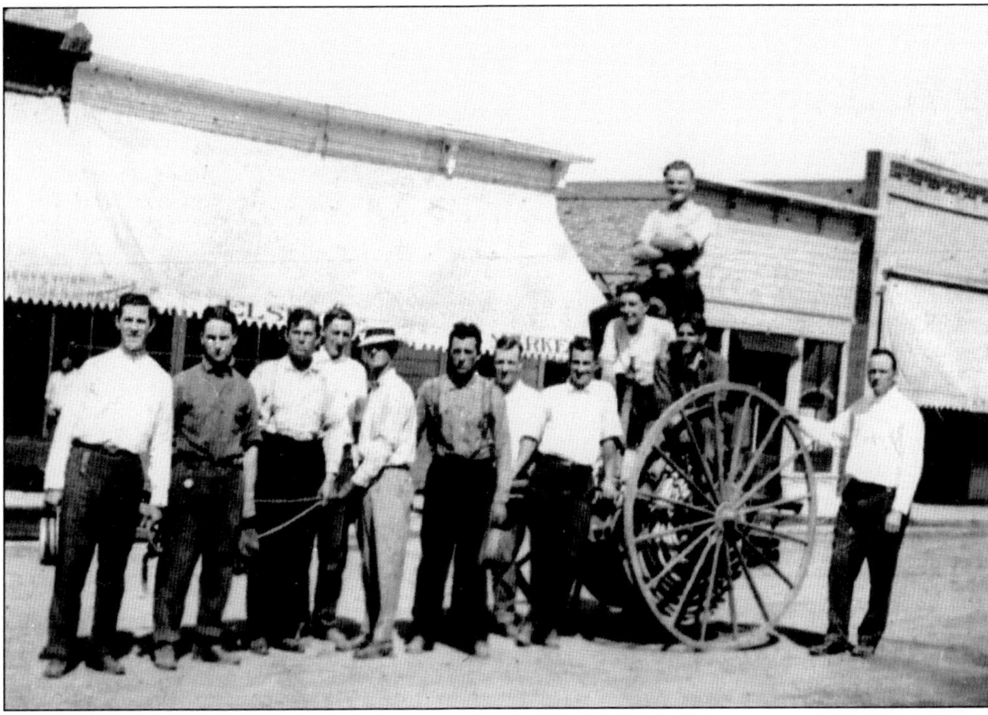

Elsinore Fire Department was formed in 1890 with a horse-drawn hose cart and 500 feet of hose. A. G. Keck was appointed by the city council to organize the fire department's hose company. (Courtesy Riverside County Library System.)

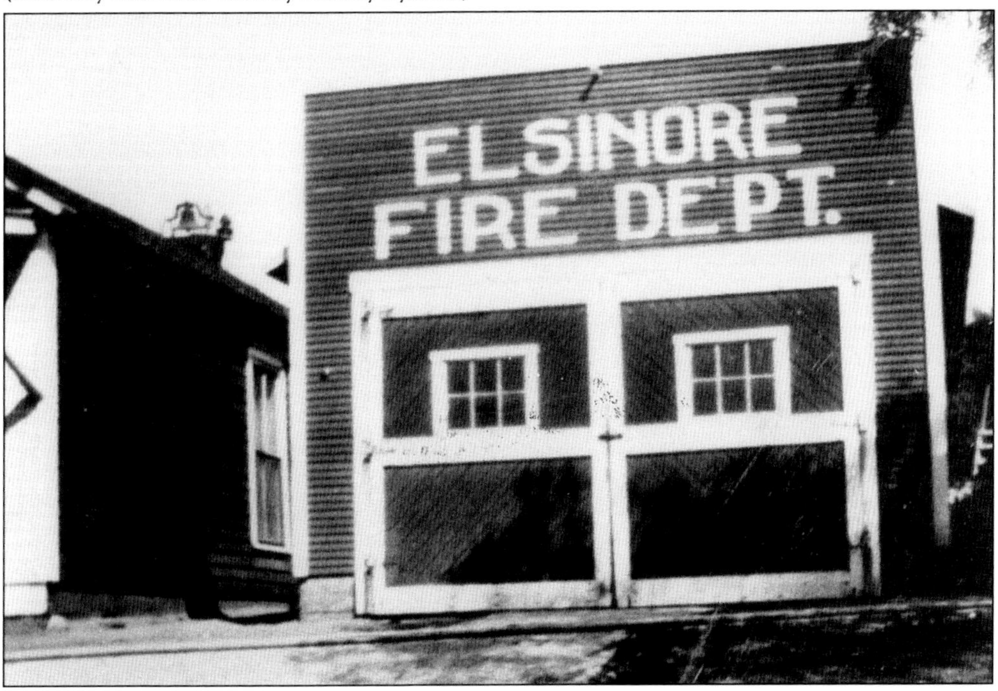


Lake Elsinore's first firehouse, a wooden building next to city hall on Main Street, housed the unique 1925 American LaFrance fire engine. (Courtesy Dr. Timothy Kimble, D.C.)

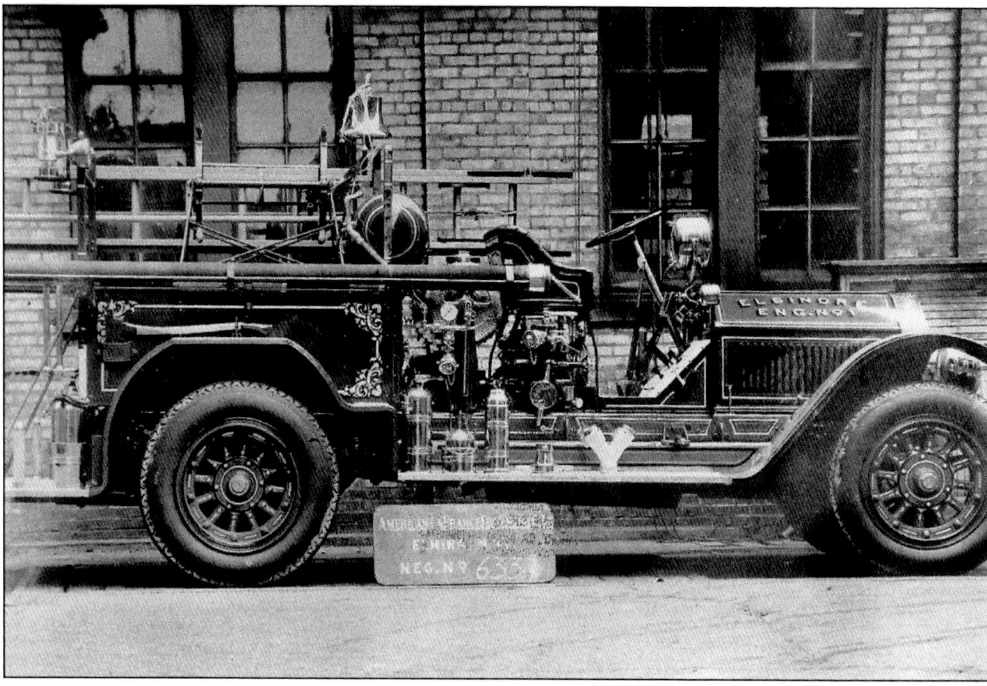

In 1925, the City of Elsinore was in need of a new fire truck, and the city council asked the president of the chamber of commerce for help in obtaining one. Working together, city agencies were able to purchase an American La France fire engine. There were only three of these engines manufactured and the restored Elsinore engine is the only one still in existence. (Courtesy Dr. Timothy Kimble, D.C.)

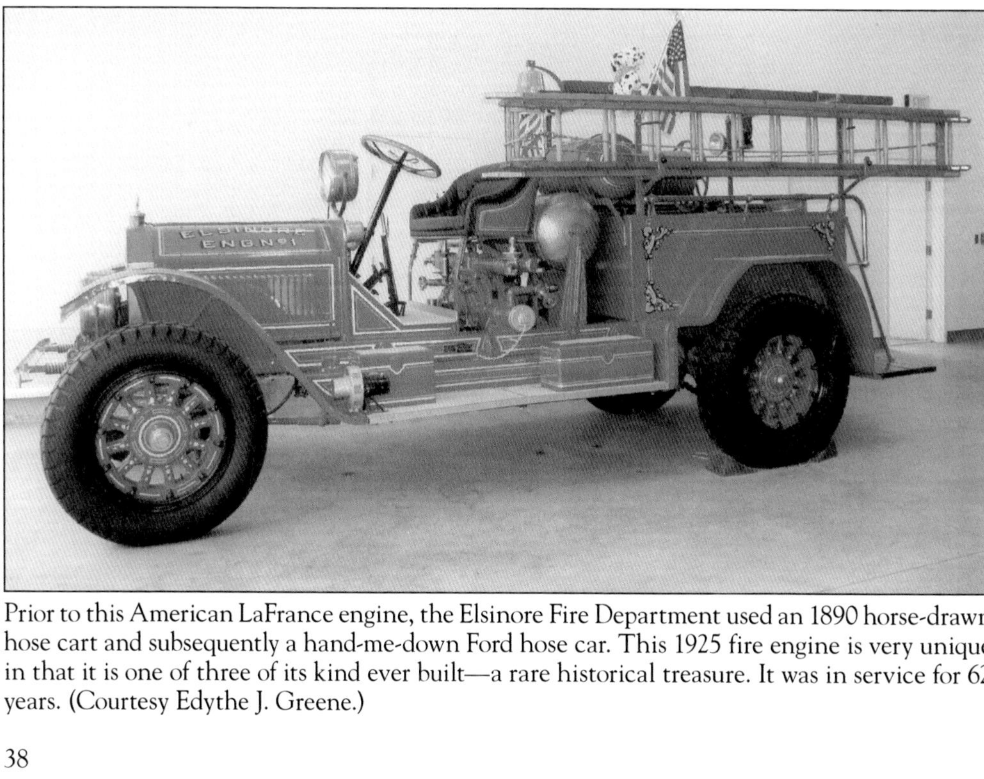

Prior to this American LaFrance engine, the Elsinore Fire Department used an 1890 horse-drawn hose cart and subsequently a hand-me-down Ford hose car. This 1925 fire engine is very unique in that it is one of three of its kind ever built—a rare historical treasure. It was in service for 62 years. (Courtesy Edythe J. Greene.)

C. S. Merrifield and D. R. Crane made the forms for the ornamental street lighting poles. The lights were designed to be used on Main Street. (Courtesy Louise Rowden.)

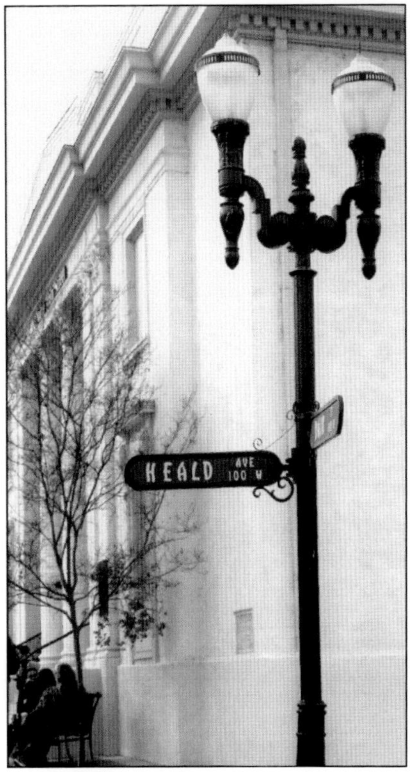


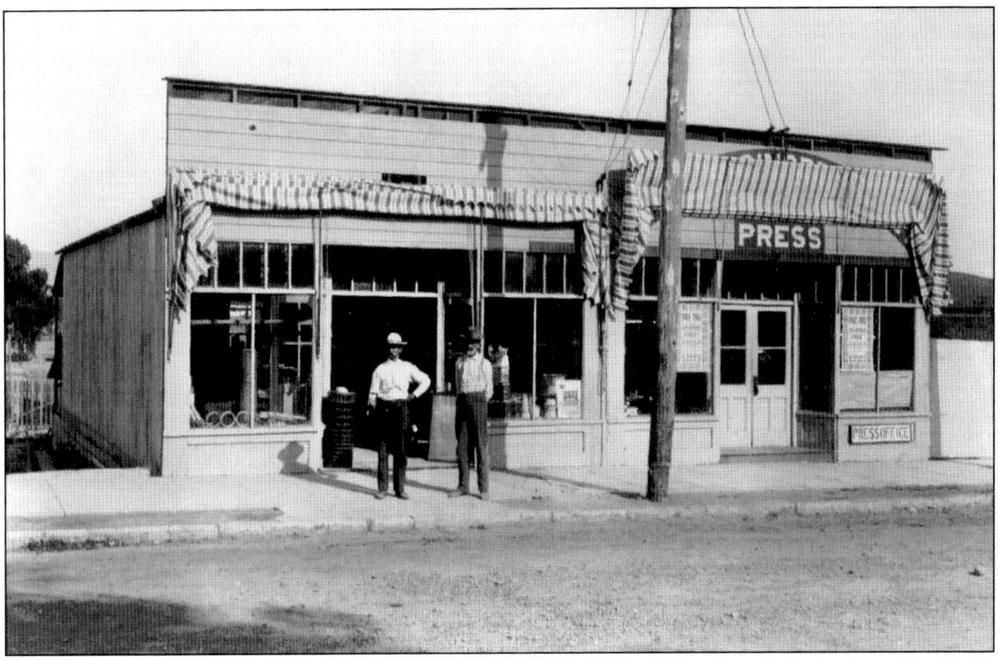


In 1911, C. S. Merrifield built this store on the south side of Main Street. Looking from the front of the building, his hardware and plumbing business was on the left side. On the right side was the *Elsinore Valley Press* with one room for offices and one for printing. (Courtesy Riverside County Library System.)

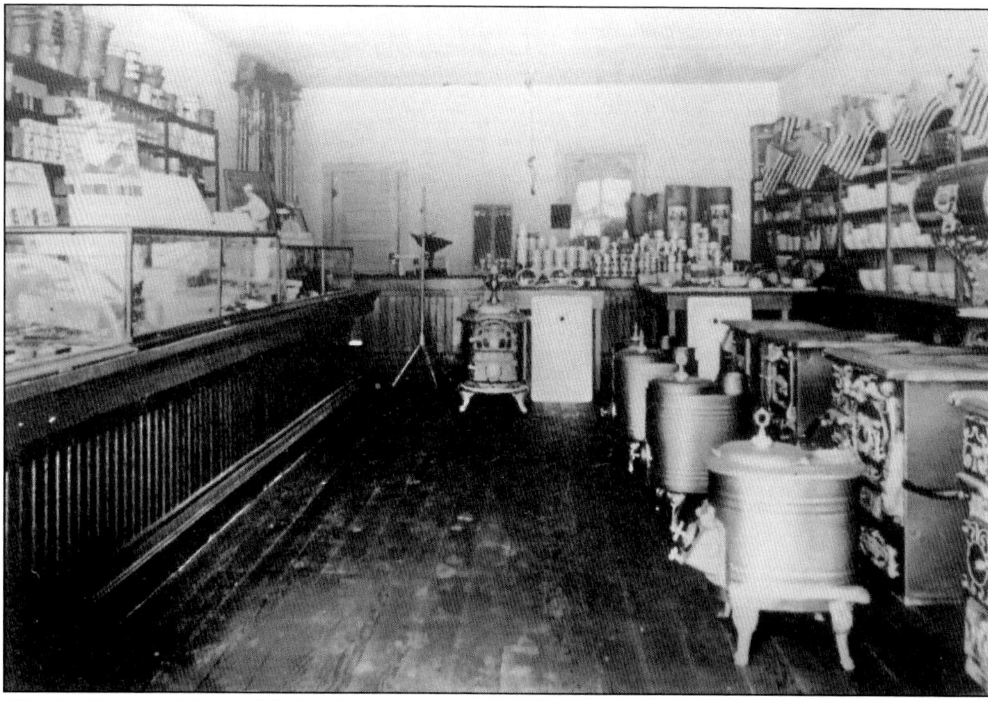

Charles Sumner Merrifield's hardware store, as seen here in 1911, served the Elsinore community by supplying building supplies and plumbing needs. (Courtesy Smoke House El Salvador.)

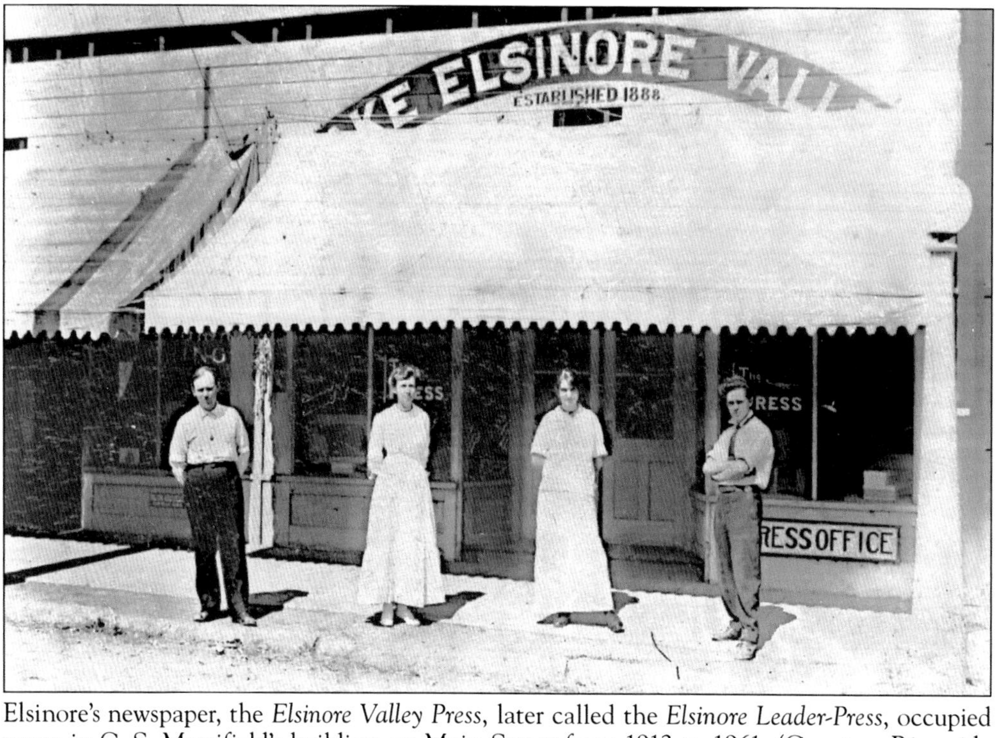


Elsinore's newspaper, the *Elsinore Valley Press*, later called the *Elsinore Leader-Press*, occupied space in C. S. Merrifield's building on Main Street from 1912 to 1961. (Courtesy Riverside County Library System.)

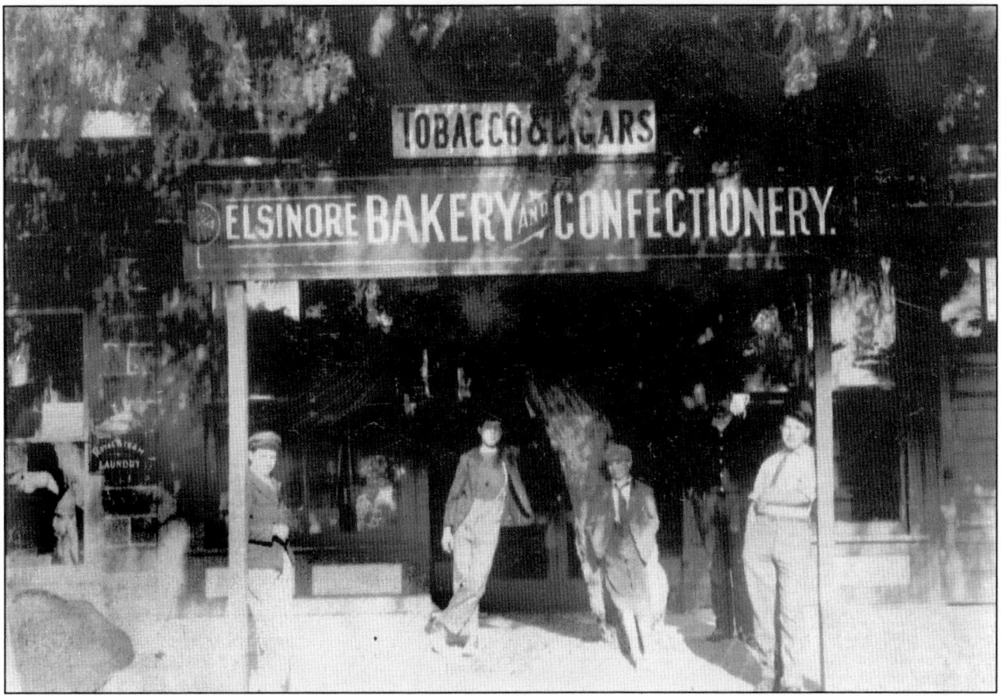


The Elsinore Bakery and Confectionery was one of the many popular early businesses in downtown Elsinore. (Courtesy the Riverside County Library System.)

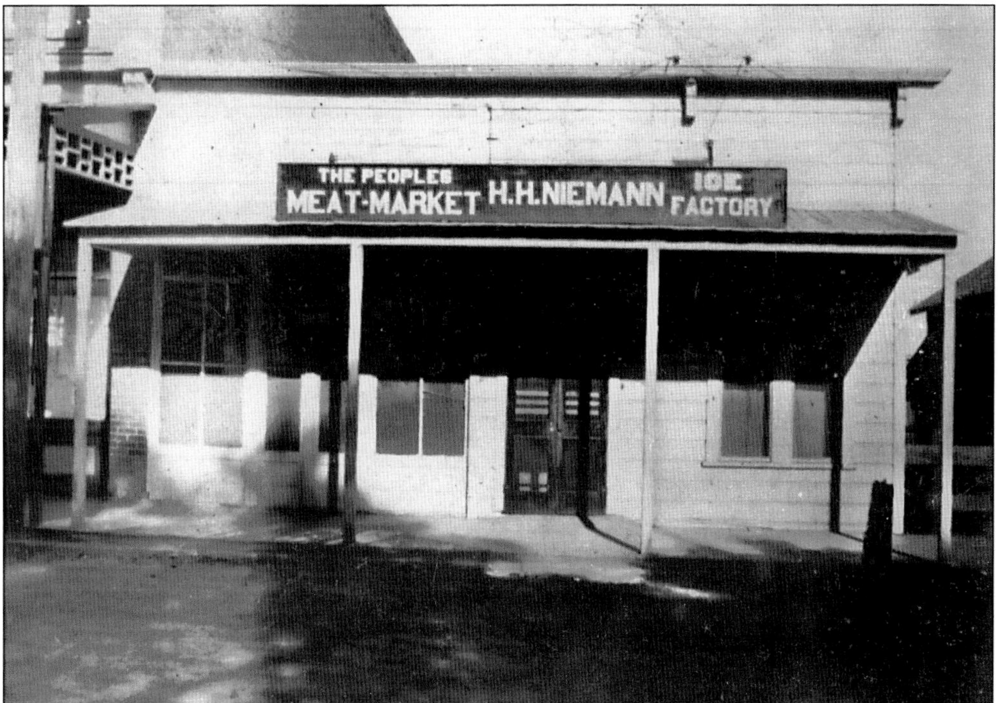


The People's Meat Market occupied the store next to Herbelin Dry Goods, *c.* 1912. Later Vernon's Bakery occupied this same site. (Courtesy Riverside County Library System.)

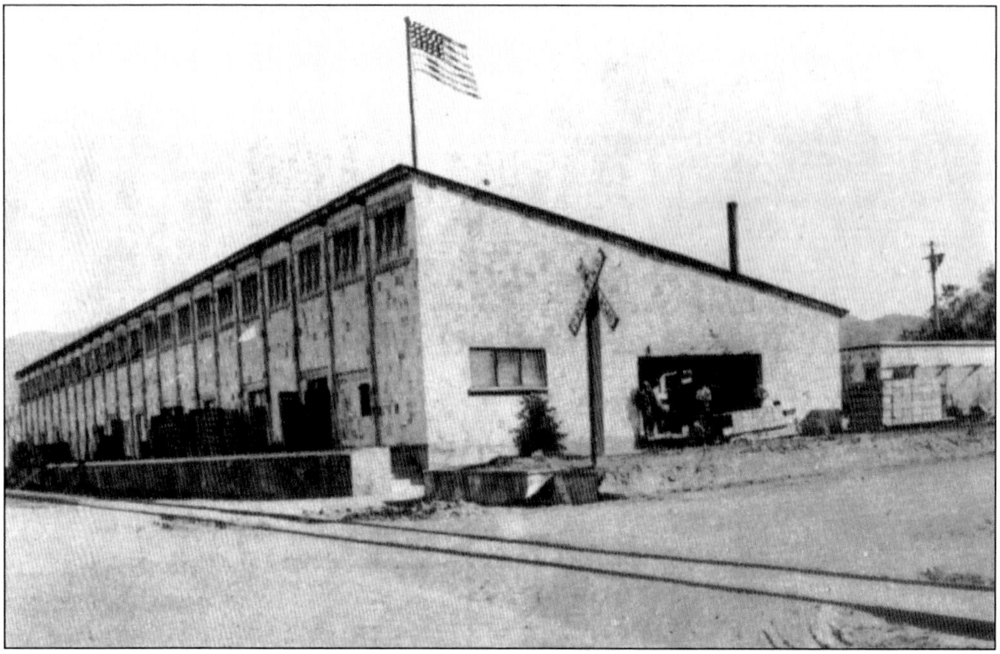

The employment of many people by the Lake Elsinore Dried Fruit Association and Cannery helped to boost the economy of Elsinore. Locally grown fruit, nuts, and tomatoes were sold by the tons for thousands of dollars. Another Elsinore export, shipped to Genoa, Italy, were the trunks of black walnut trees for use in the manufacturing of fine furniture. (Courtesy Riverside County Library System.)

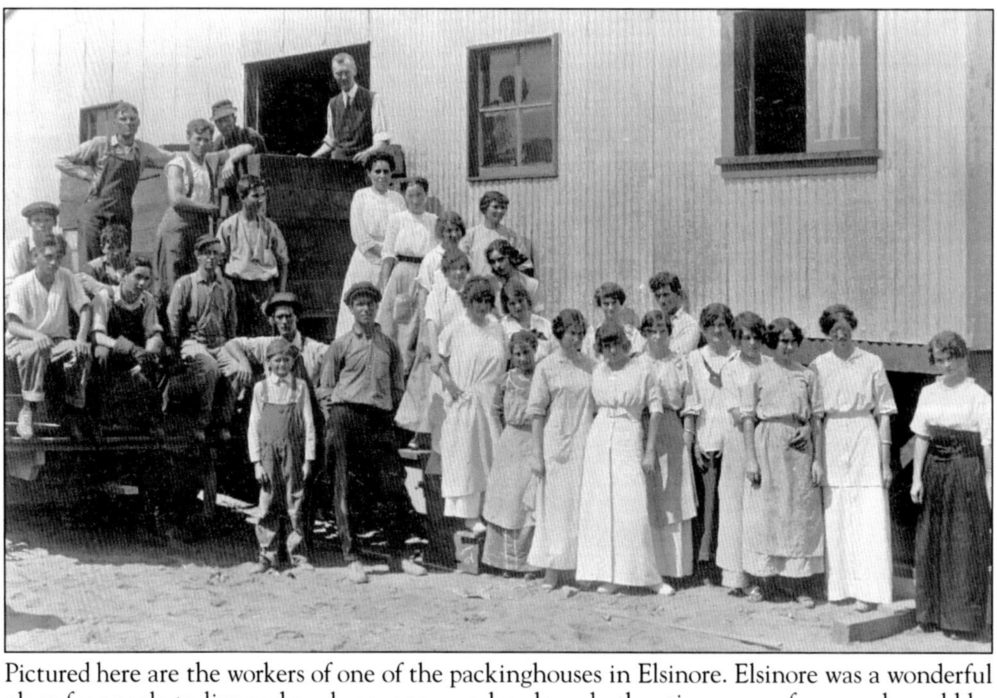

Pictured here are the workers of one of the packinghouses in Elsinore. Elsinore was a wonderful place for people to live and work, as many weekends and other times away from work could be spent at the lake. (Courtesy Riverside County Library System.)

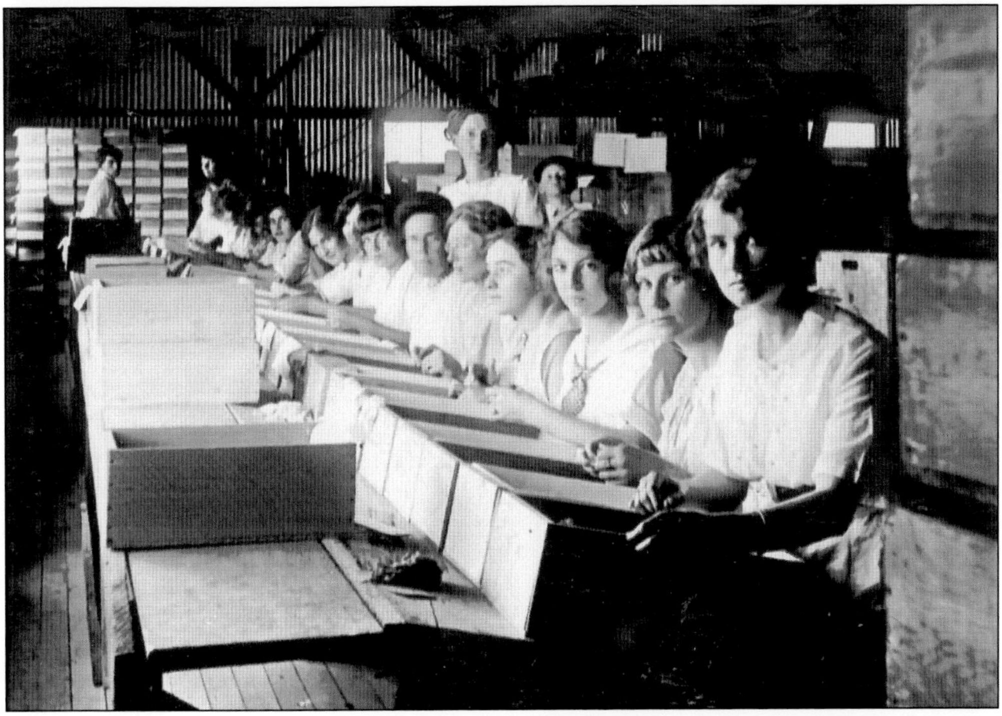

Preparing the fruits and nuts for packing took a lot of people. Here is a row of young women sorting and sizing different items according to the season. (Courtesy Riverside County Library System.)

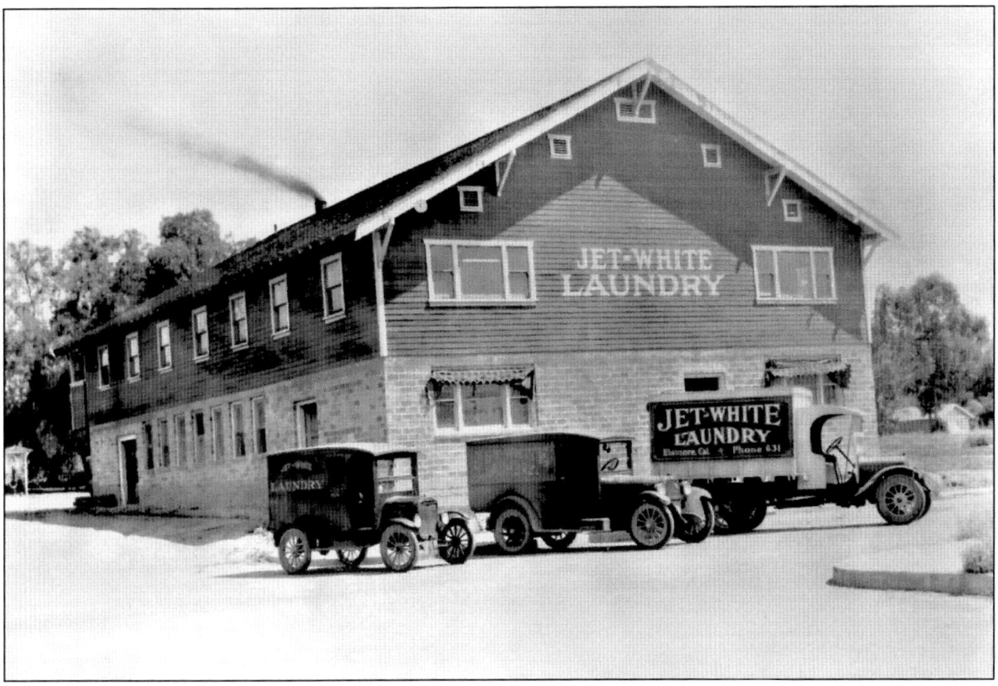


The Jet-White Laundry Company was a successful business in Lake Elsinore in the early 20th century. Here we see the company's delivery trucks ready for pickups and deliveries. (Courtesy Riverside County Library System.)

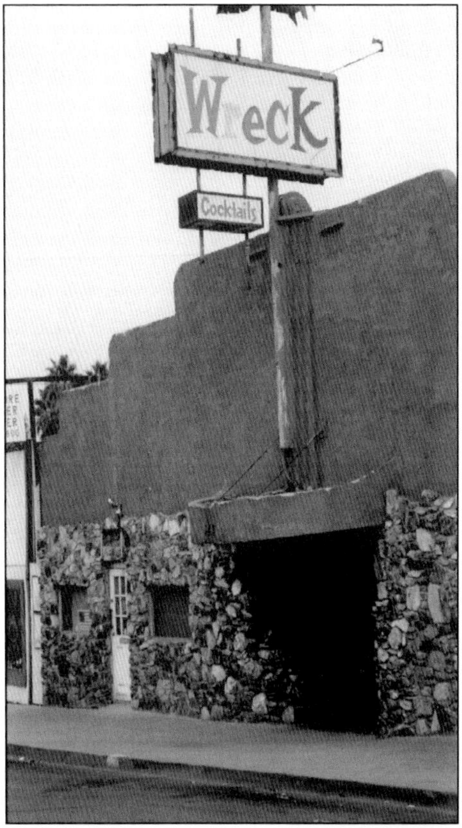


The Wreck has seen many uses in Elsinore since its opening in 1913 as a livery stable. It was changed to a garage when automobiles were introduced to the area. It was later remodeled into a bowling alley, and is now a place to play pool and reminisce about the old days of Elsinore. The Wreck is located on Graham Street. (Courtesy Louise Rowden.)

In 1922, the Clewett and Graham City Garage, located at Main and Sulphur Streets, was built by Clewett and Perty C. Graham. The building was later taken over by John's Ambulance Service and Western Auto. (Courtesy Riverside County Library System.)

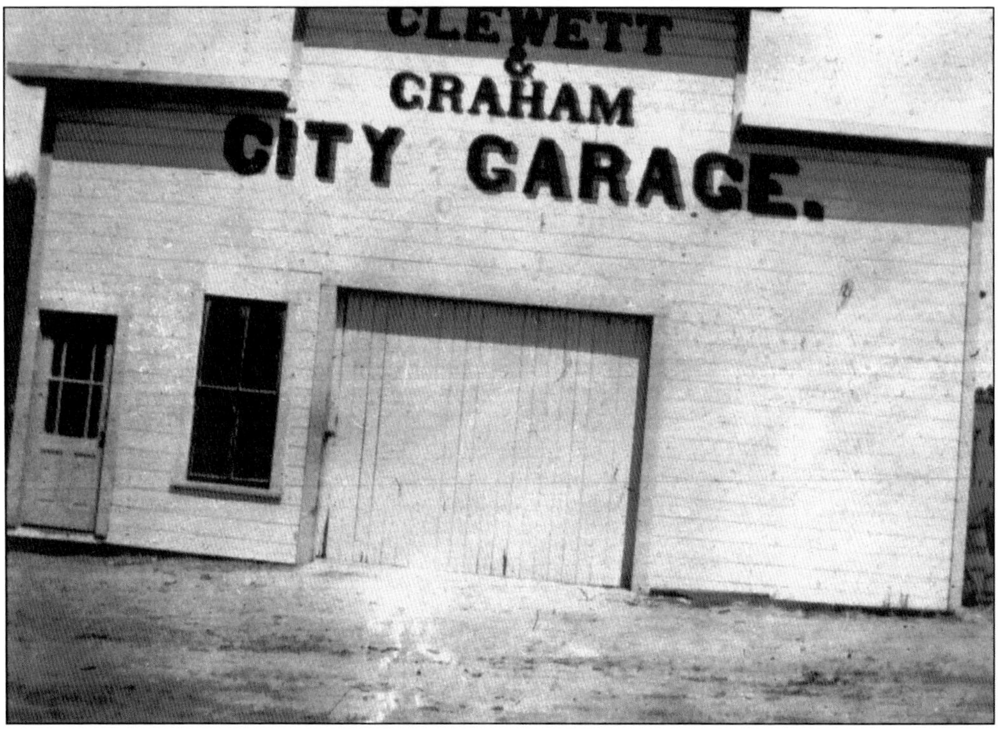

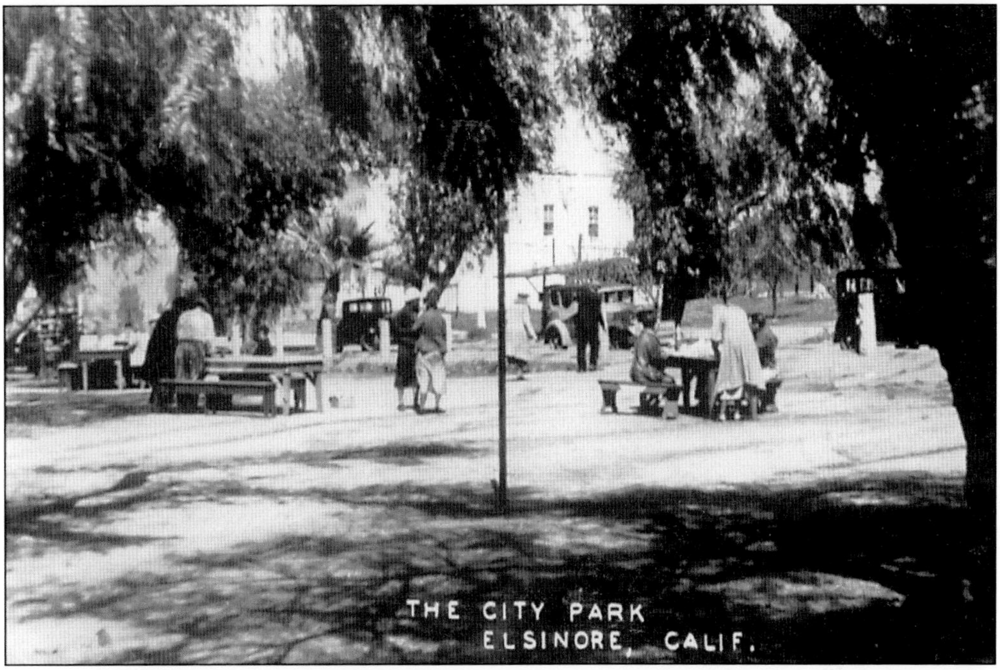


In 1906, Heald donated land to be used for a city park. More land for the same park was also deeded by Hattie and C. S. Traphagen. Some Elsinore citizens planted trees and, together with band members, built a wooden bandstand. A masonry barbeque stove was contributed later by the Elsinore Women's Club. In 1938, when the country was recovering from the Great Depression, the Works Progress Administration (WPA) built a retaining wall around the park. (Courtesy Riverside County Library System.)

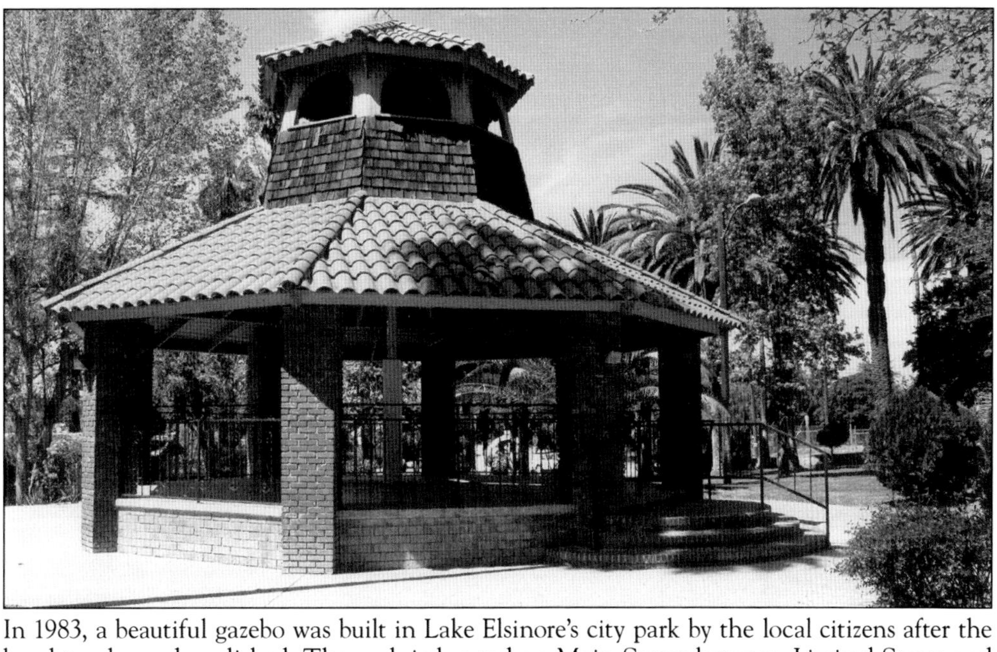

In 1983, a beautiful gazebo was built in Lake Elsinore's city park by the local citizens after the bandstand was demolished. The park is located on Main Street between Limited Street and Library Street. (Courtesy Edythe J. Greene.)

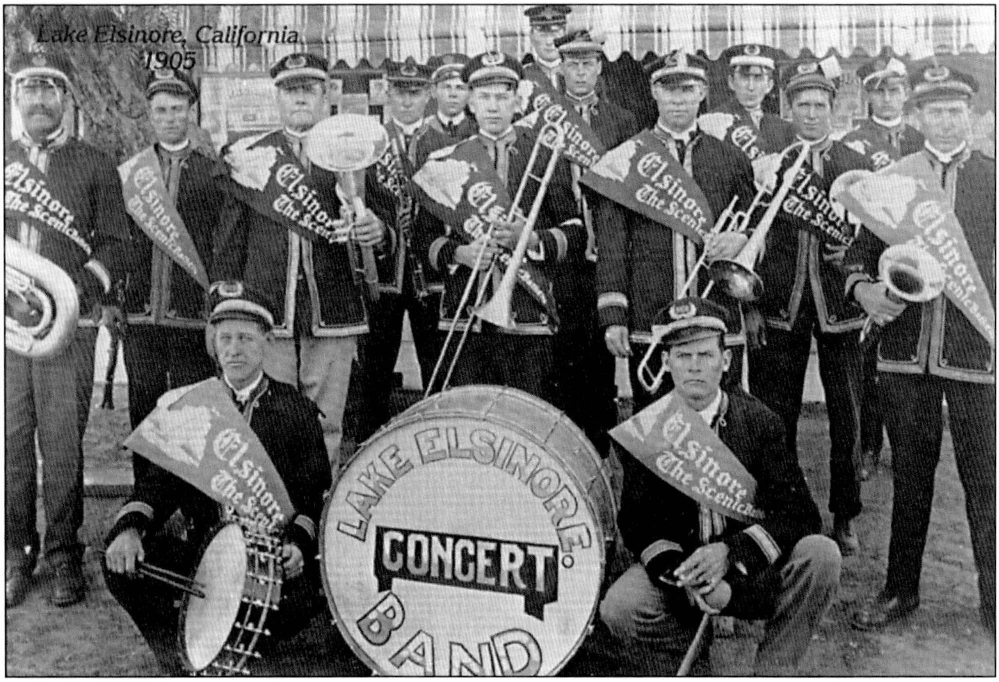


The Lake Elsinore Concert Band played at the local park. Here in this 1905 photograph we see the band's leader, Elmer Michener, in the top row, second from the left. John Graham is fifth from the right in the same row. (Courtesy Dr. Timothy Kimble, D.C.)

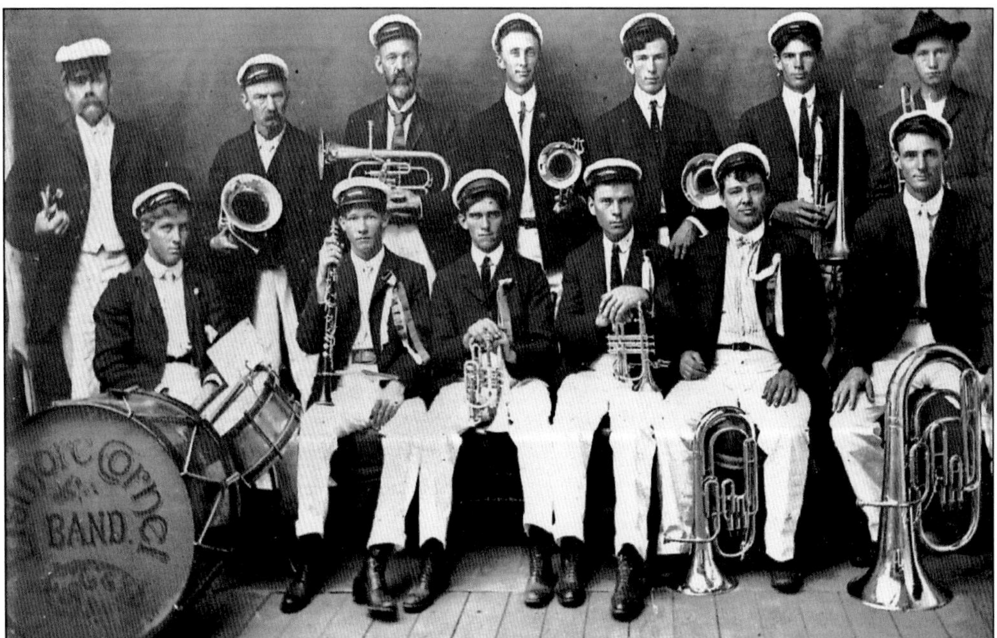


Elmer Michener was secured as leader and instructor of a band formed in 1904 and named the Elsinore Cornet Band. It leased the Bank Hall for a year. In 1905, the Grand Ball was given by the band boys at the Bank Hall. Admission, including supper, was $1. (Courtesy Riverside County Library System.)

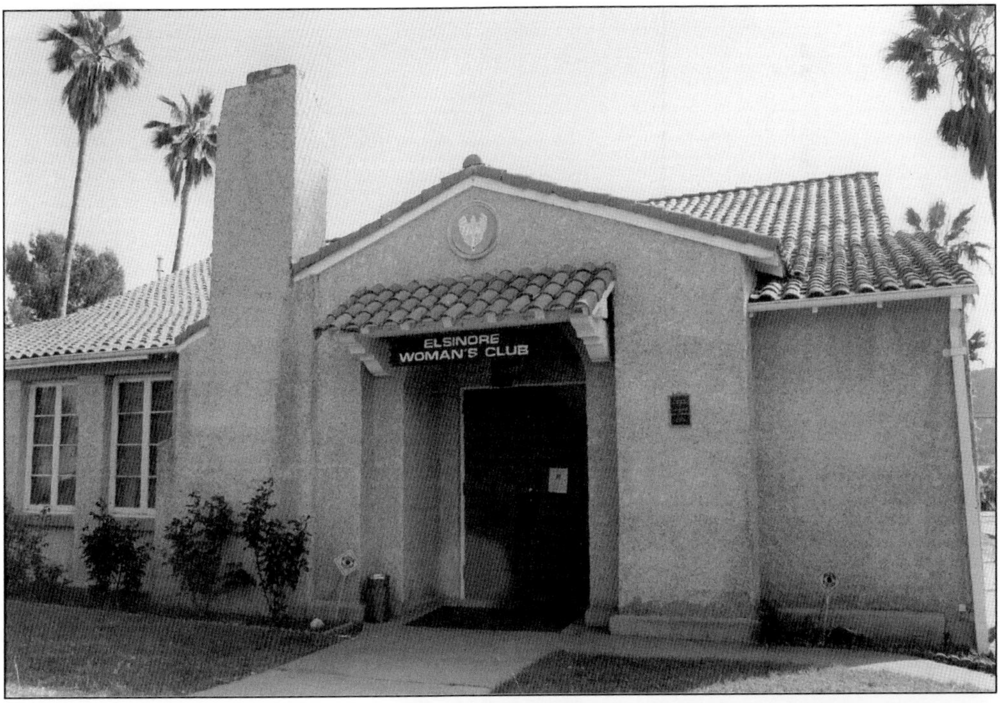


The Elsinore Woman's Club will celebrate its 100th anniversary on February 9, 2006. It was formed to extend the sphere of the club's influence in education, philanthropy, welfare, moral and social values, civic duties, and the fine arts to its members and to the public. The dream of a clubhouse came true when Mrs. Isabel J. Norris deeded a lot at Lowell and Graham Avenues, and pledged $1,000 a year for five years to build the structure. (Courtesy Edythe J. Greene.)

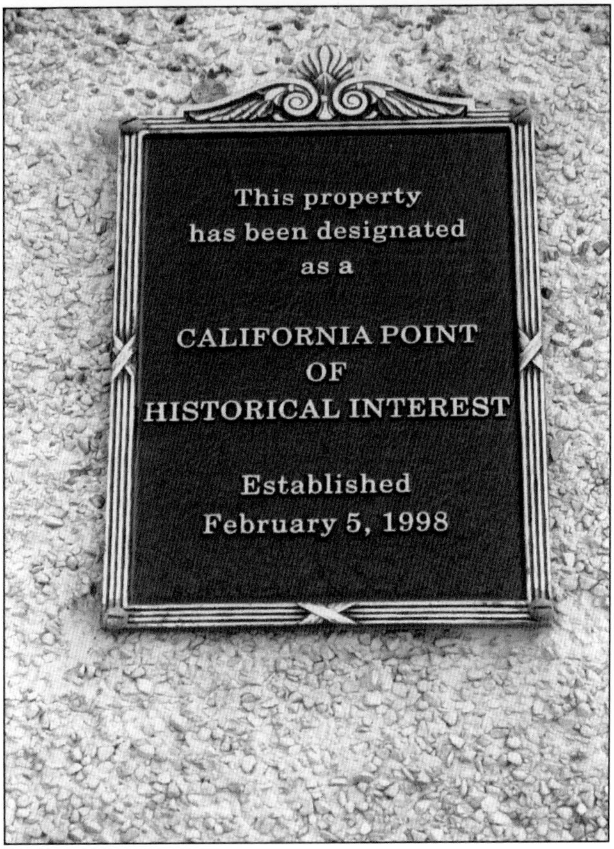


The attractive clubhouse of the Elsinore Woman's Club at 710 West Graham Avenue is Mediterranean/Spanish in style with a Spanish tile, gabled roof, stucco siding, and arched windows. The interior has hardwood floors, a large meeting room with a stage, and a large kitchen for banquets. It has been designated as a California Point of Historical Interest. (Courtesy Edythe J. Greene.)

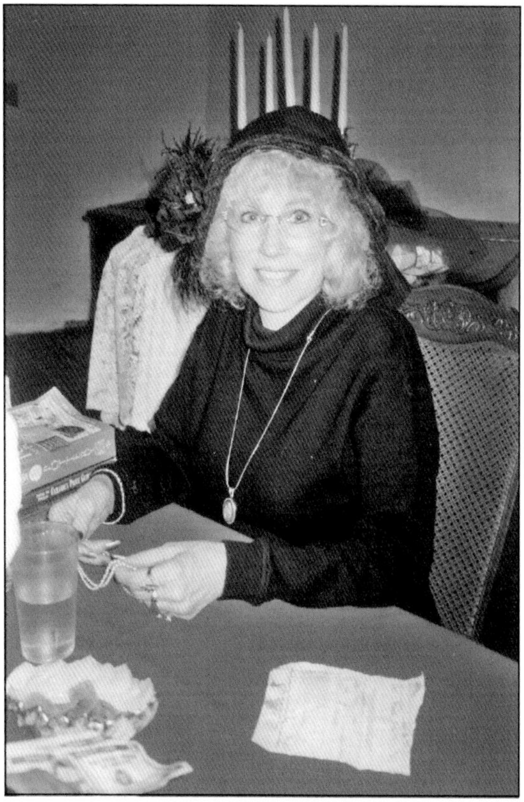

The Heritage Dinner and Antique Road Show is one of the many types of fund-raising benefits held by the Elsinore Woman's Club. Knowledgeable antique dealers, such as Nancy Collins, pictured here, appraise treasures at the fund-raisers. (Courtesy Louise Rowden.)

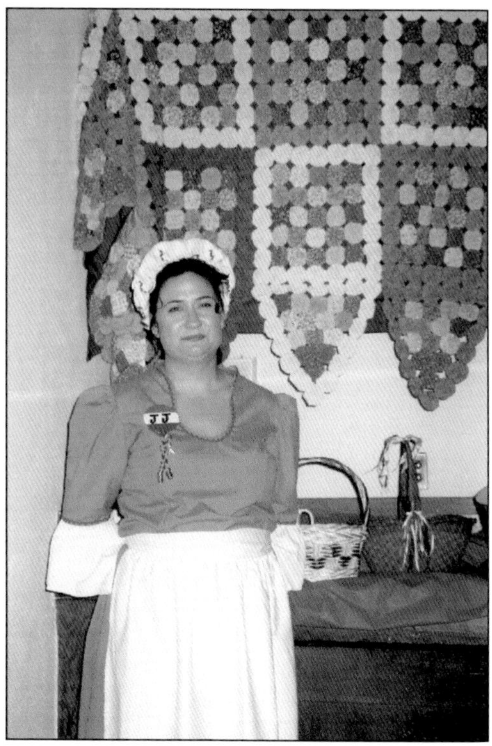


J. J. Swanson stands in front of a handmade quilt that was raffled along with many other items at a recent Heritage Dinner, cooked and served by Elsinore Woman's Club. (Courtesy Louise Rowden.)

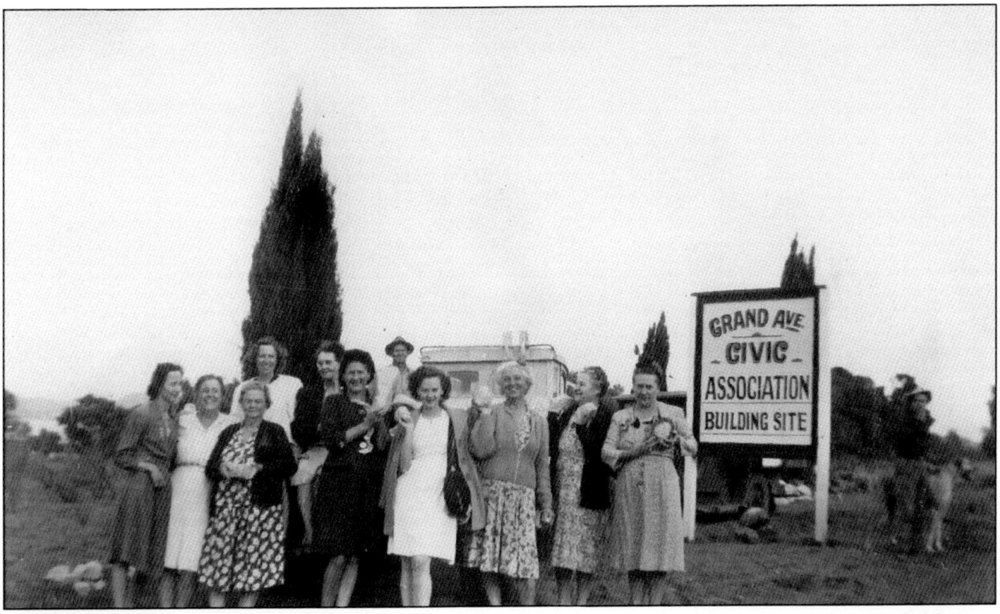


Grand Avenue was such an active place during Elsinore's mid-20th century that a clubhouse seemed to be needed. Its construction became a community voluntary project and, by May 1948, the first social event took place there. The same building still serves the community. (Courtesy Betty Burke.)

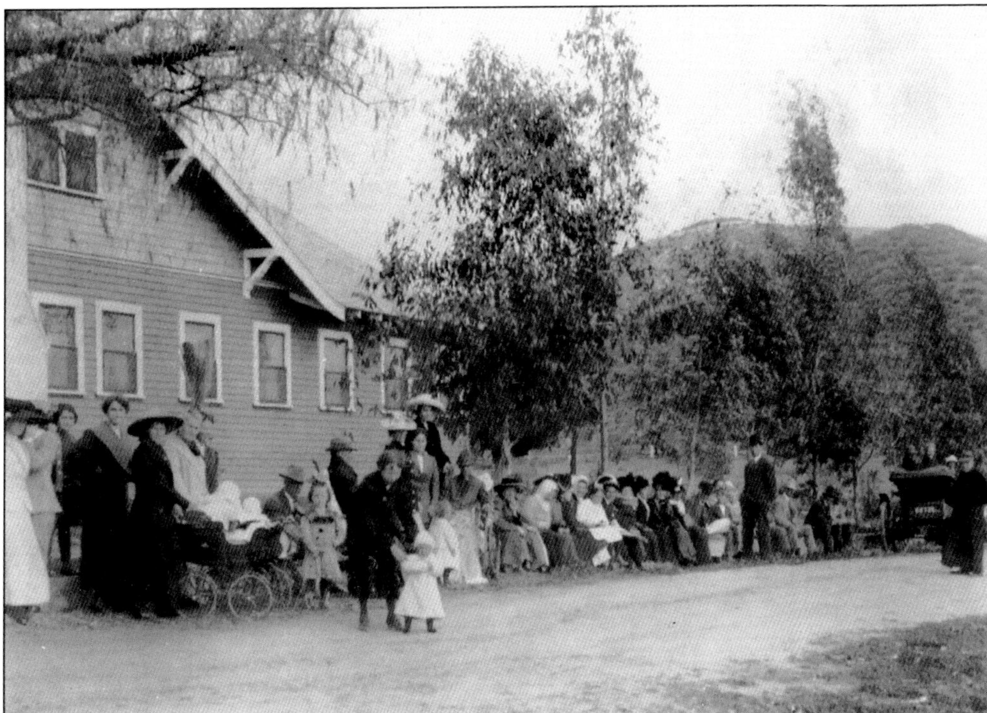

Elsinore has been a town of parades since its very early days. People lined along the dirt streets to get a good view. (Courtesy Riverside County Library System.)

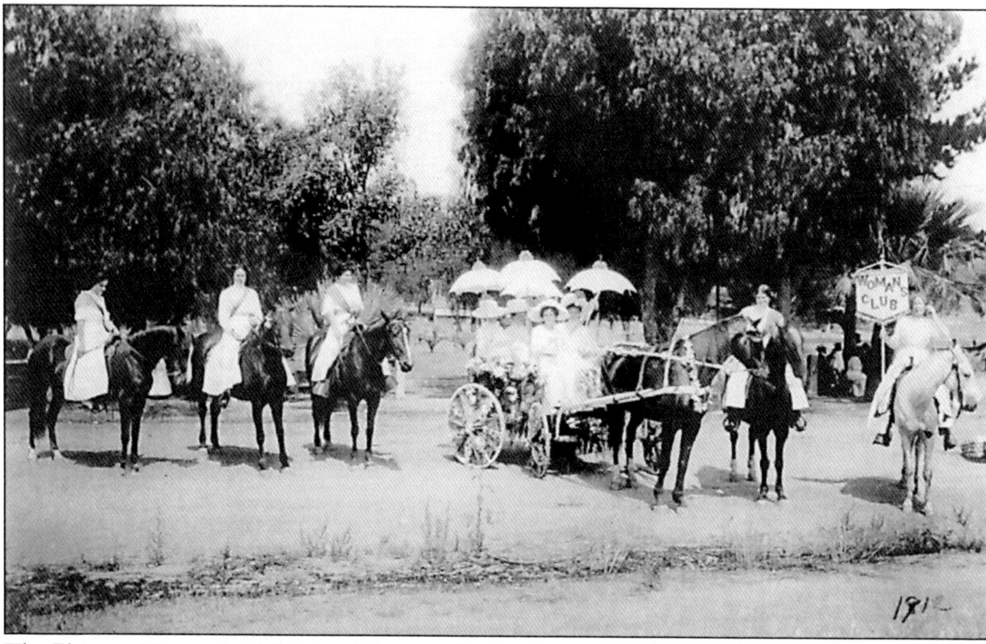


The Elsinore Woman's Club joined the parade clutching parasols—some riding in a horse-drawn carriages while others rode horses. (Courtesy Elsinore Historical Society.)

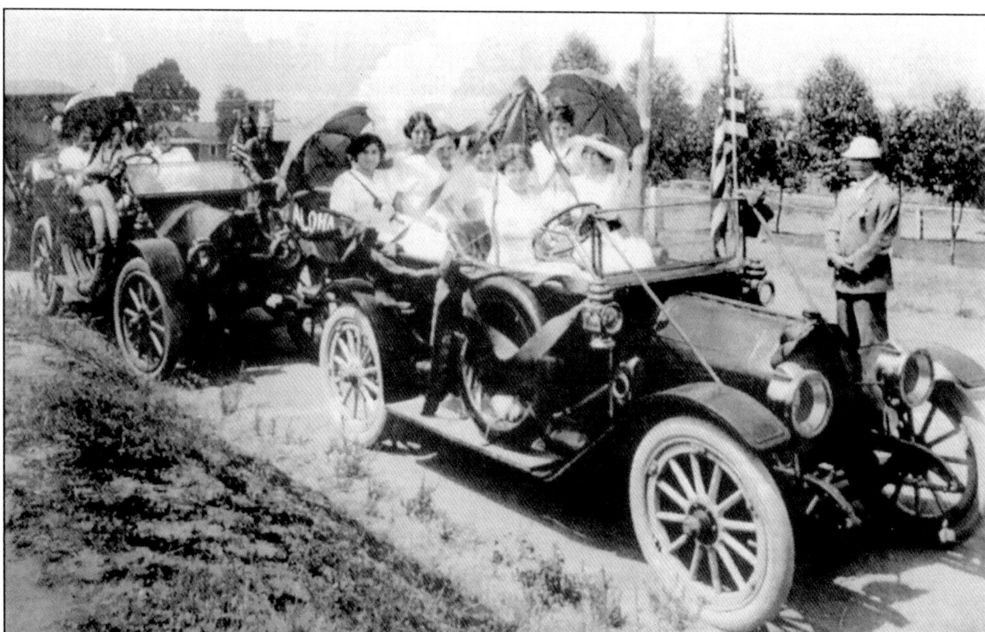


The parade horses were replaced by cars in the first decades of the 20th century. Here the automobiles, filled with women, are elaborately decorated with an American flag and festive ribbons. (Courtesy Elsinore Historical Society.)

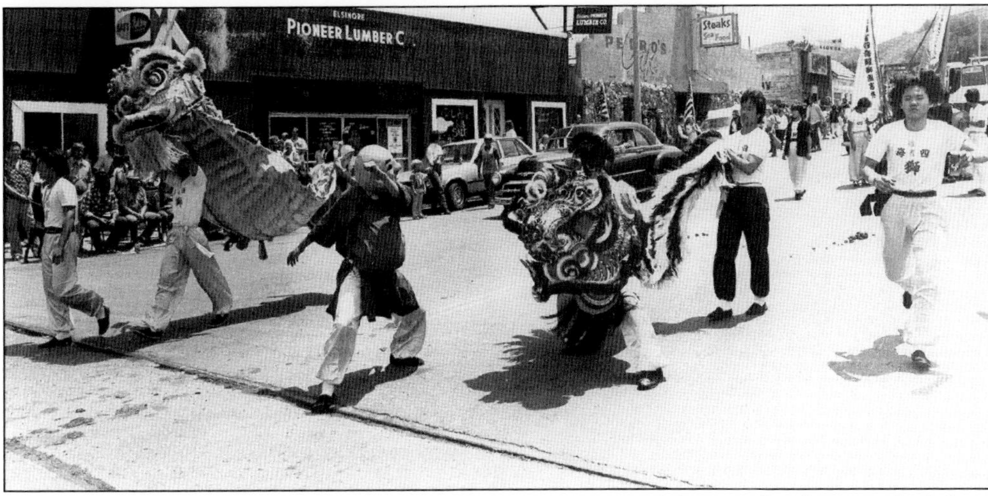


As years passed, more groups wearing elaborate costumes joined the parades that marched down Graham Street. (Courtesy Jeanie Corral.)

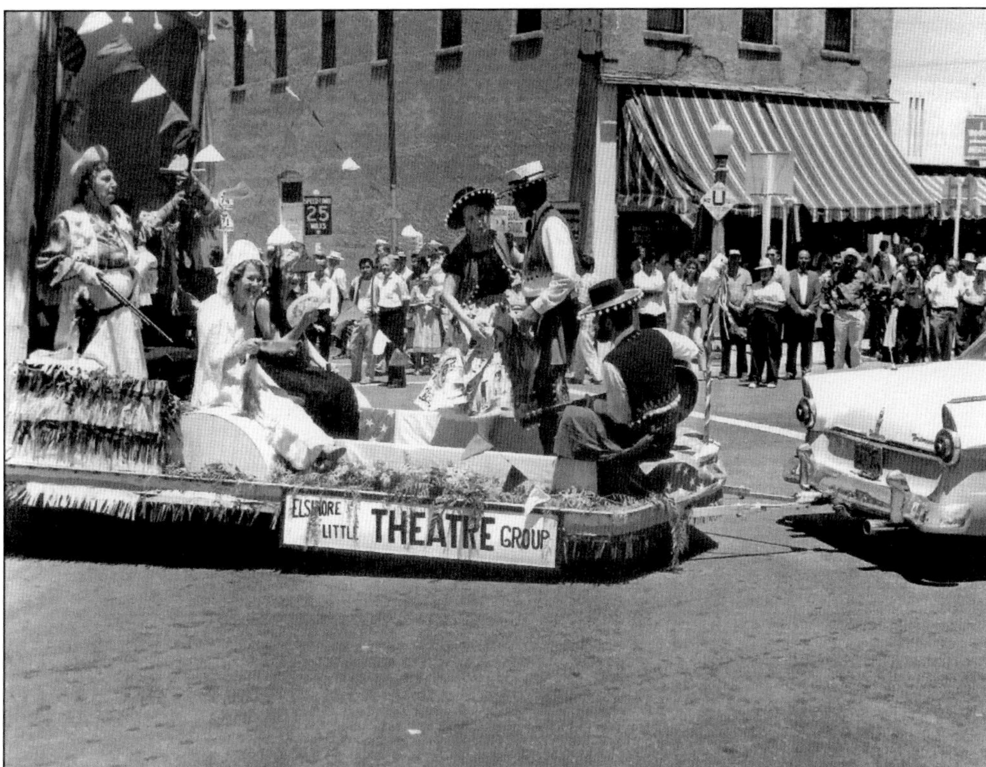


The Elsinore Little Theatre Group has a large, beautiful float with many people dancing and playing music. (Courtesy Main Street Mercantile.)

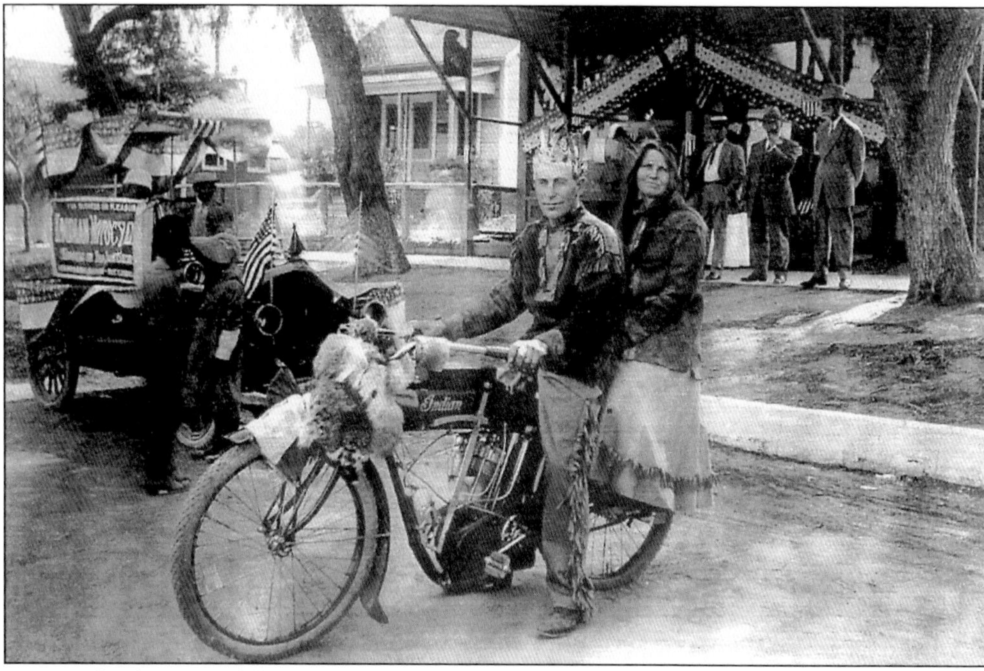

Waiting for the start of the parade is a couple on an Indian motorcycle. The man is dressed in a Native American costume with feathers on his head. (Courtesy Jeanie Corral.)

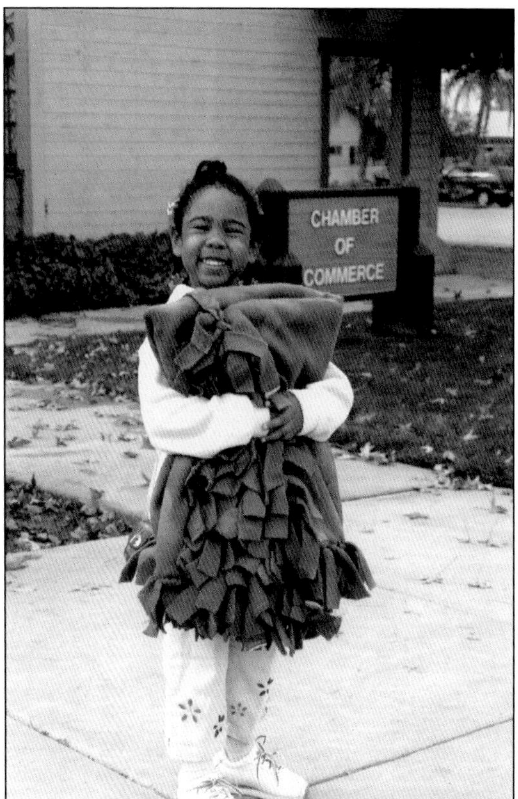


To this day, the Unity Parade has been successful in bringing the residents of Elsinore together. Waiting in front of the chamber of commerce on Graham Street is this young girl, obviously happy to be there. (Courtesy Louise Rowden.)

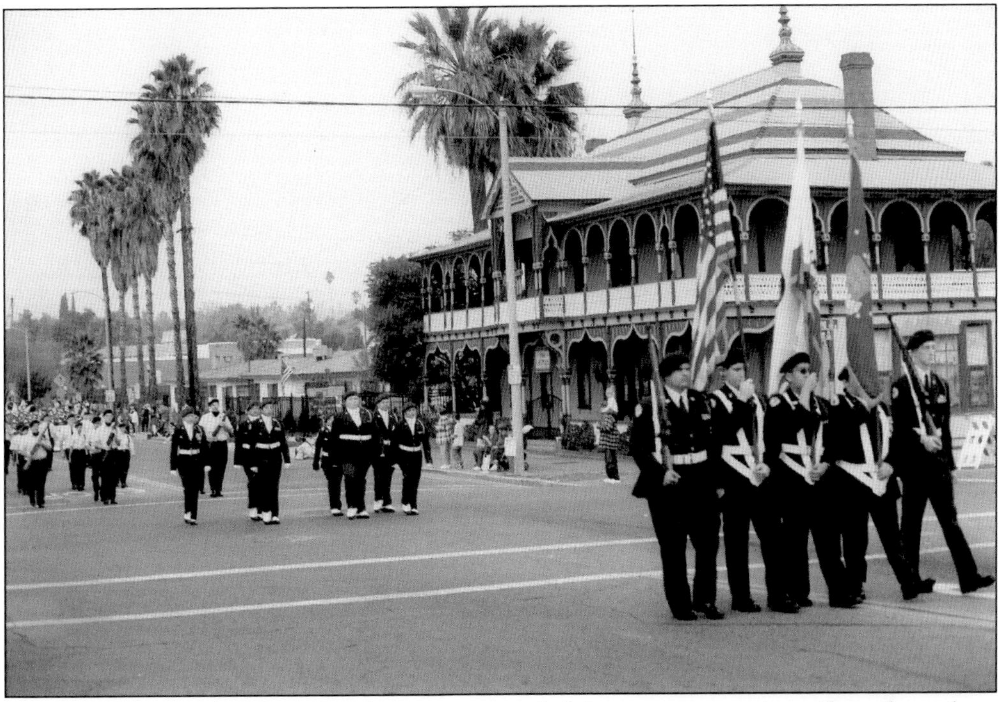

One assemblage in the Unity Parade was comprised of these young men in uniform shown here passing the historic Chimes Building on Graham Street. (Courtesy Louise Rowden.)

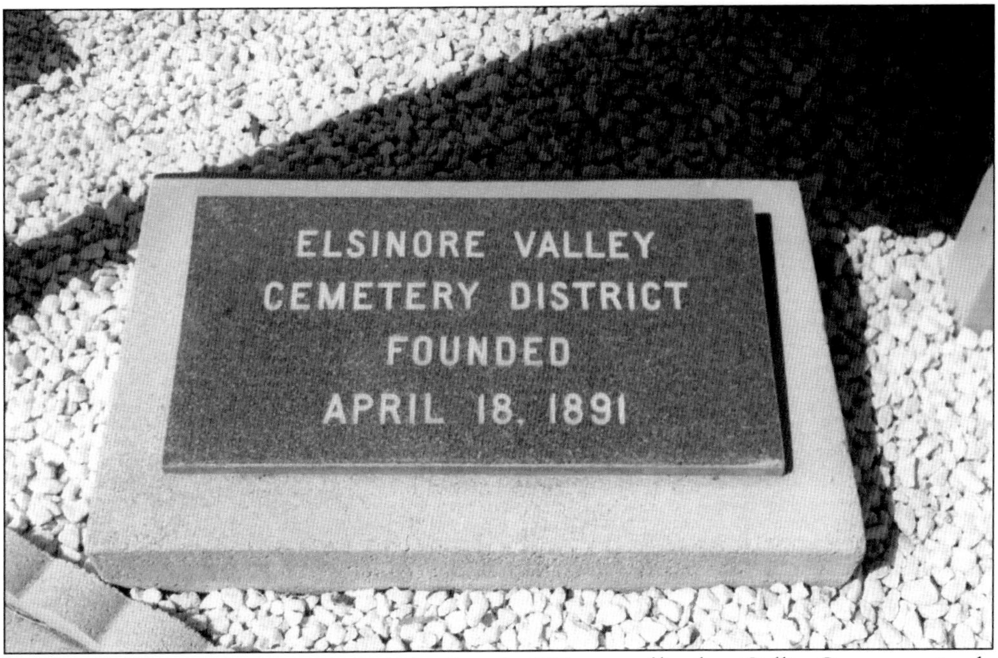


In 1891, the Elsinore Cemetery Association bought 12½ acres of land on Collier Street, previously used to grow eucalyptus trees, from Peter Wall for $1,250. (Courtesy Louise Rowden.)

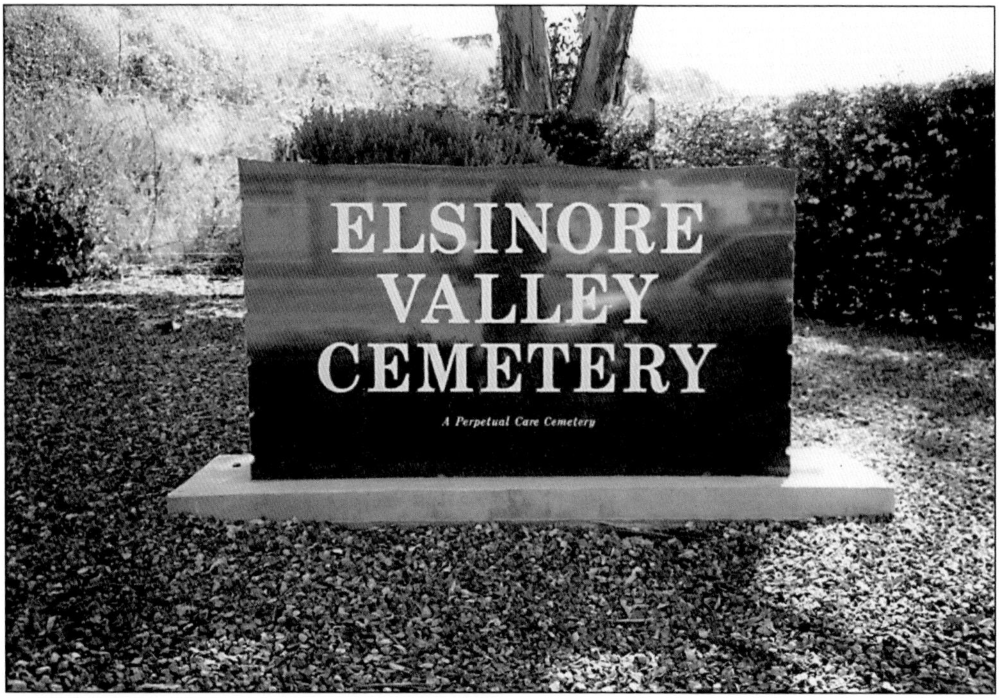


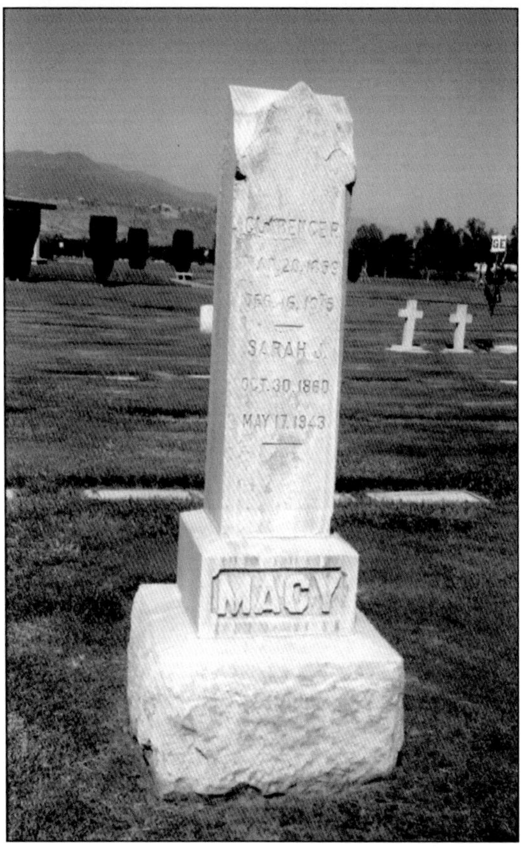


The Elsinore Valley Cemetery was originally named the Greenwood Cemetery. C. S. Merrifield was its superintendent until 1934 when he was succeeded by his son, Leslie Merrifield, who served until his retirement in 1974. Father and son operated the cemetery for 83 years. (Courtesy Louise Rowden.)

This old tombstone is still standing, contributing to a beautiful, peaceful atmosphere in the cemetery. (Courtesy Louise Rowden.)

# *Four*

# Historic Houses and Schools

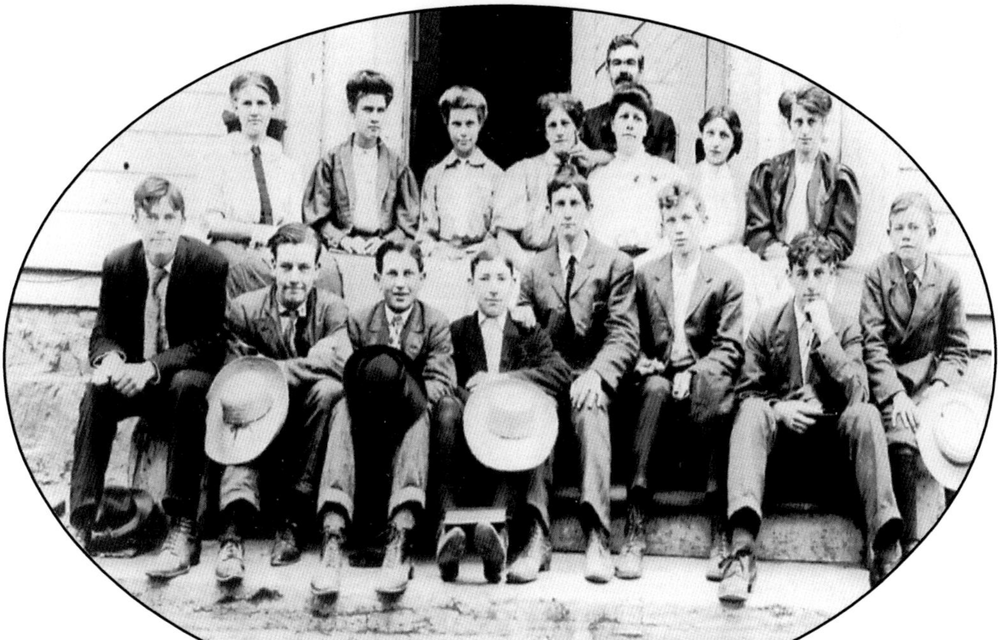

This group of elementary school children in 1907 poses on the front steps of the Grammar School building of Lake Elsinore. Pictured, from left to right, are (first row) Carswell McIntyre, George Keck, Earl Ellis, Ray Bohannan, Claude Craft, John Miles, Harry Pool, and Arthur Ramodale; (second row) Ruth Stewart, Altha Merrifield, Jessie Hanna, Altha Strickland, Rose Ellis, William Dunning, and Julia Strickland. The teacher, Malcolm McLean, is standing in the back. (Courtesy Riverside County Library System.)

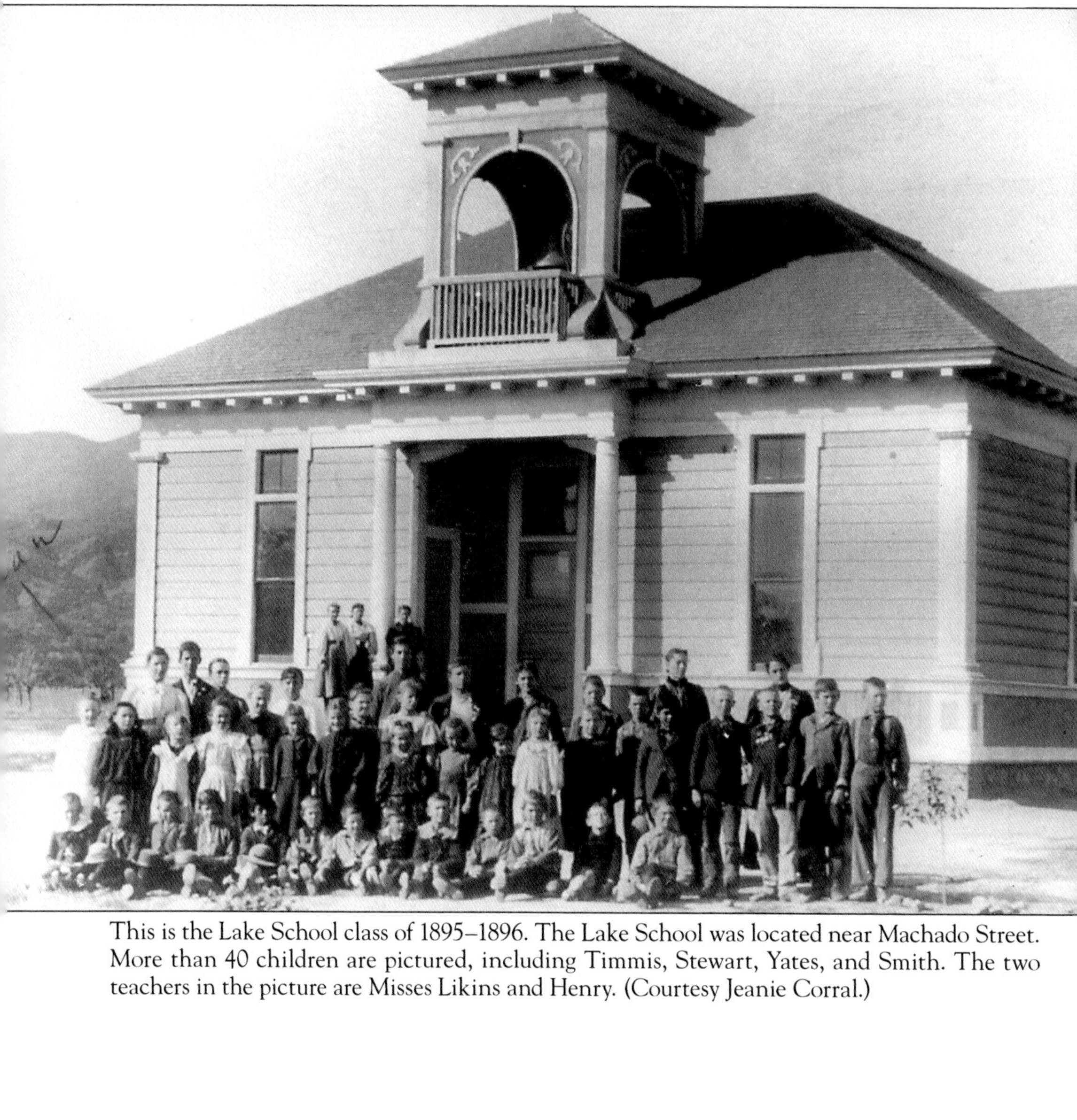

This is the Lake School class of 1895–1896. The Lake School was located near Machado Street. More than 40 children are pictured, including Timmis, Stewart, Yates, and Smith. The two teachers in the picture are Misses Likins and Henry. (Courtesy Jeanie Corral.)

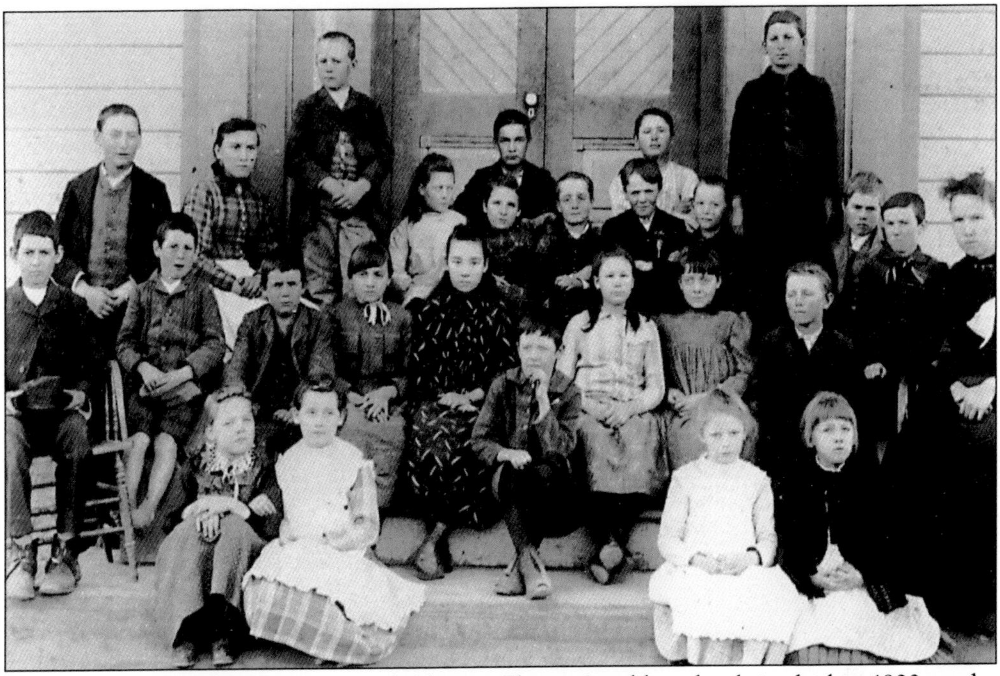

This is a class picture of elementary children in Elsinore's public schools in the late 1800s or the early 1900s. (Courtesy Riverside County Library System.)

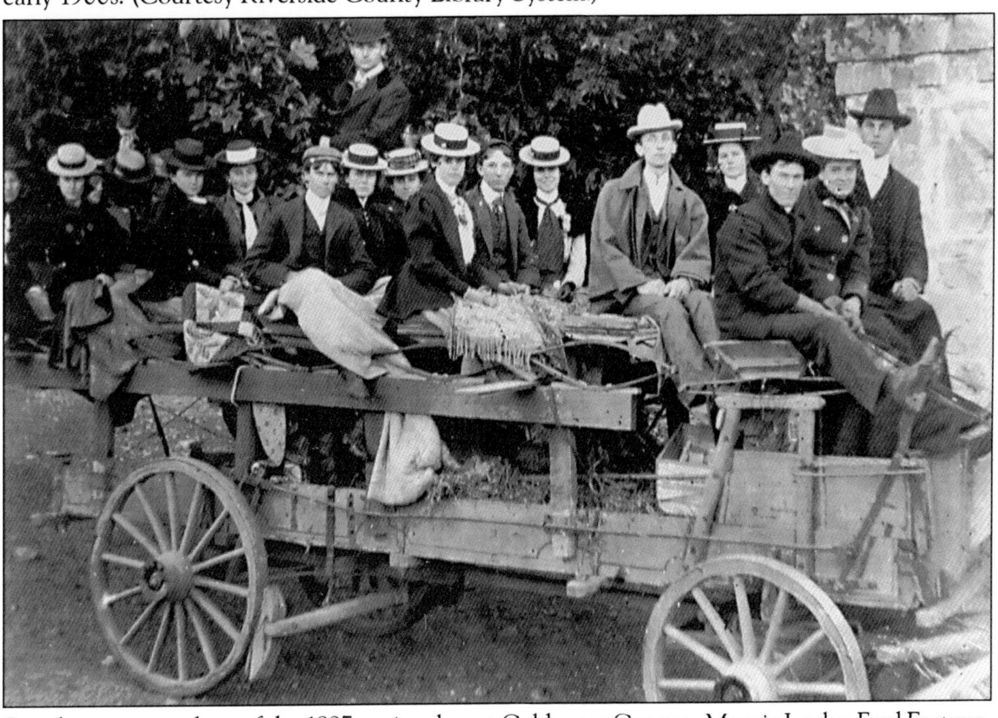

Seen here are members of the 1897 senior class at Coldwater Canyon: Maggie Lauler, Fred Fortune, Maud Minthorn, Carrie Lewis, William Lavayea, May Gilman, May Ward, Harry Hoag, Estelle McClintock, Leslie Wall, Olive Yates, John Peck, Stewart Clark, Guy Wilsey, Edith McConnell, and Harry Henderson. (Courtesy Riverside County Library System.)

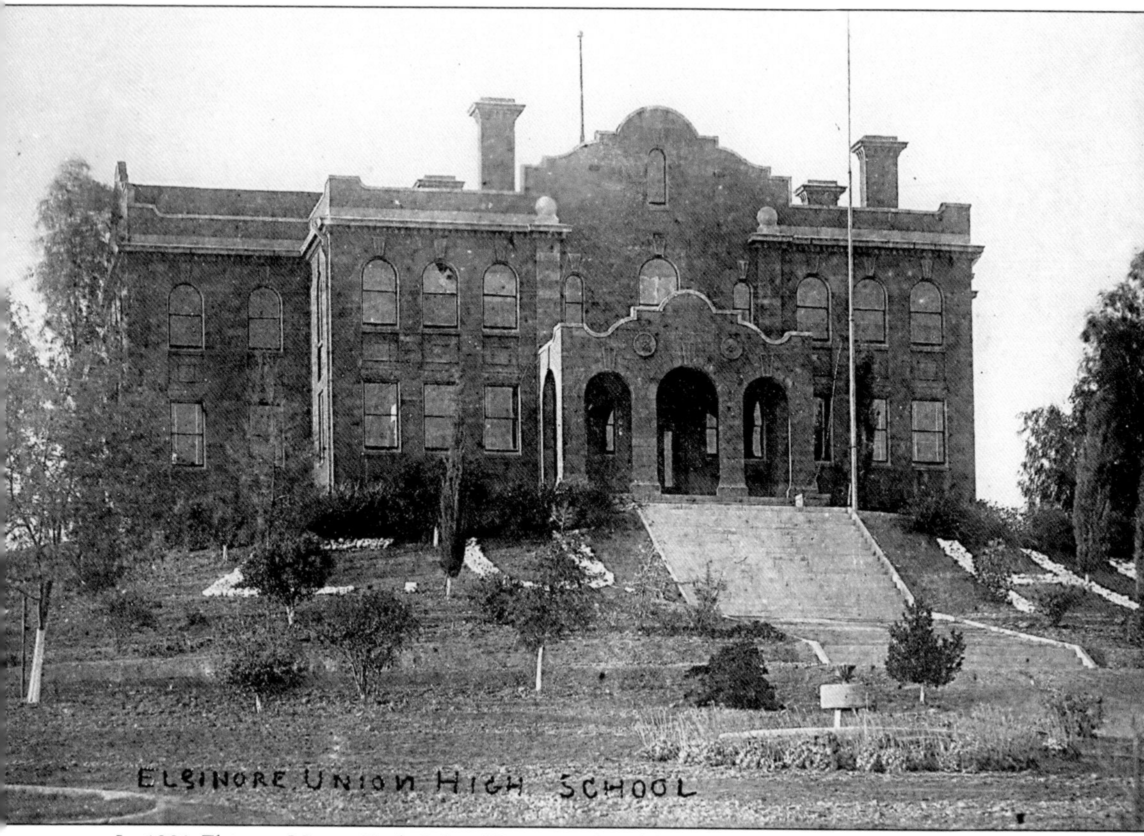


In 1891, Elsinore Union High School District, the oldest high school district in Riverside County, was formed. The first school had 10 students in attendance, and five were in the first graduating class of 1894. Pictured is the new high school building on West Graham Avenue in 1912 on a hill overlooking the lake. (Courtesy Jeanie Corral.)

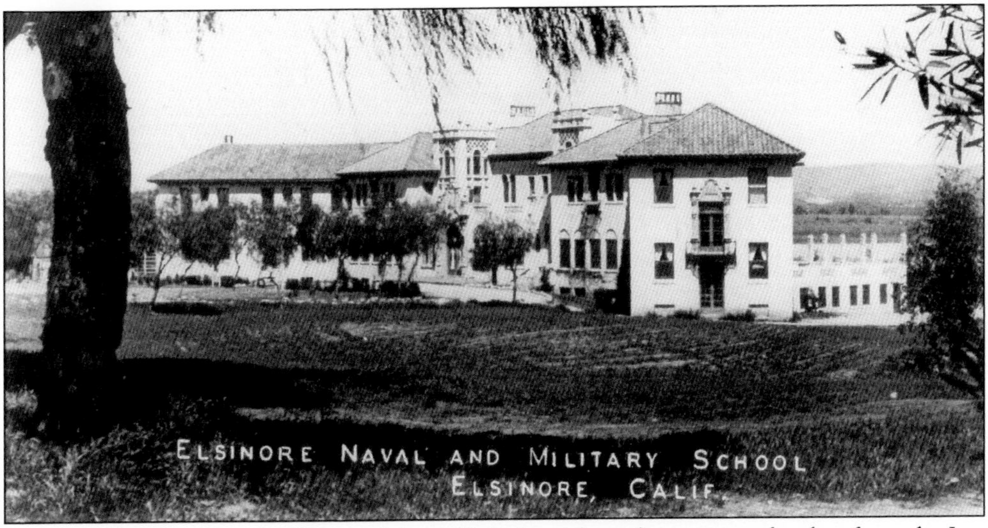


In July 1933, Maj. Glen Conklin and Capt. P. A. Jones brought a group of cadets from the Los Angeles Pacific Military Academy to Lake Elsinore for a summer session. They stayed at the old Heald home. During this session, it was determined that the Lake Elsinore Southern California Athletic and Country Club would be an ideal home for a military academy. The Elsinore Naval and Military School was then established at this location. (Courtesy Jeanie Corral.)

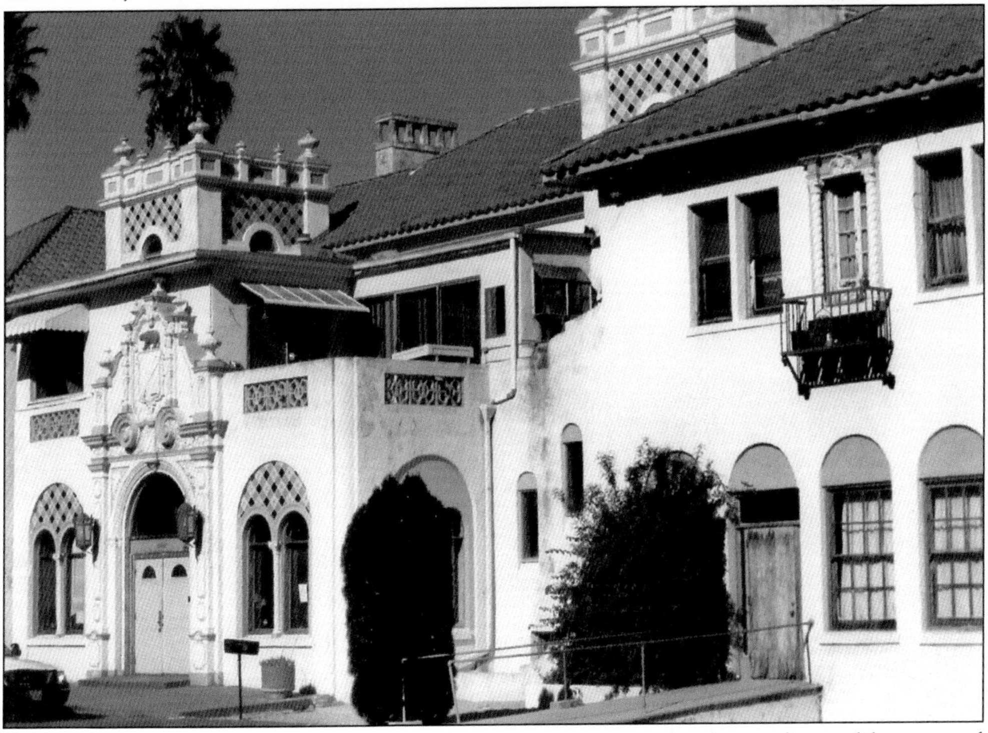

Most graduating seniors from the Elsinore Naval and Military School were thoroughly prepared for entering college. One such student was Bela Lugosi Jr., whose well-known father had played the elegant vampire count in the 1931 movie *Dracula*. The Lugosi family owned two homes near the lake where they spent vacations from 1944 to 1952, as well as other quiet times on weekend getaways from the glitter of Hollywood. Bela Lugosi Jr. became a lawyer. (Courtesy Louise Rowden.)

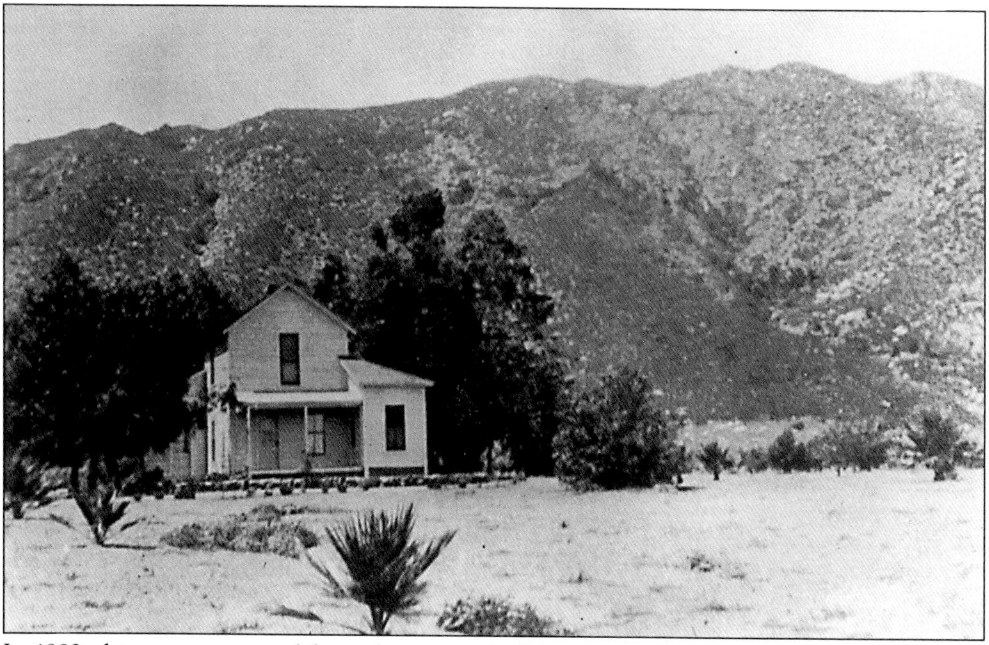

In 1883, this two-story wood frame house was built near Grand and Rio by Wilson Heald and his wife, Sara Macy Heald. They were the parents of Franklin and Charles Heald. Dr. Franklin Heald lived here until he built his new home in 1888. (Courtesy Jeanie Corral.)

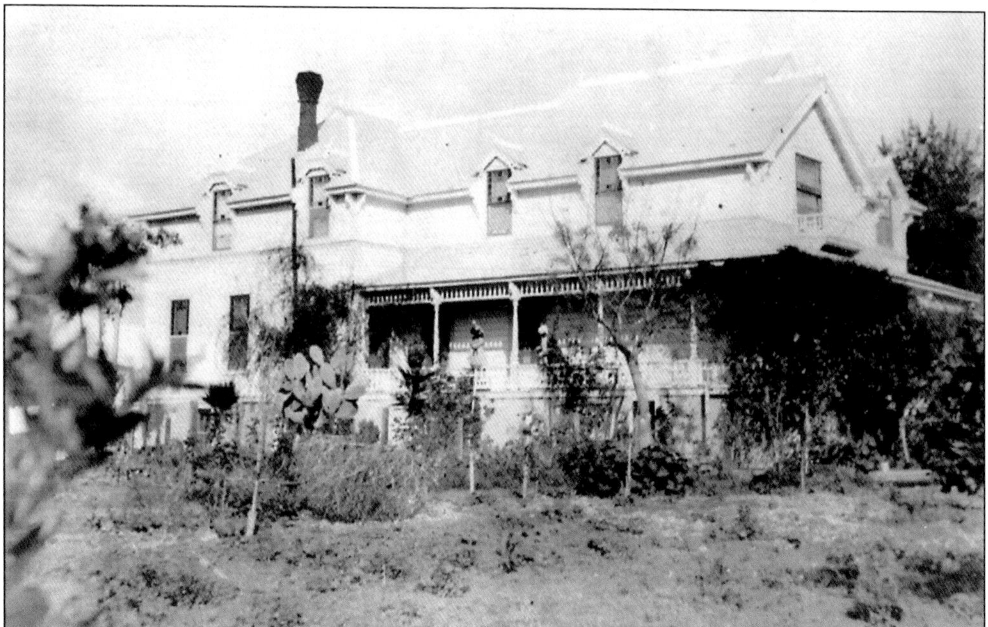

This attractive 19-room, three-story colonial house was at one time located on the west side of Poe Street and commanded an outstanding view of the lake and the mountains. However, Dr. Franklin Heald vacated the house when his view of the lake became obstructed by olive and pepper trees. During World War II, the home was used as the headquarters for the Women's Land Army and was named Casa de Campo or Camp House. Unfortunately Casa de Campo was razed in April 1951 when the lake was dry. (Courtesy Riverside County Library System.)

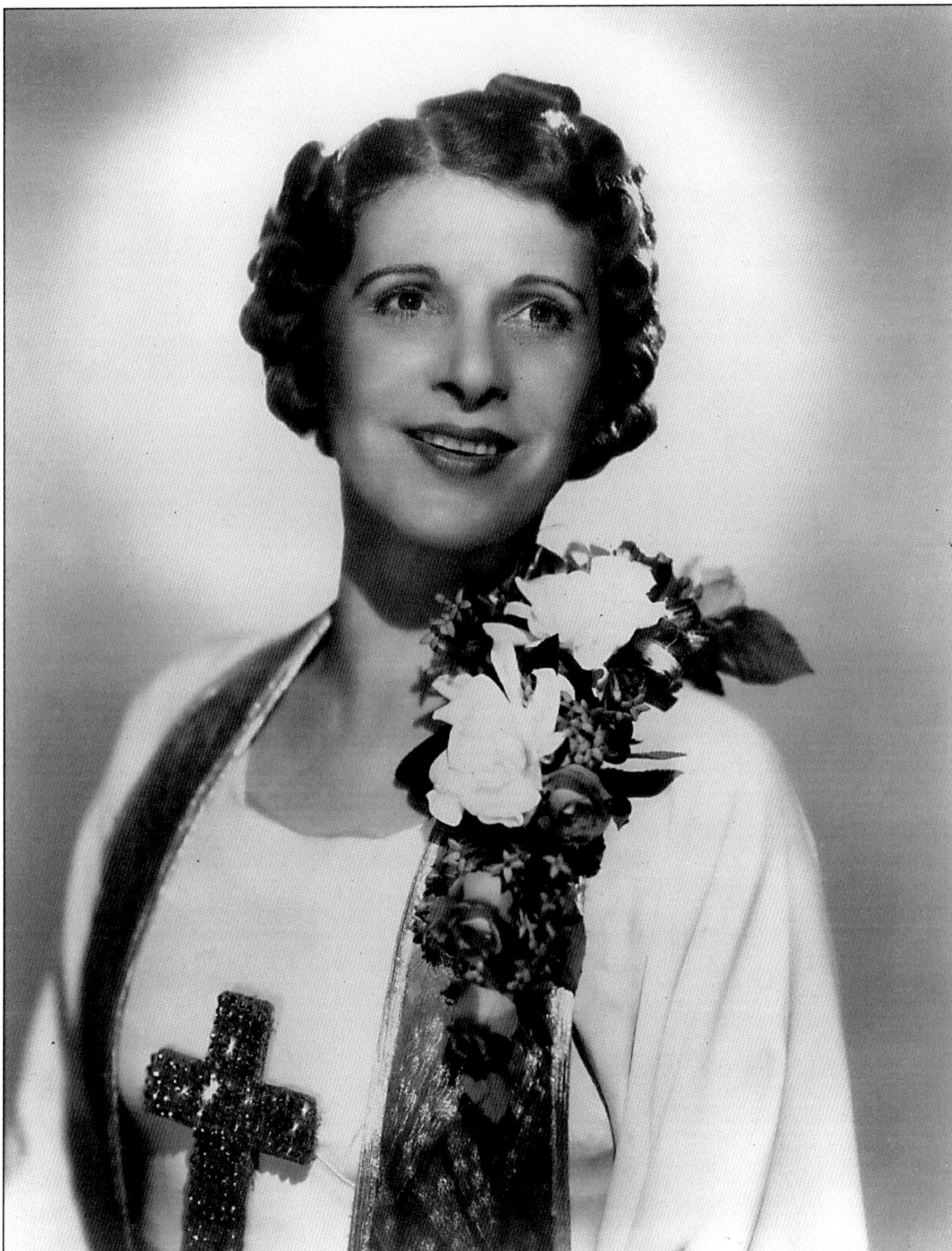

Aimee Semple McPherson (1890–1944) was a well-known evangelist based in southern California from the 1920s through the 1940s. Her Angelus Temple in the Echo Park area of Los Angeles became well-known across the nation and throughout the world. During these years, she enjoyed living in her ornate castle overlooking Lake Elsinore. (Courtesy Heritage Department, International Church of the Foursquare Gospel.)

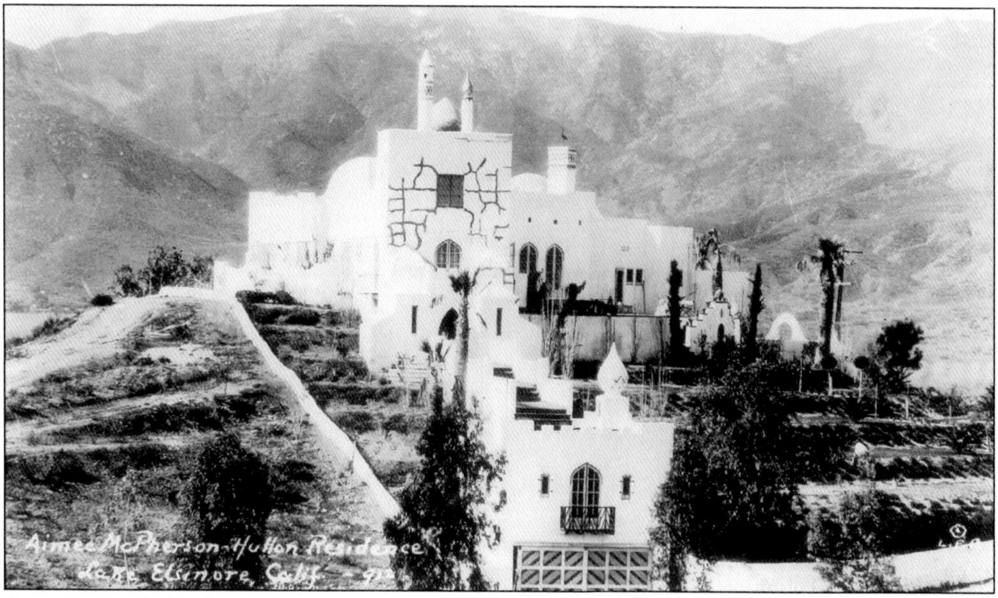


Aimee's Castle, built in 1929, belonged to Aimee Semple McPherson, the renowned evangelist. With its Moorist arches, a minaret, and dome, this ornate residence in the hills above Lake Elsinore had many rooms, including three bedrooms, two-and-a-half baths, maid's quarters, a library, and an 18-by-30-foot salon. This unusual home has been called one of the wonders of Riverside County and an architectural treasure. (Courtesy Jeanie Corral.)

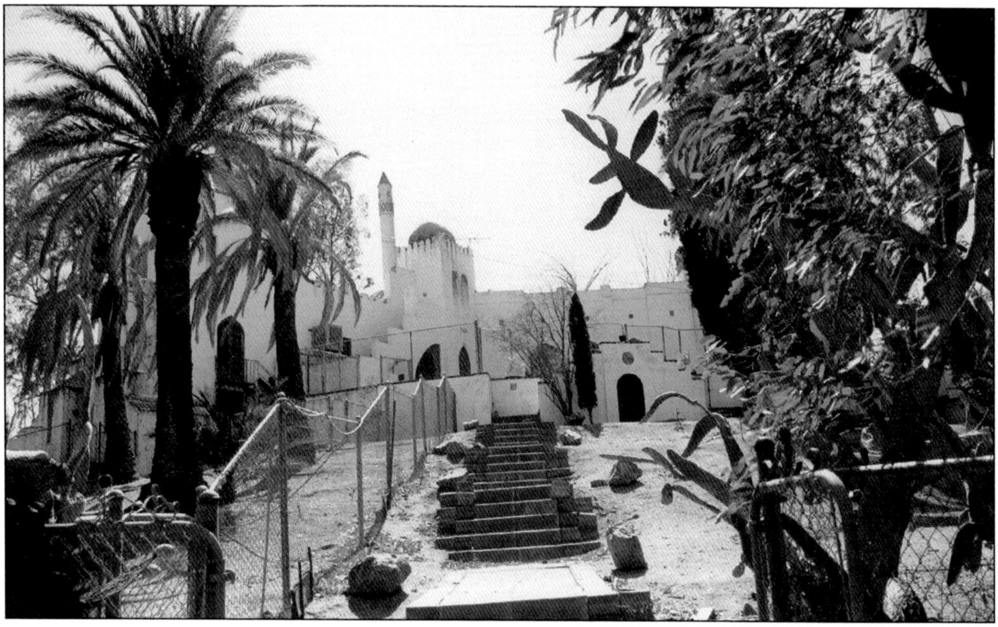

In earlier days, Aimee Semple McPherson toured through the southern United States in her "Gospel Car," a 1912 Packard with religious slogans painted on the side. She would sometimes stand in the backseat of this convertible giving sermons through a bullhorn. Above is a view of the steps leading up to Aimee's Castle overlooking Lake Elsinore. An unusual feature of this ornate castle is the underground catacombs where one could sit undisturbed and meditate. (Courtesy Edythe J. Greene.)

This is the entry way to the castle owned by Aimee Semple McPherson, founder of the worldwide Foursquare Gospel Church. McPherson's Moorish-style, 5,000-square-foot home is situated high on a hill overlooking Lake Elsinore. The ornate structure is known to the town of Lake Elsinore simply as Aimee's Castle. For many years, it served as a retreat from the world for this well-loved evangelist. (Courtesy Edythe J. Greene.)

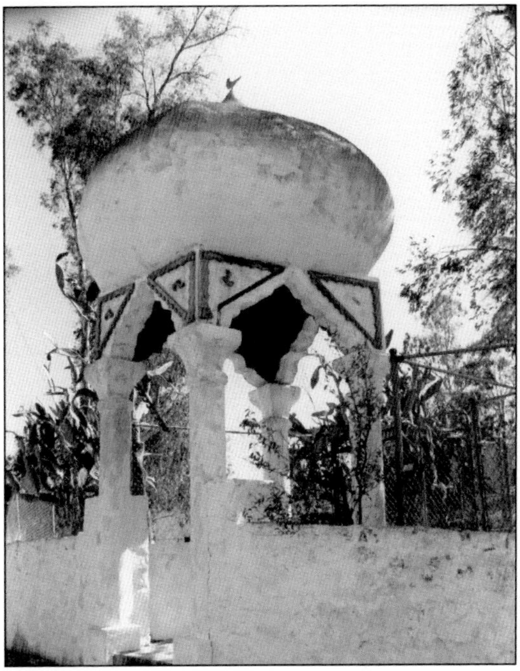

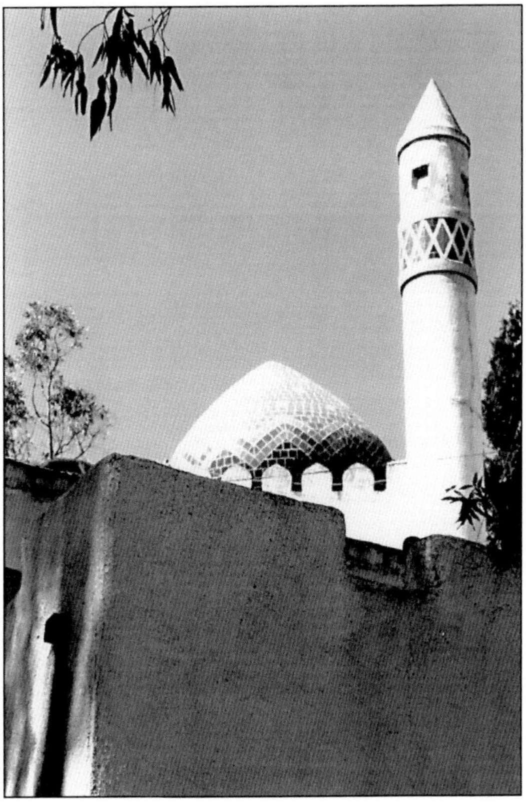

The dynamic Aimee Semple McPherson attracted a large following to her Pentecostal preaching, and in 1923 supervised the construction of the large domed church, Angelus Temple, with a seating capacity of over 5,000, in the Echo Park area of Los Angeles. The ornate minaret and dome of Aimee's Castle is shown overlooking Lake Elsinore. Built in 1929 at a cost of $229,000, the castle featured real gold and imported marble from Europe. (Courtesy Louise Rowden.)

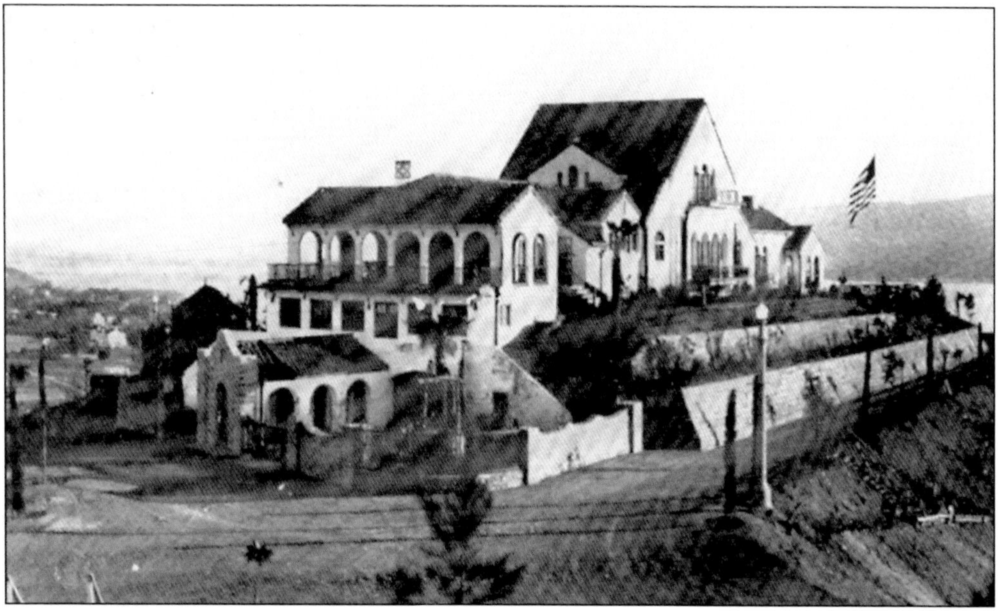

The Bredlau Castle in Lake Elsinore was built in 1926 by Henry Schultz, who had originated the Clevelin development and the Country Club Heights subdivision. Originally this beautiful building overlooking the lake from the top of a hill was called the Henry Schultz house. This unique building was the scene of many social gatherings in the 1920s and 1930s. (Courtesy Jeanie Corral.)

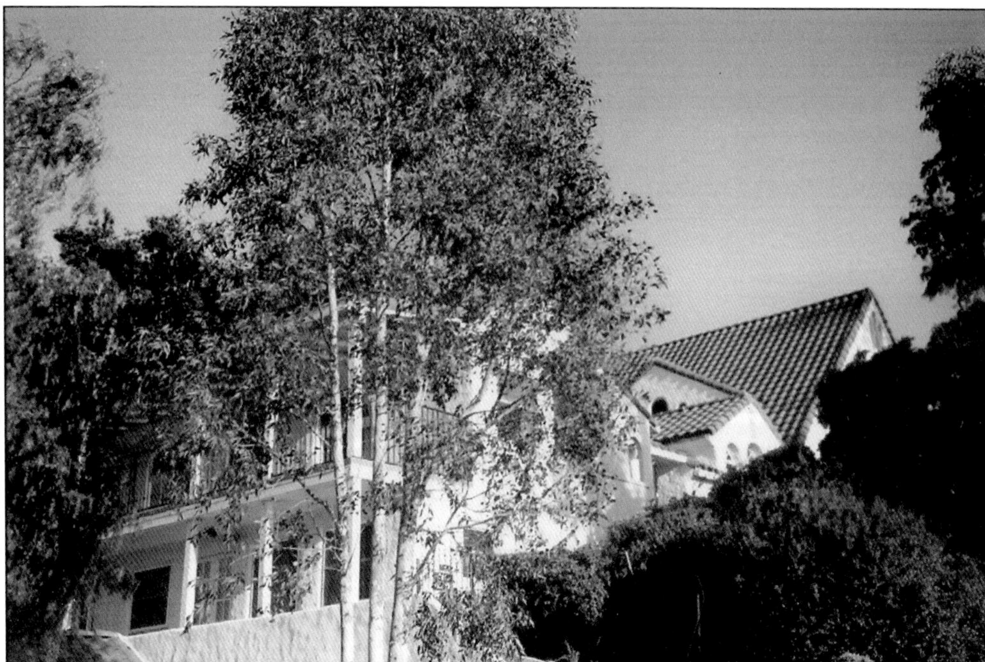

The Bredlau Castle has two stories, but is on four different levels and includes nine bedrooms and seven bathrooms within its 9,000-square-foot floor area. Also included is a hidden room complete with a sliding bookcase door that was used during Prohibition. (Courtesy Louise Rowden.)

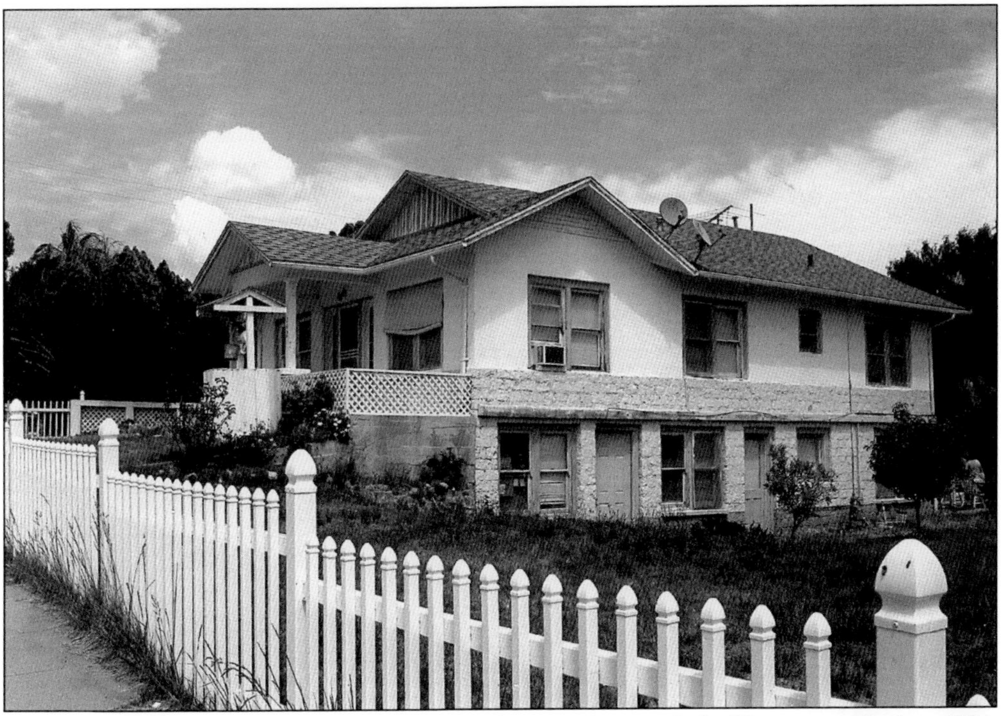

The home of the Merrifield family at 240–242 Chestnut Street in Lake Elsinore was built in 1924. Altha Couch Merrifield lived here until her demise in 1982. (Courtesy Edythe J. Greene.)

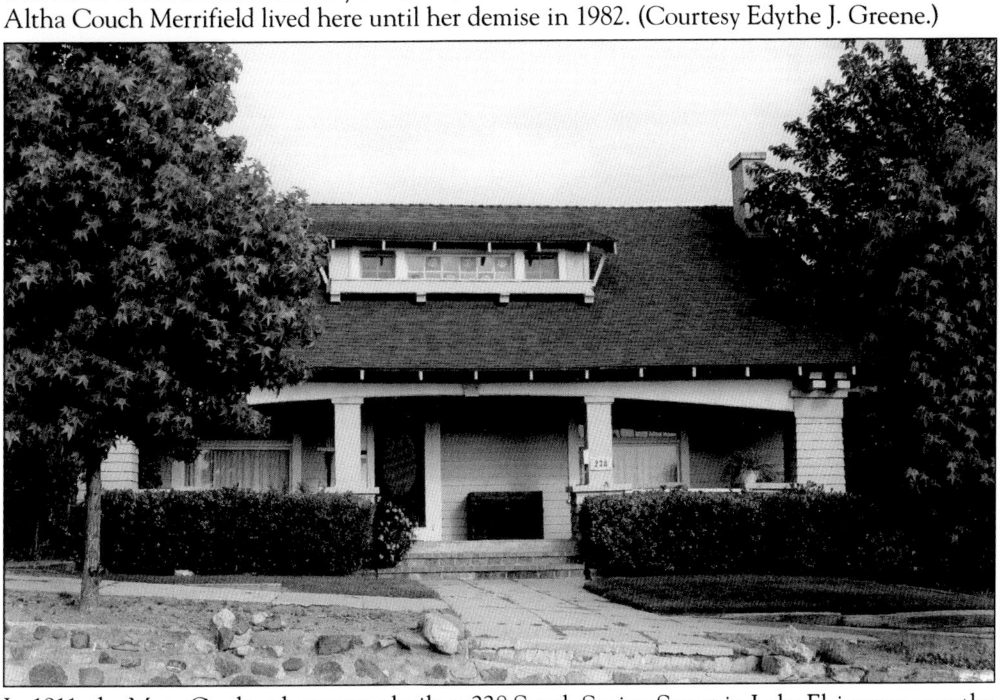

In 1911, the Mary Gardner house was built at 228 South Spring Street in Lake Elsinore across the street from the popular Lakeview Inn. Designed by architects Merrifield and March, the house has a large mantle made of granite from local quarries. The house still stands today. (Courtesy Edythe J. Greene.)

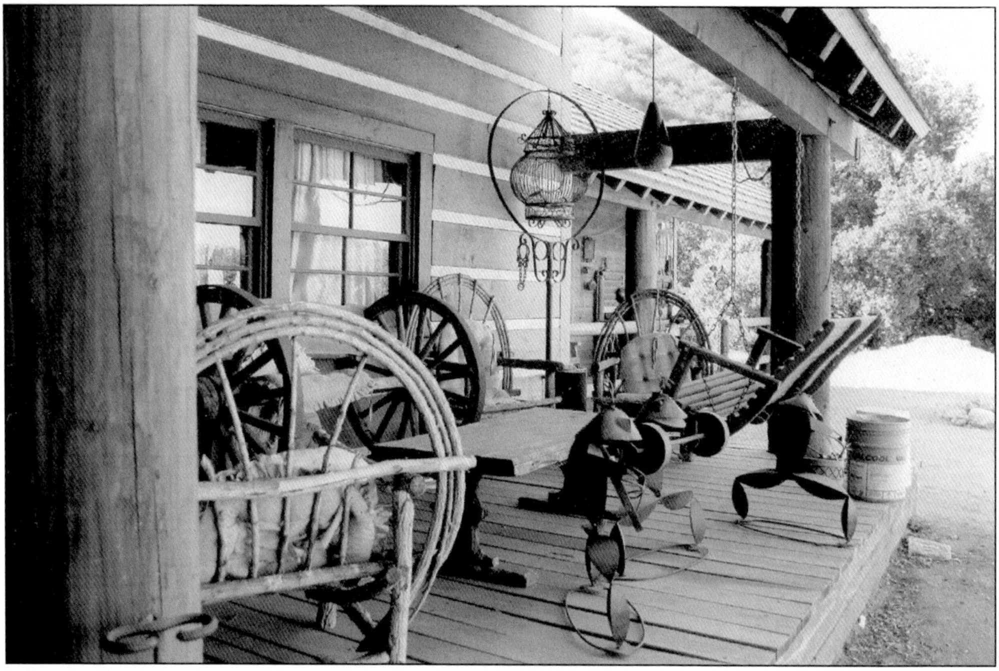

John Outhuijse, owner of the Outhouse Saloon, built his house to the exact specifications of the "Ponderosa," home of the Cartwrights on the well-known television western *Bonanza*. When walking into the large kitchen, you can almost picture Hop Sing of the show busily preparing dinner. Pictured here is the comfortable old-fashioned porch similar to the one in the old television series. (Courtesy Edythe J. Greene.)

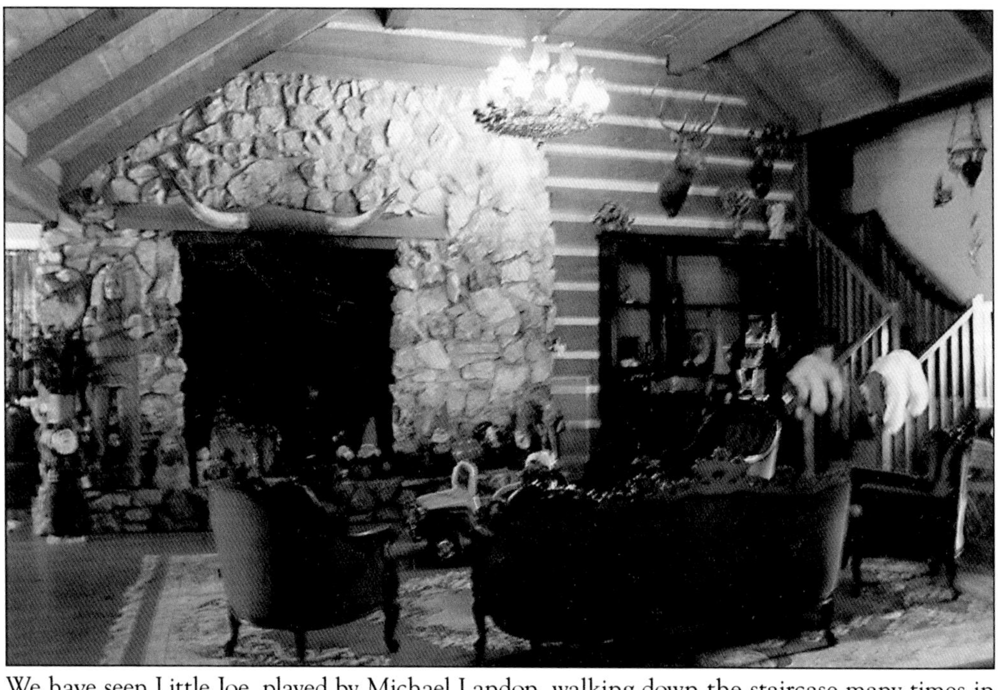

We have seen Little Joe, played by Michael Landon, walking down the staircase many times in television's *Bonanza*, and Lorne Greene resting by the huge fireplace. (Courtesy Edythe J. Greene.)

# *Five*

# Lake, Hotels, and Bathhouses

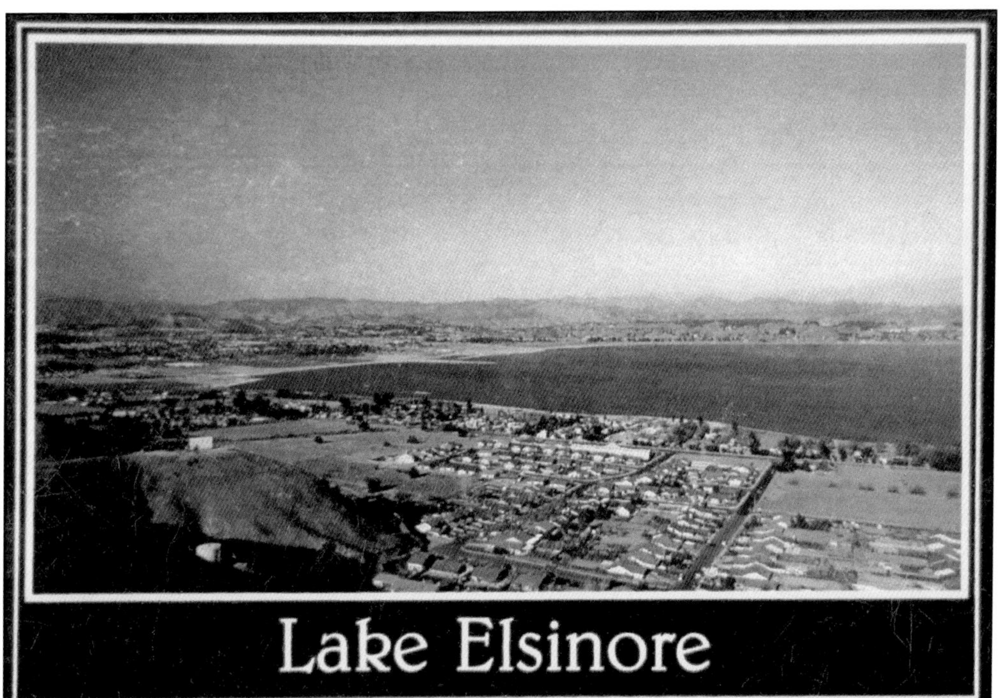


This aerial view takes in the stately panorama of Lake Elsinore.

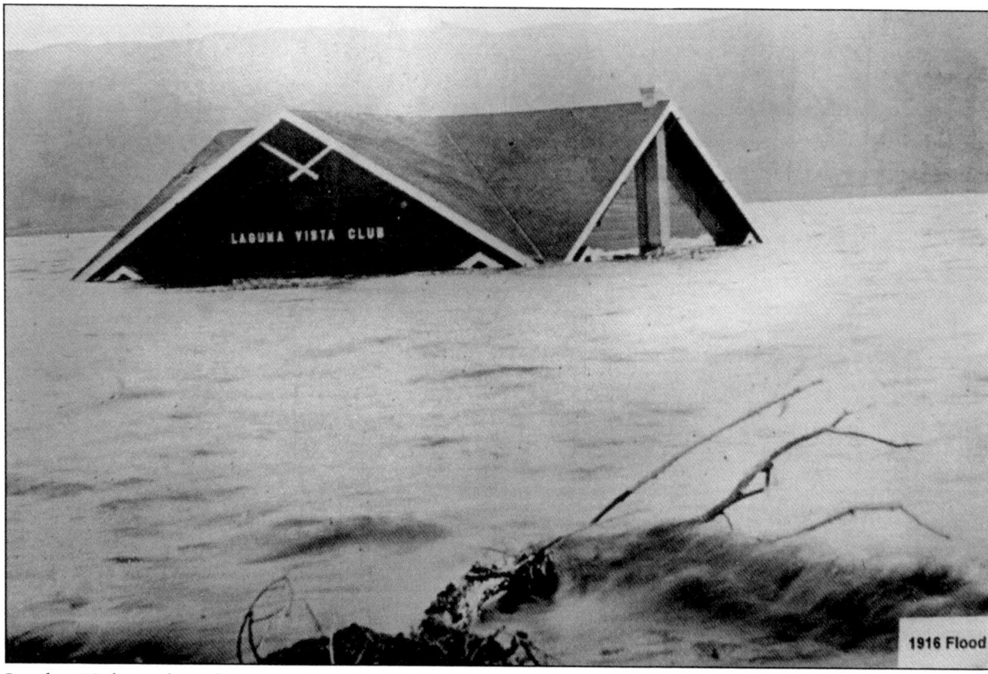


In the 19th and 20th centuries, the Lake Elsinore alternated between floods and drought. In 1884, 62 inches of rain fell in one season, turning the mountains green with flowers and ferns. In 1916, the lake rose so high that people fished from the side of Poe Street, and the Laguna Vista Club was almost totally immersed in water, as shown above. In 1969, seven inches of rain fell in 11 days and once again flooded the shores. The city has endured its share of rising shorelines. (Courtesy Smoke House El Savador.)

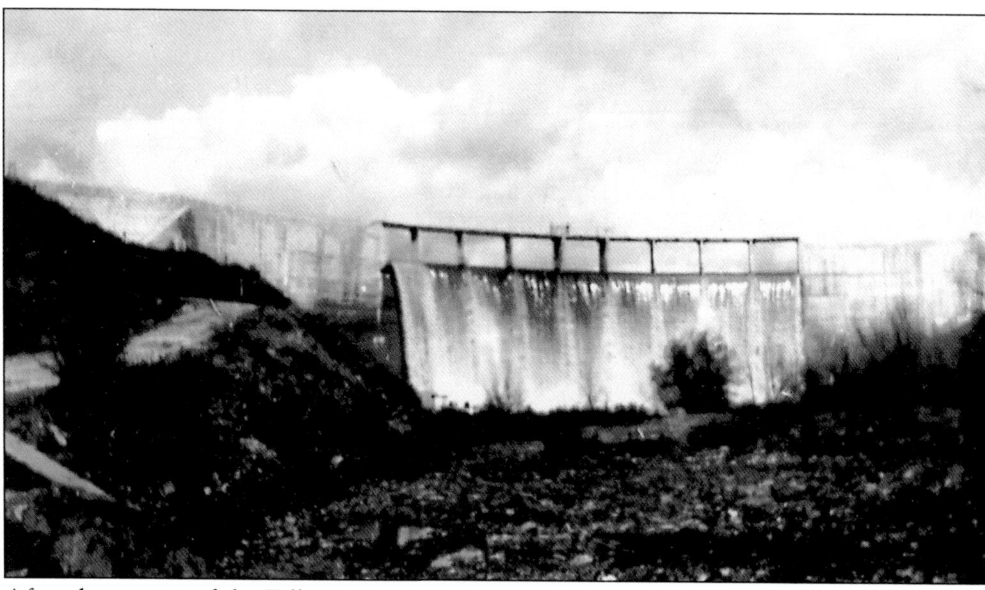

After the signing of the Tilly Agreement, the Temescal Water Company began work on the Railroad Canyon Dam, originally called the Temescal Dam. The dam, when completed in 1927, blocked the natural flow out of Railroad Canyon and thus formed Canyon Lake. (Courtesy Riverside County Library System.)

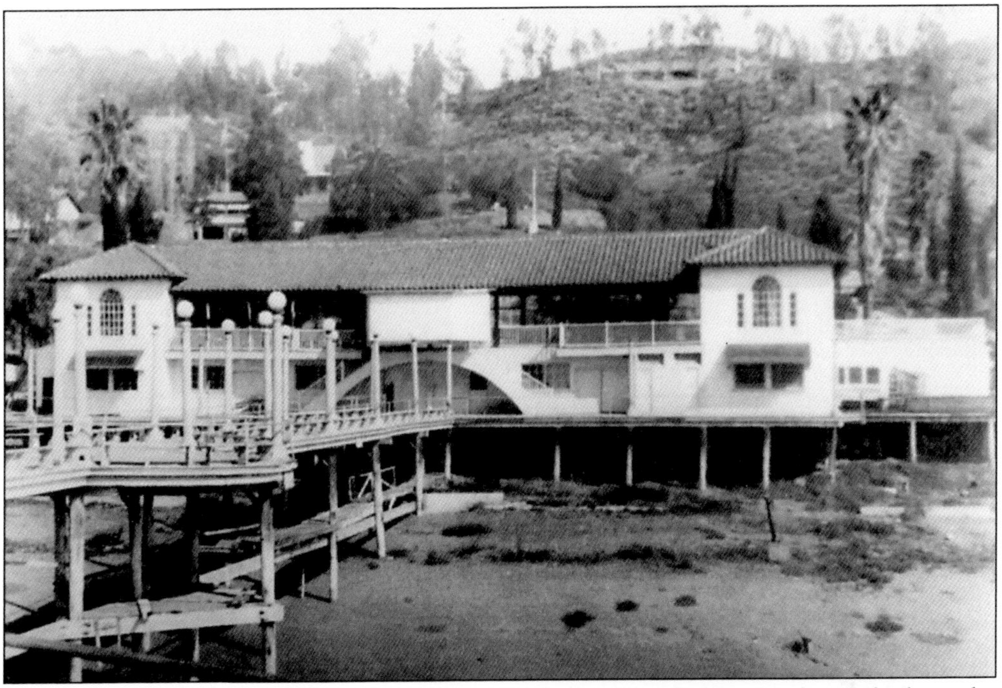

In 1926, the Aloha Pier and Pavilion, complete with swings and playgrounds, was built on the north shore of Lake Elsinore. A second story, extending over the lake, was added in 1927. A superb oval-shaped dance floor was part of the second story and orchestras performed there on weekends and holidays all summer long. This was the scene of many festive occasions. (Courtesy Smoke House El Salvador.)

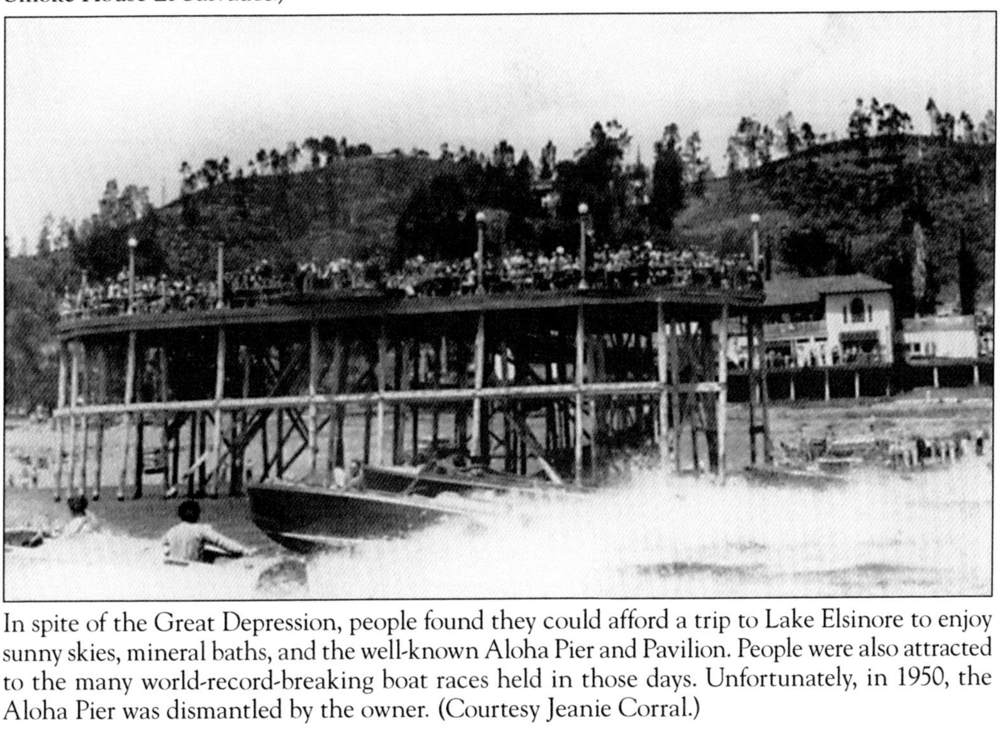

In spite of the Great Depression, people found they could afford a trip to Lake Elsinore to enjoy sunny skies, mineral baths, and the well-known Aloha Pier and Pavilion. People were also attracted to the many world-record-breaking boat races held in those days. Unfortunately, in 1950, the Aloha Pier was dismantled by the owner. (Courtesy Jeanie Corral.)

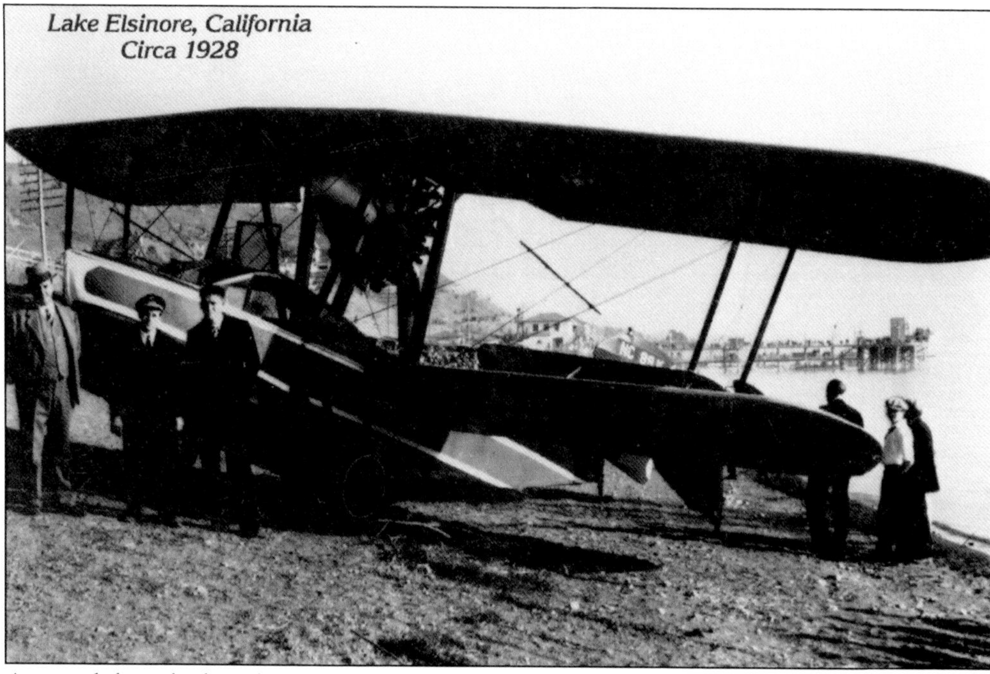


An amphibian biplane lands on Lake Elsinore at Aloha Beach in 1928. Notice the pier and restaurant in the background. (Courtesy Dr. Timothy Kimble, D.C.)

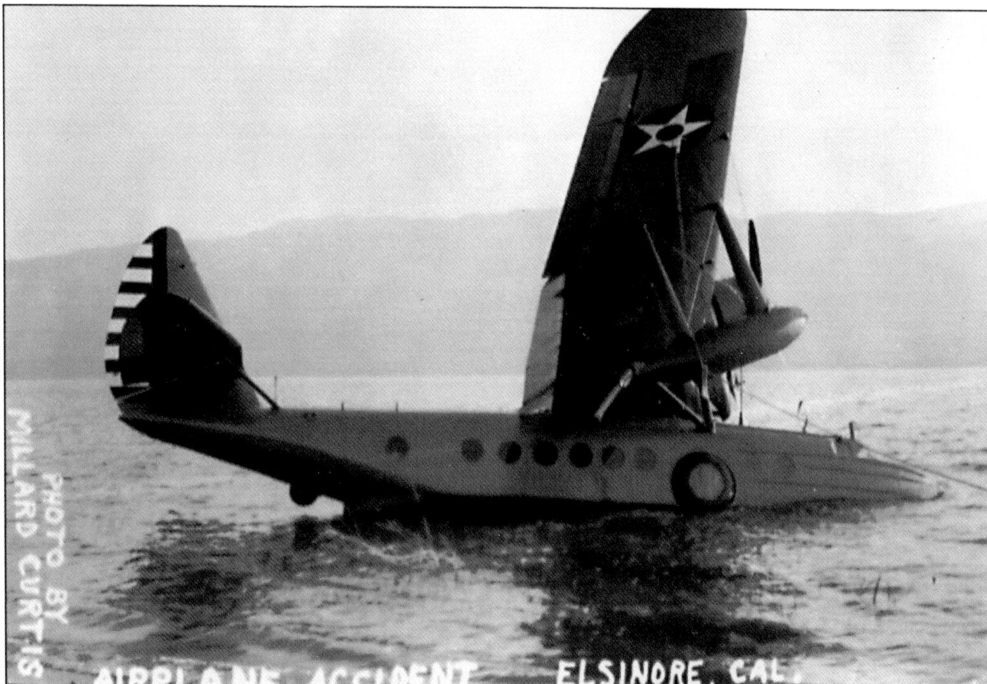


Douglas Aircraft used Lake Elsinore to test their seaplanes. Later Northrop Aircraft tested N-3 seaplane patrol bombers on the lake before they were sent to Europe for use during World War II. The one pictured here crashed into the lake during a heavy fog in 1939. The pilot survived the crash. (Courtesy Riverside County Library System.)

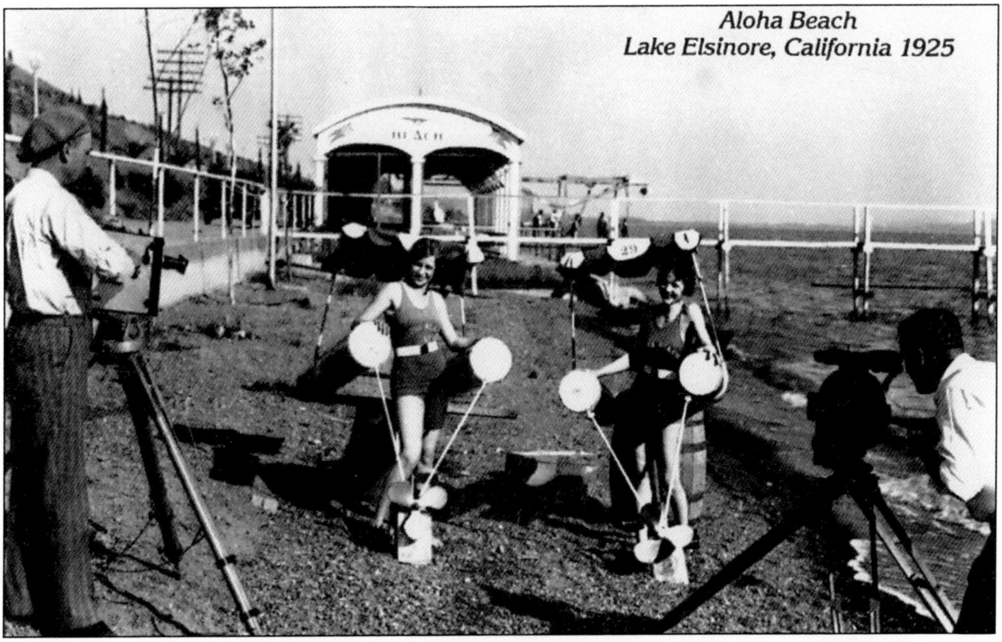


Air shows and many other events were held on Aloha Beach. In 1925, two models are posing for photographs using the Aloha Pier and Lake Elsinore for a beautiful background. (Courtesy Dr. Timothy Kimble, D.C.)

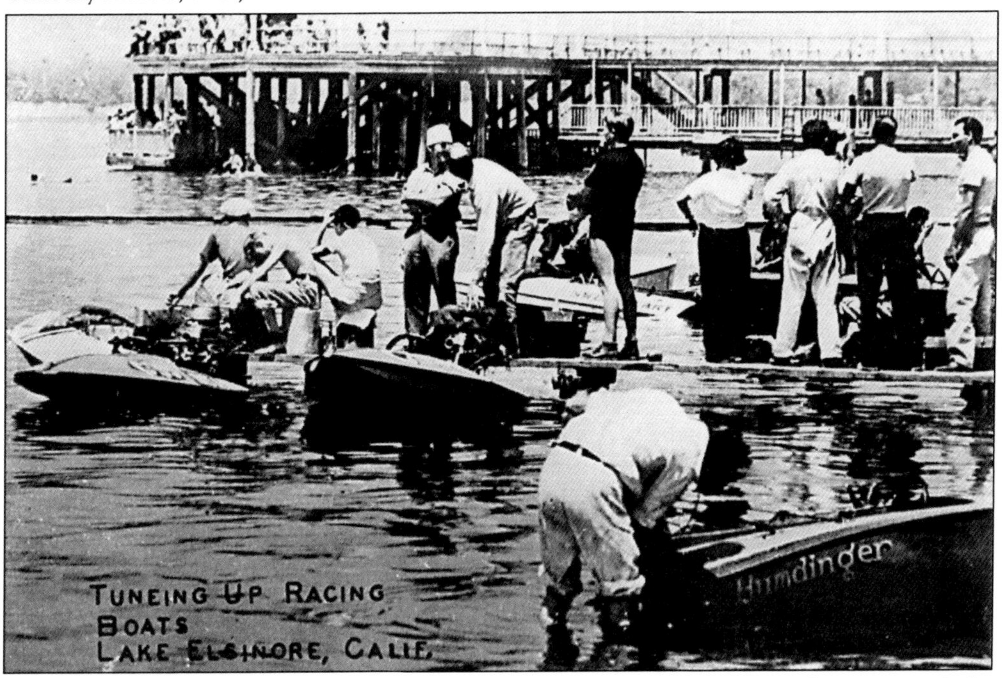


On June 9, 1928, Floyd Pierce set a world's record of 33.74 miles per hour in a boat race on Lake Elsinore. His boat, named *Miss Elsinore*, was a Class C outboard. Here people are preparing for the historic event with the Aloha Pier, seen in the background. Boat racing was in its heyday during the 1920s and 1930s and continued even through the war years of the 1940s. (Courtesy Dr. Timothy Kimble, D.C.)

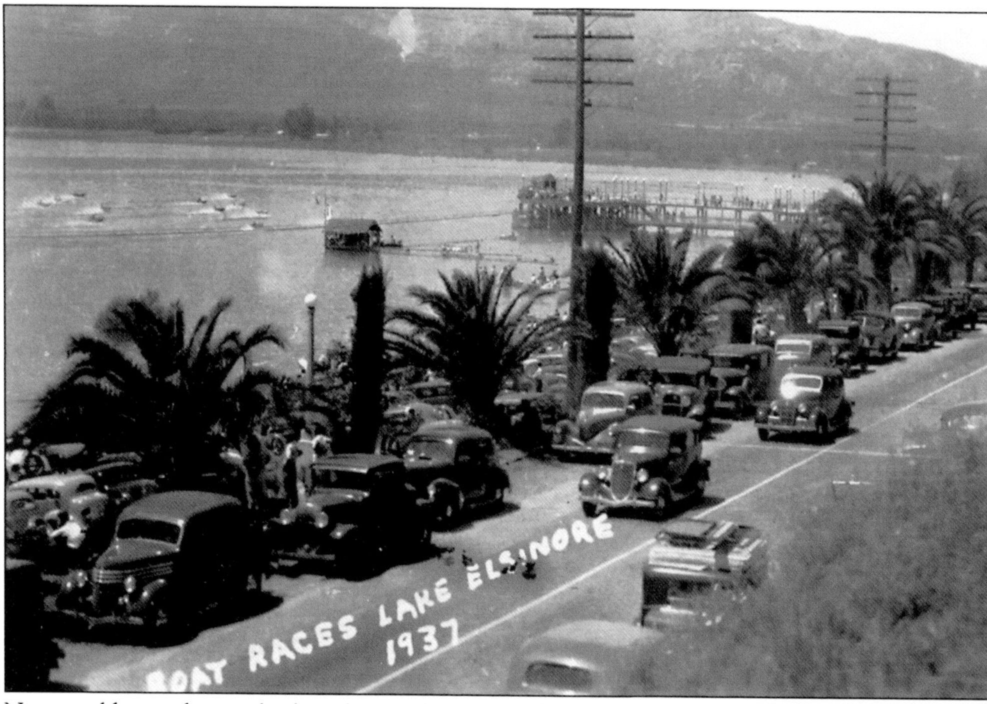


Nine world records were broken during the National Speed Boat Races held at Lake Elsinore on December 8 and 9, 1928. Speed boat racing brought throngs of people here until the new sport of water skiing took over the lake in the early 1940s. (Courtesy Riverside County Library System.)

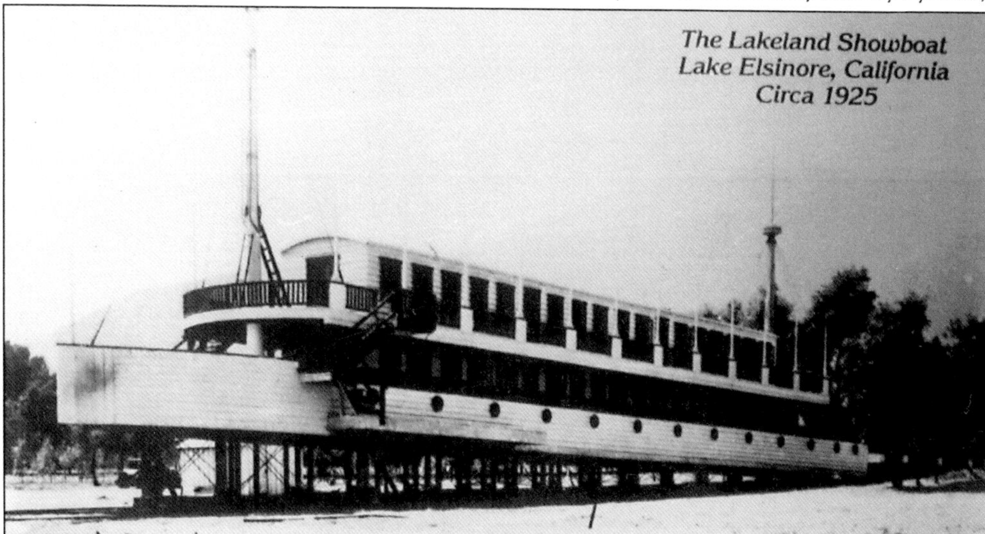


The Lakeland Showboat was actually a ship pier built by the Clevelin Realty Corporation. At 200 feet long and 200 tons, it resembled a ship complete with portholes and a 100-foot-long, lavishly appointed room on the top deck. It was mounted on wheels that transported it easily from the water's edge onto dry land, then to steel rails when repairs were needed. Since it was actually a pier, small boats would dock along both sides of it. It was dedicated with much hoopla, and even an air show with 30 aviators, on June 14, 1931. Pleasure seekers found it a favorite place for their rendezvous for many years. (Courtesy Smoke House El Salvador.)

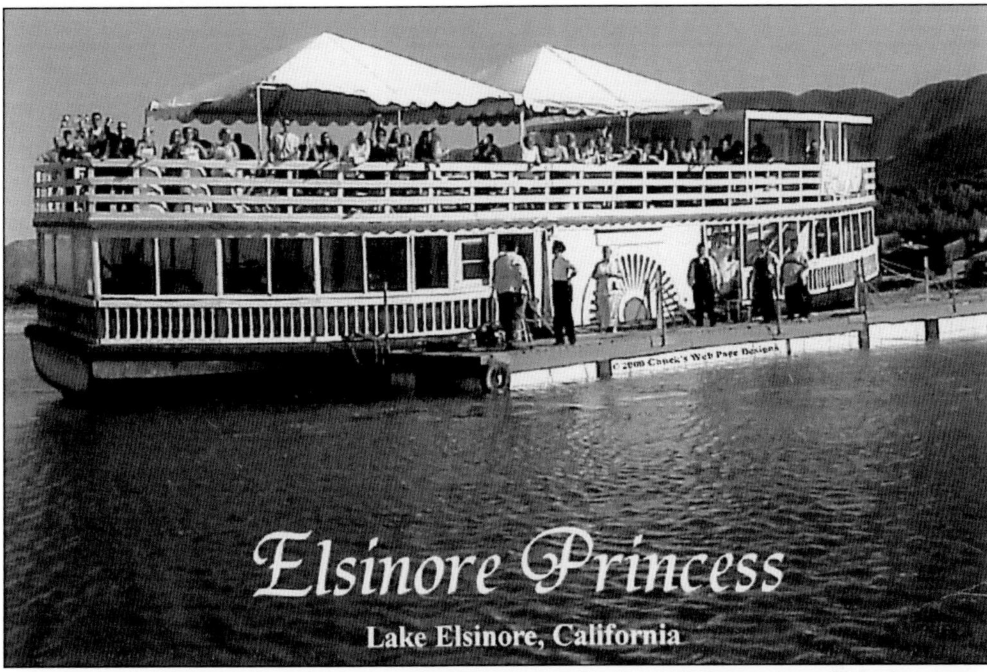


When the glass-bottom boat known as the *Princess* was built in 1921, it was used to take visitors on tours around Santa Catalina Island. The steamer became the title subject of the Doris Day/Rod Taylor movie, *The Glass Bottom Boat* (1966), and made the *Princess* famous. Then in 1999, it was renamed the *Elsinore Princess*. It went through a lengthy restoration process after being hauled overland from Long Beach to Lake Elsinore. Since its restoration, the people of Lake Elsinore have used it for gala weddings and other celebrations.

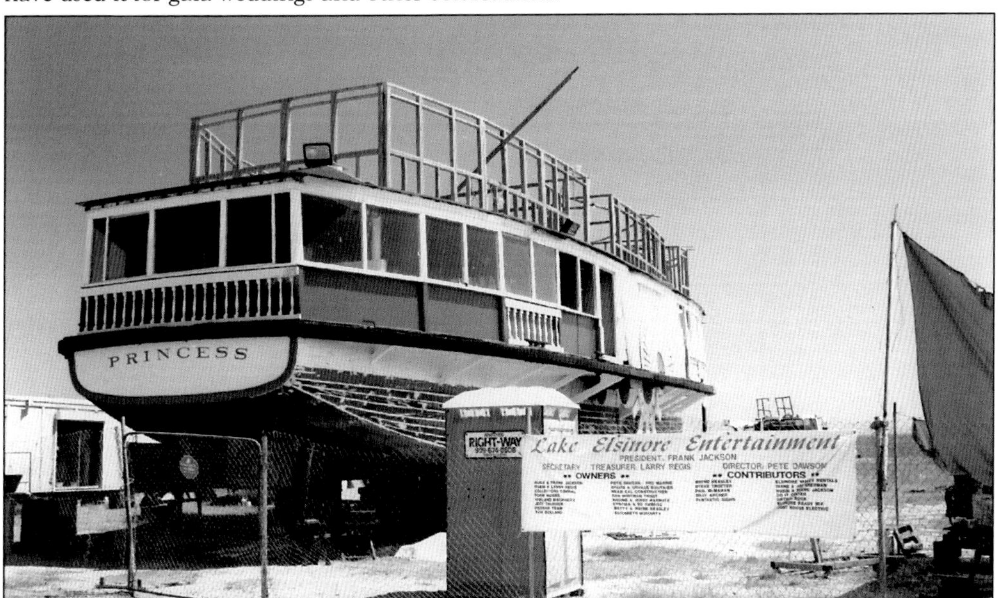


Here the *Elsinore Princess* is moored at the Elsinore West Marina with two new motors and hand-crafted paddle wheels. Since more refurbishing is necessary to make it seaworthy once again, it has been moved from the West Marina. (Courtesy Edythe J. Greene.)

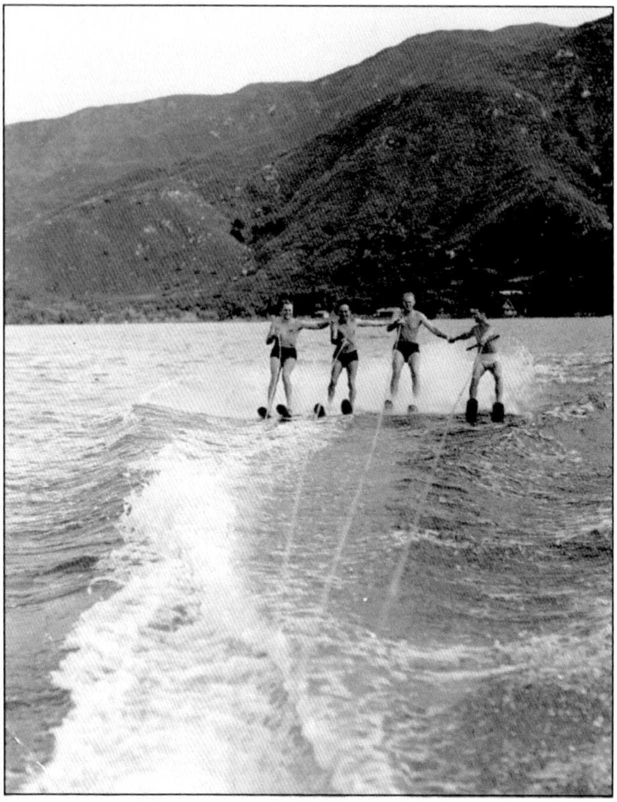

Fred Ashbridge started building boats in 1903, earning $1 a day, before starting his own business. From 1929 to 1931, he rode aquaplanes and won races in Elsinore and Long Beach. In 1936, he began water skiing, making his own skies, originally using two skis. In 1942, one of the first ski jumps was built by him in Lake Elsinore. He water skied from the California mainland to Santa Catalina Island when he was 75. No other water skier of any age could make that claim at that time. Fred is the third from the left in the above picture. (Courtesy Chad Mora.)

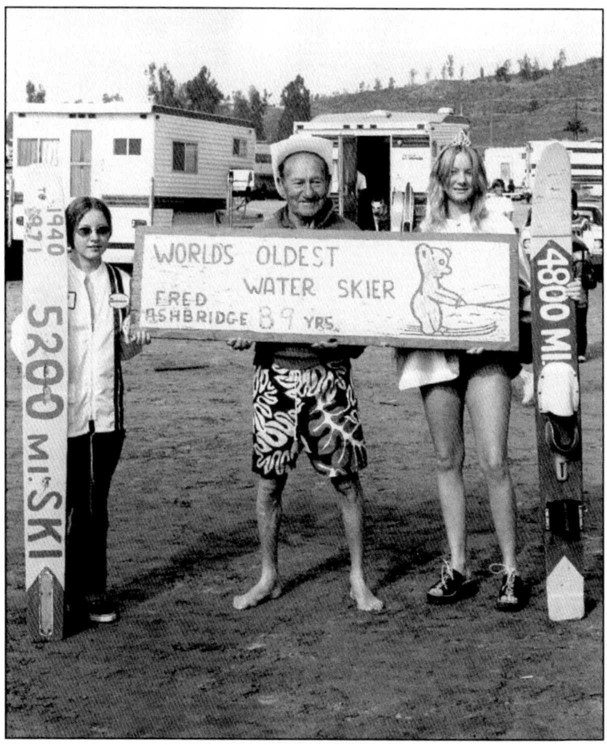


Fred Ashbridge, who was actively water skiing at the age of 89, had the distinction of being the world's oldest water skier. Every year, during his later years, he water skied from the Southern California mainland to Santa Catalina Island. Water skiing has been a favorite water sport on Lake Elsinore since the early 1900s. The first water ski was shaped like a box and was used in the ocean. Recent fads include boarding, single boarding, and board jumping. (Courtesy Betty Burke.)

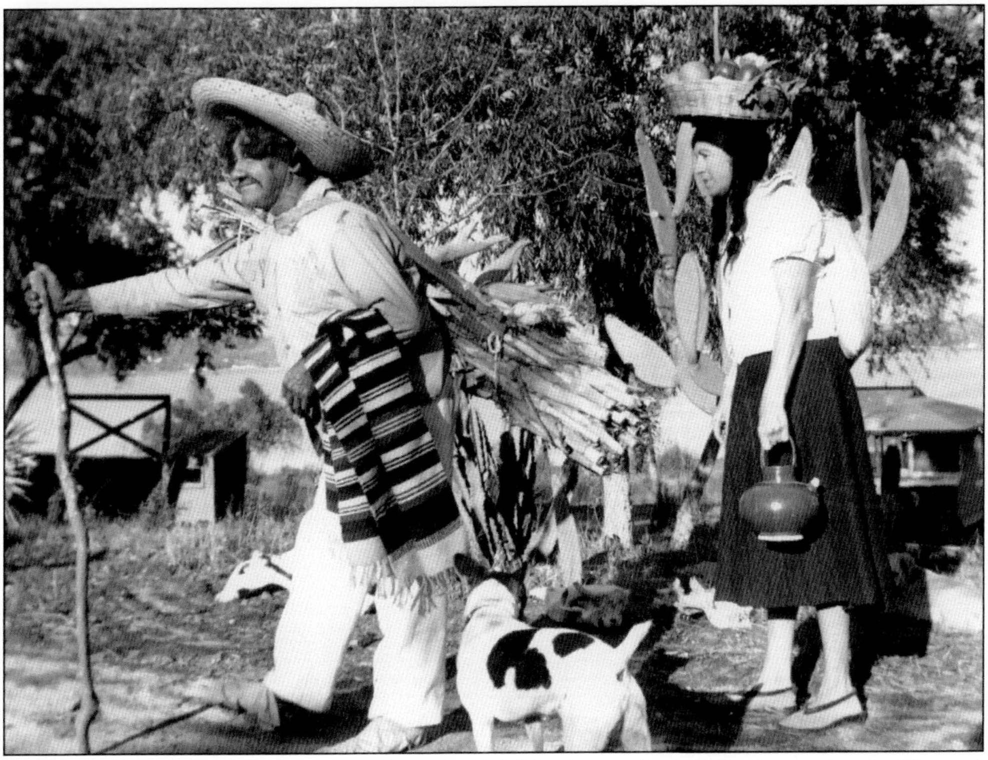

The December 1968 El Señor Parade shows Fred Ashbridge on the left. Fred was a boatbuilder and built his house in the shape of a yacht, calling it the Blue Waters Ranch. (Courtesy Chad Mora.)

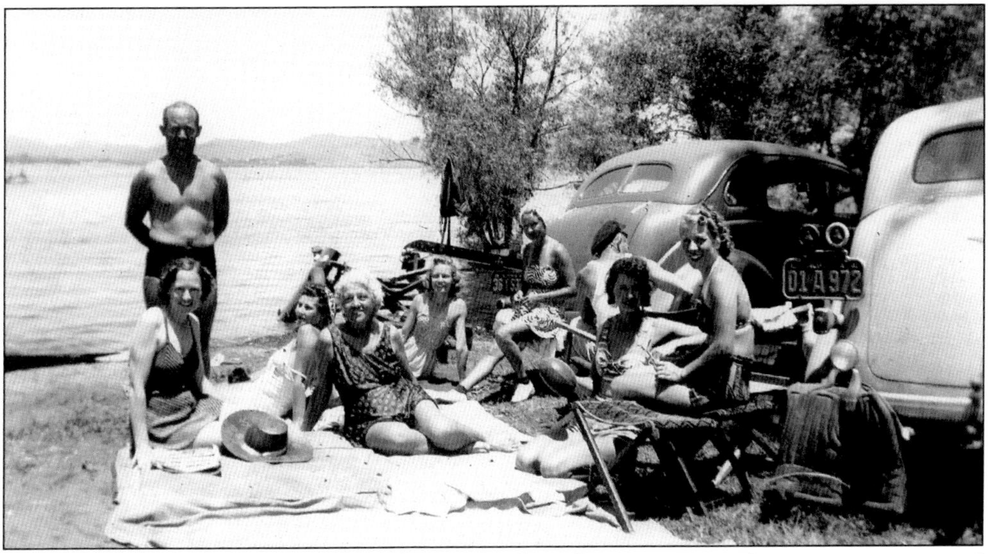


During the 1920s and 1930s, Lake Elsinore, with its boating, water skiing, swimming, and fishing, attracted many visitors. The average daily temperature of 78.5 degrees Fahrenheit was ideal for this water playground. All summer long crowds were magnetized by the lakeshore and parking places were at a premium. People often ate their lunches sitting on the running boards of their automobiles. Today Lake Elsinore attracts about 1.5 million tourists each year. (Courtesy Main Street Mercantile.)

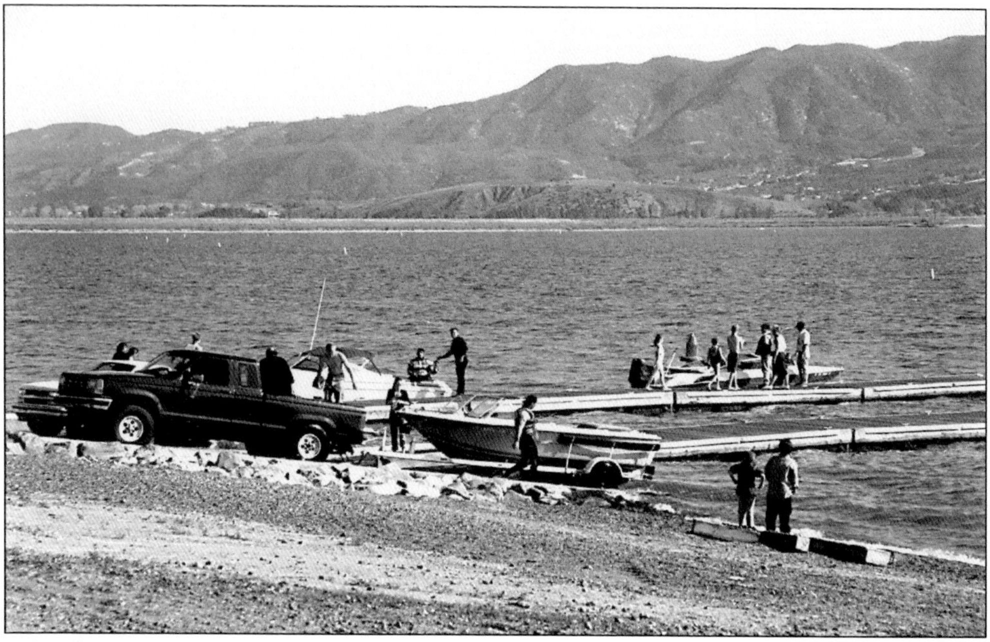

Lake Elsinore is still the playground of the Inland Empire. People come as they have in the past, some for recreation and some to settle. Fishermen and boats of various sizes and shapes as well as bird-watchers and a wide variety of water birds can be seen in the water and along the shore. (Courtesy Edythe J. Greene.)

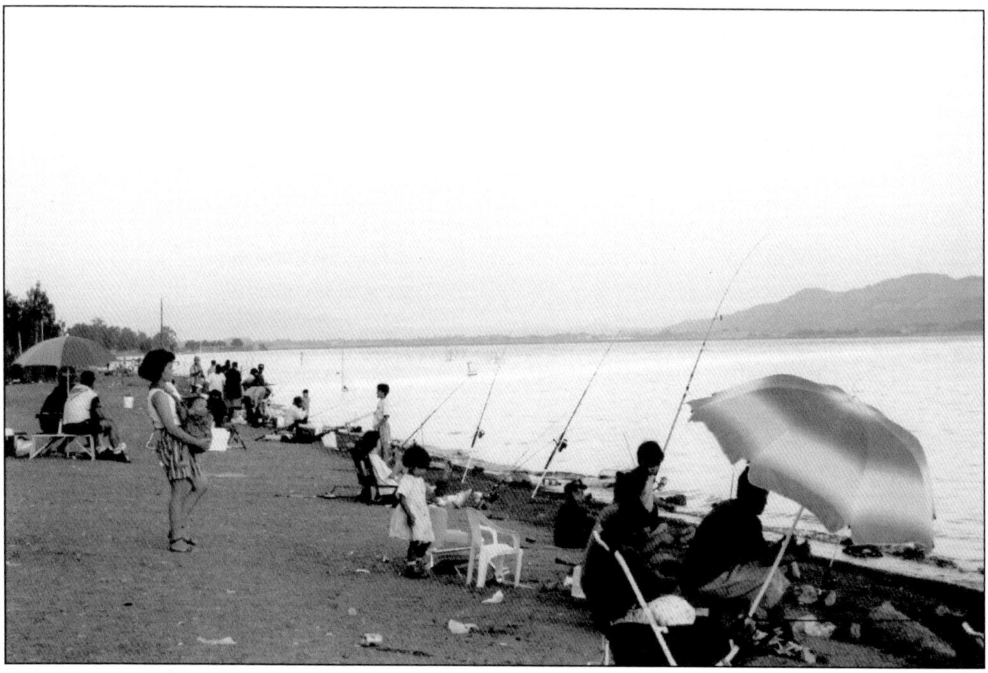

Fishermen can be seen along the shores of Lake Elsinore on any day of the week. (Courtesy Edythe J. Greene.)

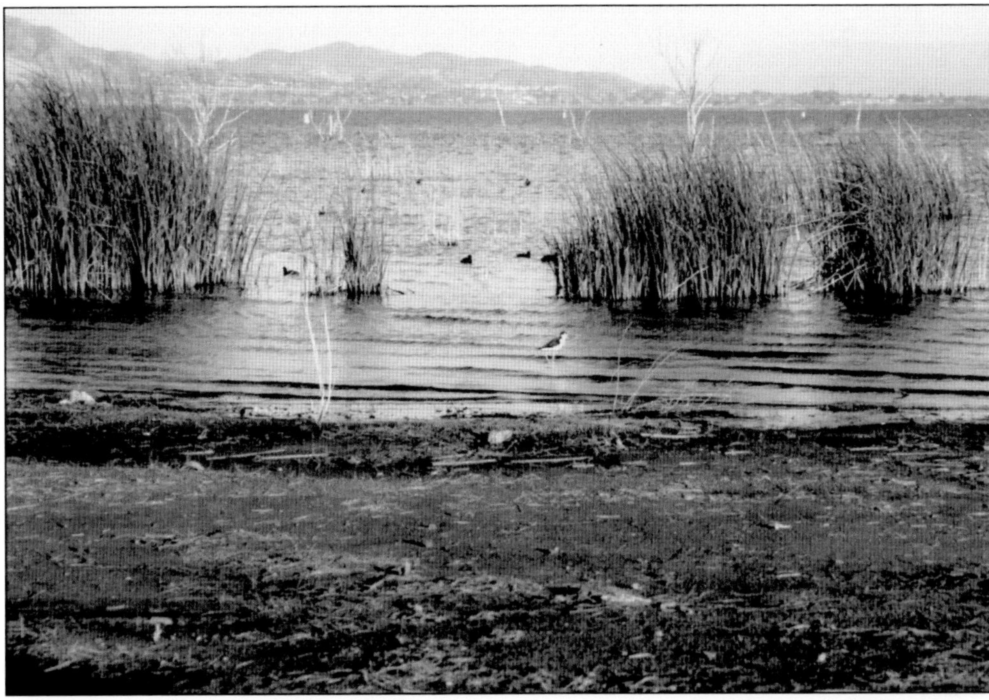

Many lagoons are located along the lake's shores where a variety of wading birds find sanctuary. (Courtesy Edythe J. Greene.)

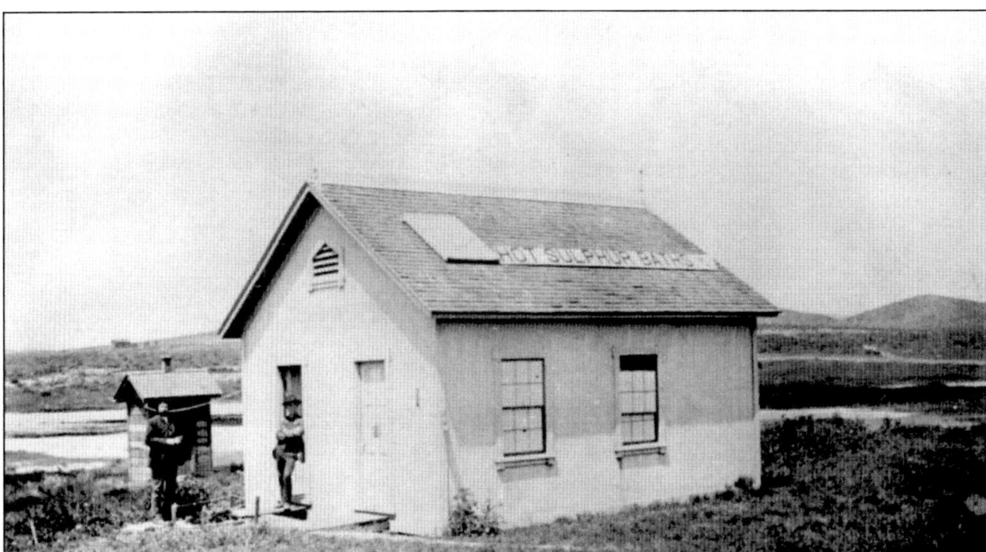


The first bathhouse in Elsinore, pictured above, was located on Peck Street behind the Chimes Building. People came from all over the world to enjoy the hot sulphur baths that were believed to have healing qualities. (Courtesy Jeanie Corral.)

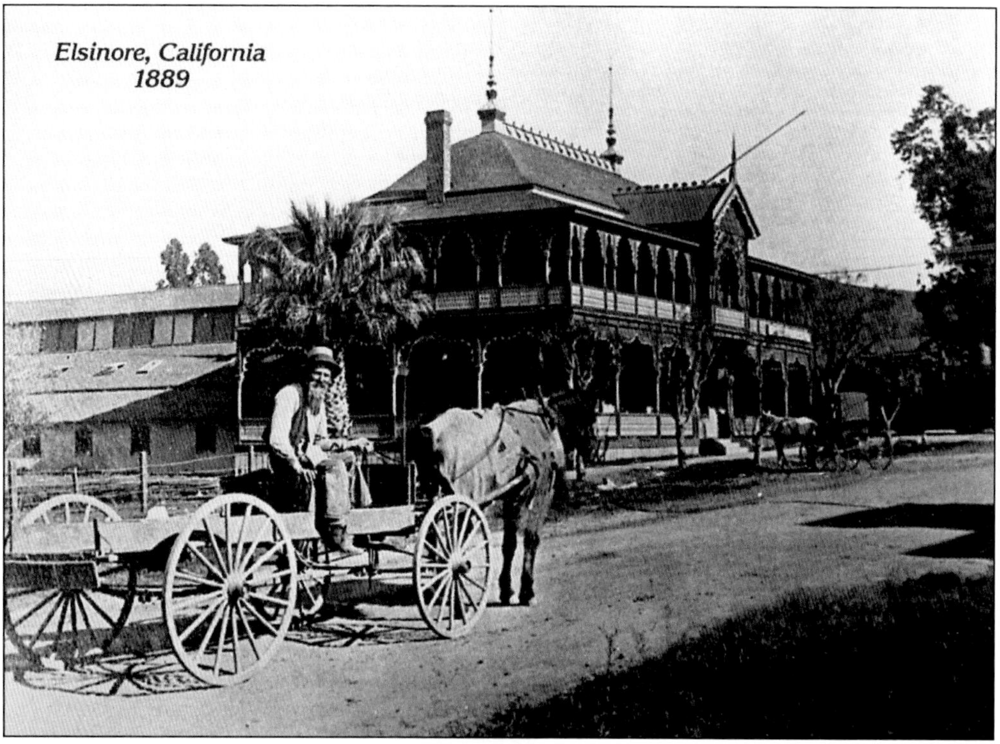


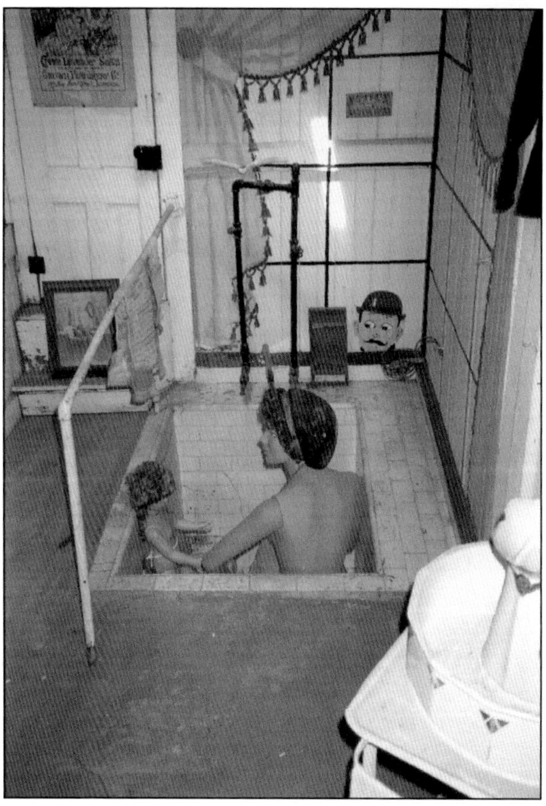

The Crescent Bath House was located at the site of Lake Elsinore's first artesian well, where hot sulfur mineral water flowed in abundance. The bathhouse was built in 1887 by Franklin Heald, the founder of Lake Elsinore, and was designed by his partner, Frank Feris. A two-story, Moorish-style building, its second floor contained bedrooms. People came to the spa to seek relief from rickets, arthritis, and other ailments using the hot mineral water baths. A historic photograph shows an unidentified man at the Crescent Bath House in 1889.

The elaborate Crescent Bath House contained Roman-style bath tubs and Moorish-style sunken tubs. The original tubs and massage area for men and women are still intact. There were areas for mud baths, massage therapy, and a large enclosed mineral water pool. (Courtesy Louise Rowden.)

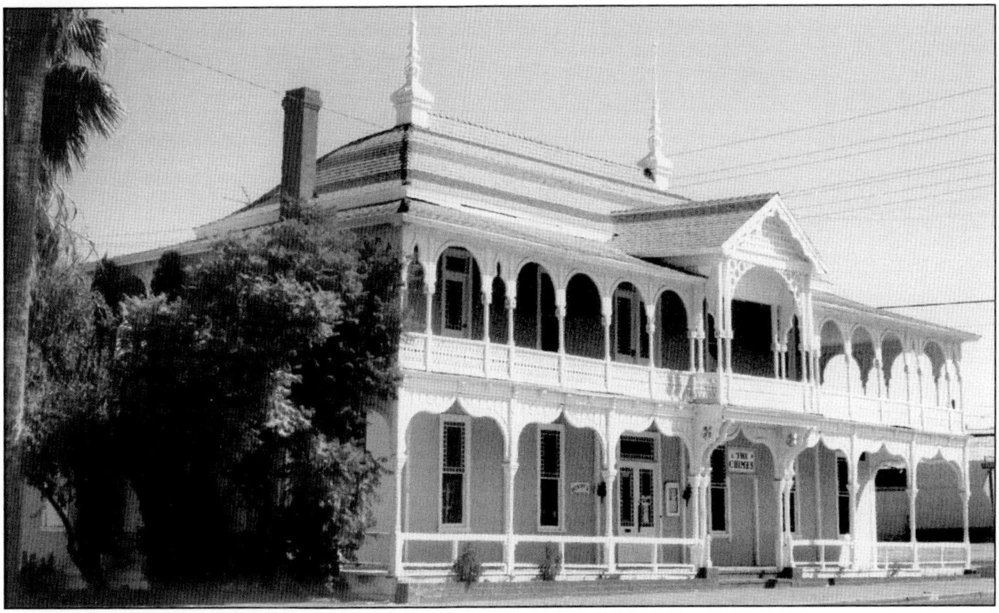

In 1945, the Crescent Bath House stopped operating its 10 Roman-style baths, steam room, and therapy rooms. It was then renamed The Chimes when Galal and Bonnie Gough bought the structure in 1949, and turned it into an office for Bonnie's interior decorating service. In 1963, another owner created an antique store within the building. Lory and Wilma Watts acquired the building in 1970 and operated it as an antique store for 32 years. In the summer of 2002, it was repurchased and refurbished with the hopes of it becoming a museum. Stories of the building being haunted by apparitions and poltergeists still circulate. The Crescent Bath House, aka The Chimes, was listed as a National Historic Landmark in 1975. It is located at the corner of Graham Avenue and Spring Street. (Courtesy Louise Rowden.)

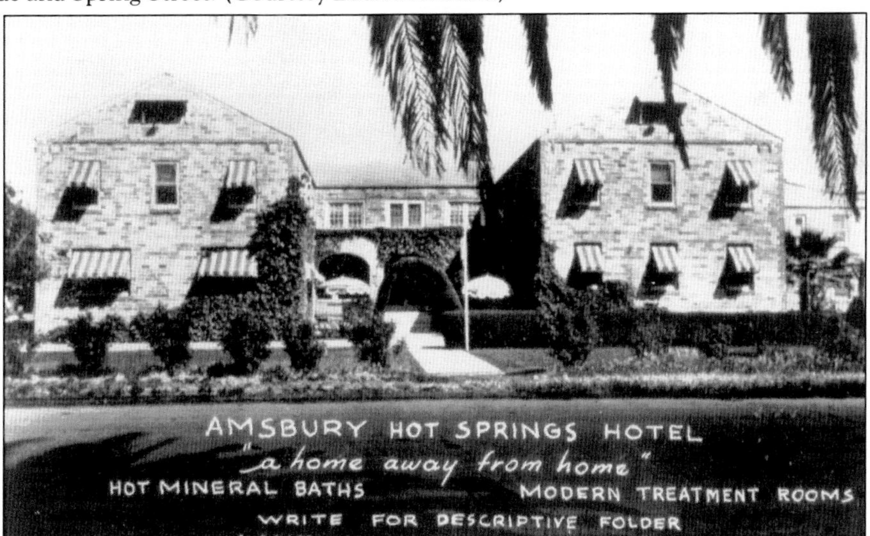


The Amsbury Hotel and Bath House faced Spring Street. Built of hollow tile, it occupied the entire block from Heald to Franklin. Will Rogers, then with Hal Roach Productions, was one of the Amsbury's noted guests. He was cast in one of many motion pictures made in and around Elsinore. (Courtesy Riverside County Library System.)

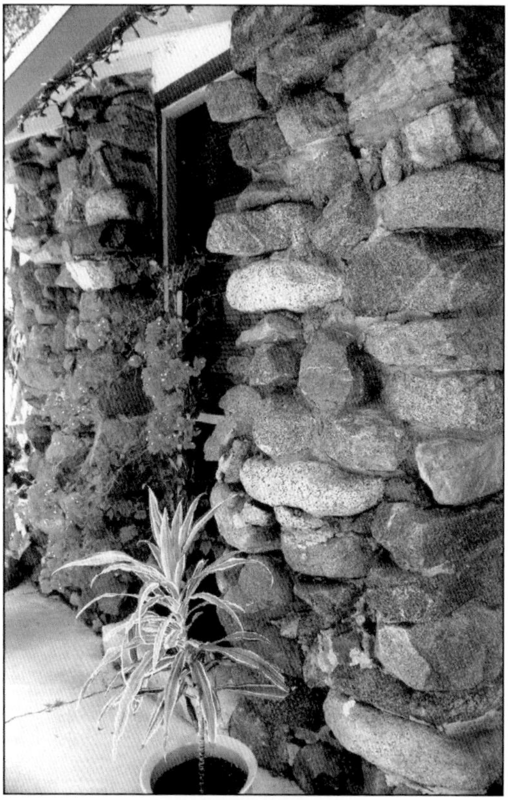

This picture shows the entrance to the Duck Lodge, which was built in 1890 on Lake Elsinore. The lodge had very small rooms with only a bed for the hunter and a place for his dog to sleep. Lighting was provided by a kerosene lamp placed in cutouts in the rock wall. (Courtesy Edythe J. Greene.)

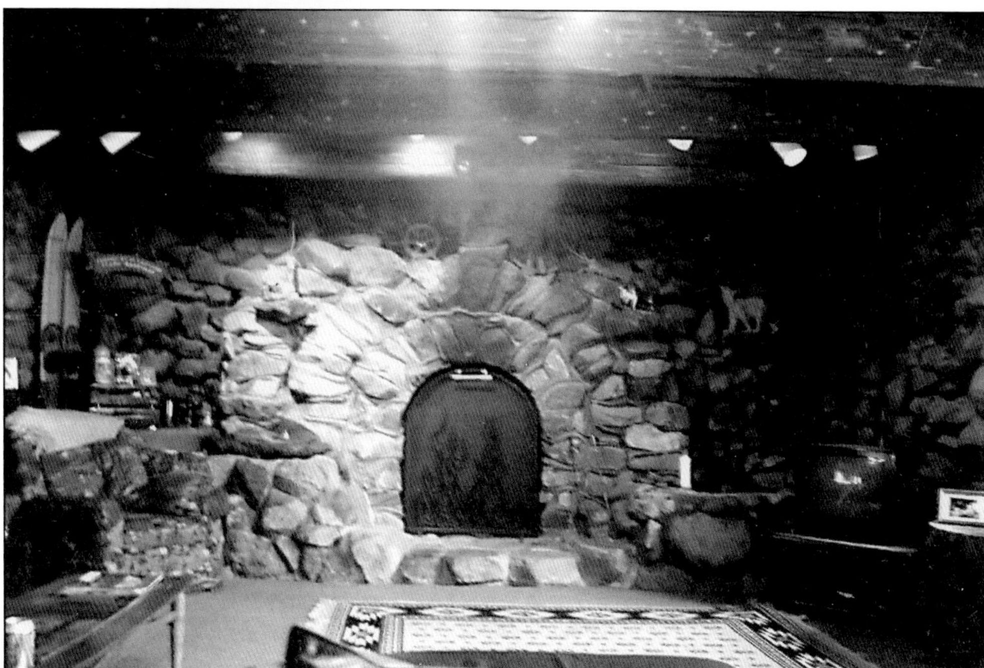

Lodges of the day contained a gathering room with a large fireplace, which was the place for the hunters to relax and tell stories of their adventures. (Courtesy Edythe J. Greene.)

Pictured here is the rock chimney of the gathering room fireplace. Constructed in 1890, it is still standing. (Courtesy Edythe J. Greene.)

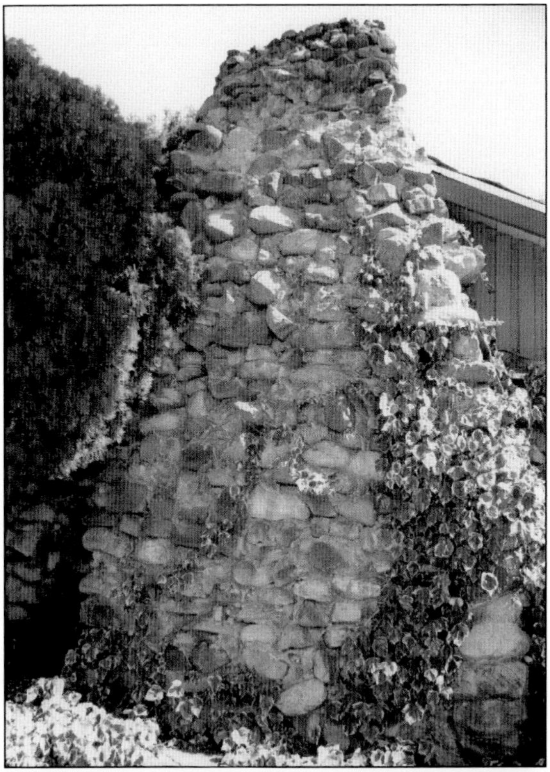

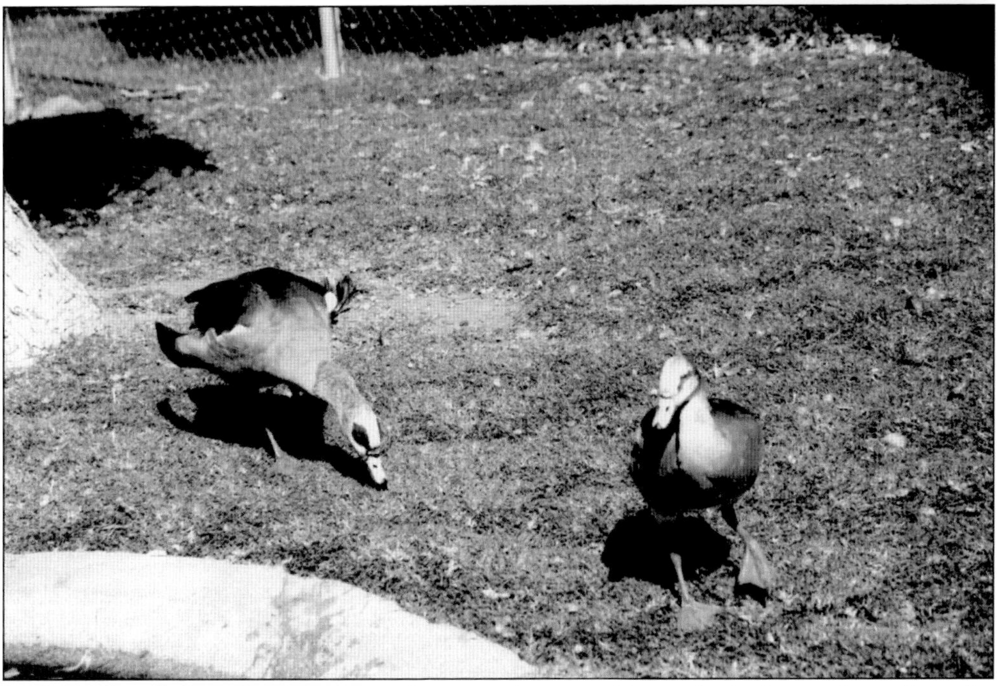

In the backyard of the Duck Lodge is a large pond, a second home for ducks wandering from the lake. Clark Gable and Andy Devine, who were avid duck hunters, came regularly in the 1930s and 1940s to hunt ducks. (Courtesy Edythe J. Greene.)

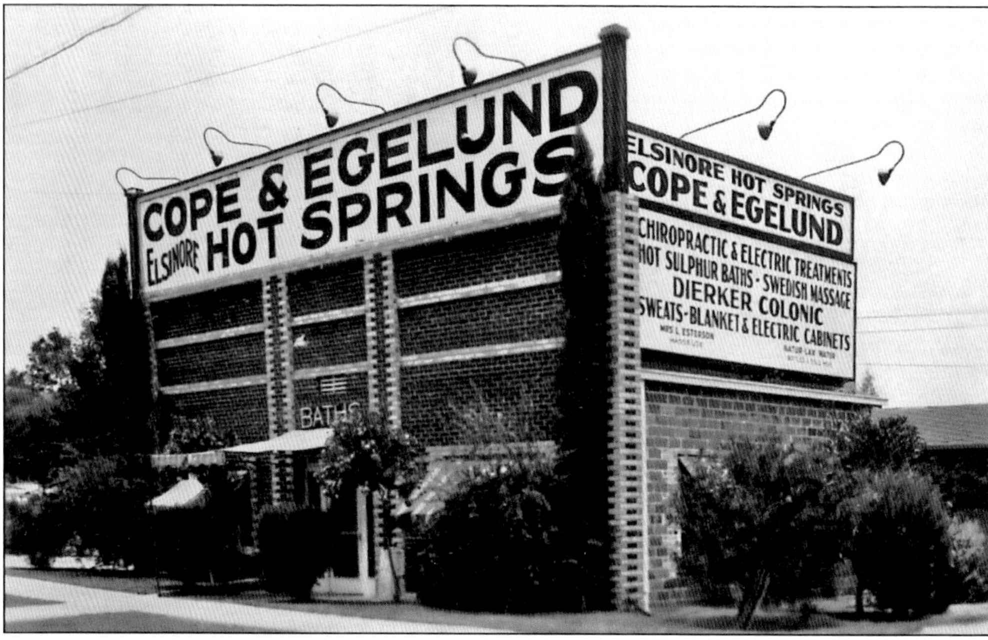


In 1938, the Cope and Egelund Elsinore Hot Springs was more than just a bathhouse. It was the place to go to cure all of your ailments, whatever they may be. (Courtesy Riverside County Library System.)

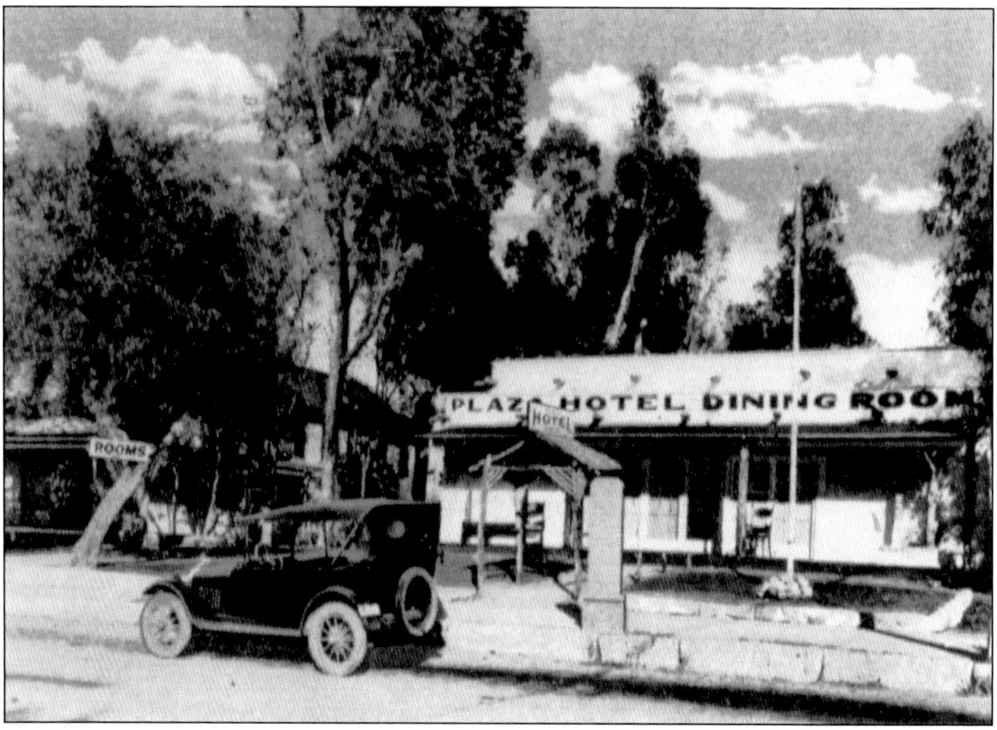


The Plaza Hotel was one of the many hotels that came into being during the heyday of Lake Elsinore in the early 20th century. (Courtesy Riverside County Library System.)

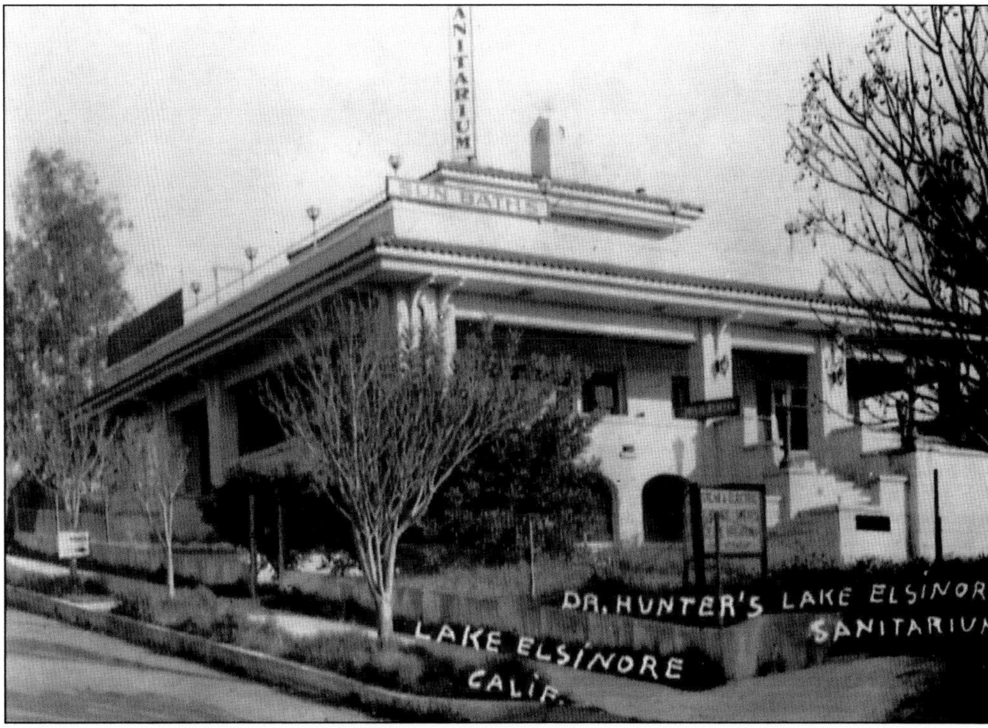


In 1928, Dr. Joseph Hunter opened Hunter's Elsinore Sanitarium in a building that had previously housed the Woodruff Sanitarium. People came from all over the world to enjoy the health benefits of the hot springs and sun bath. (Courtesy Riverside County Library System.)

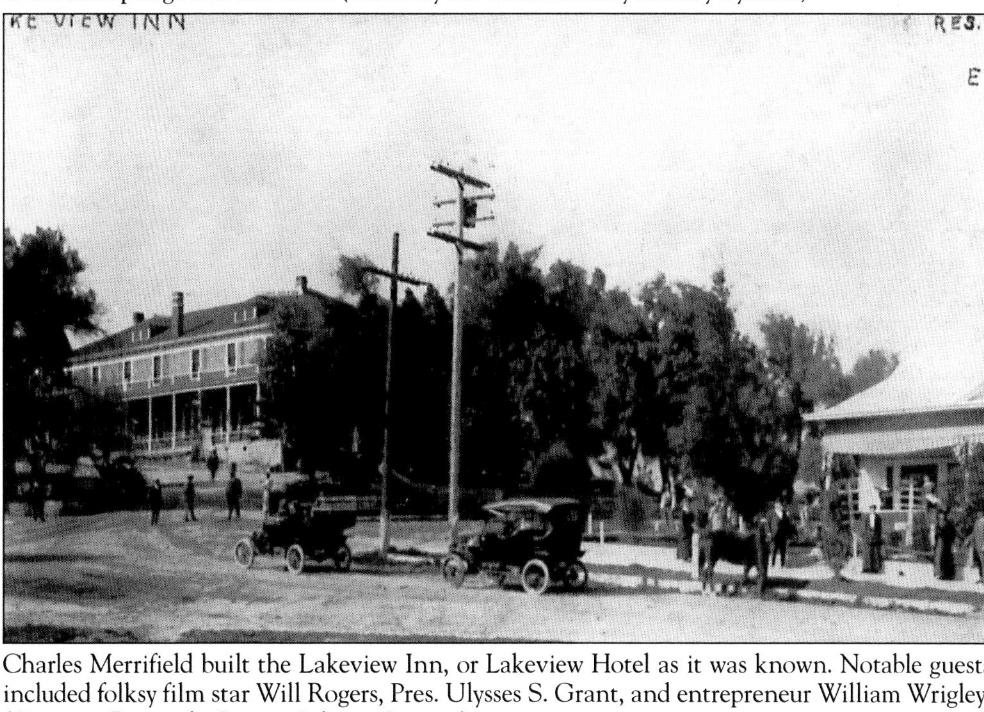


Charles Merrifield built the Lakeview Inn, or Lakeview Hotel as it was known. Notable guests included folksy film star Will Rogers, Pres. Ulysses S. Grant, and entrepreneur William Wrigley. (Courtesy Riverside County Library System.)

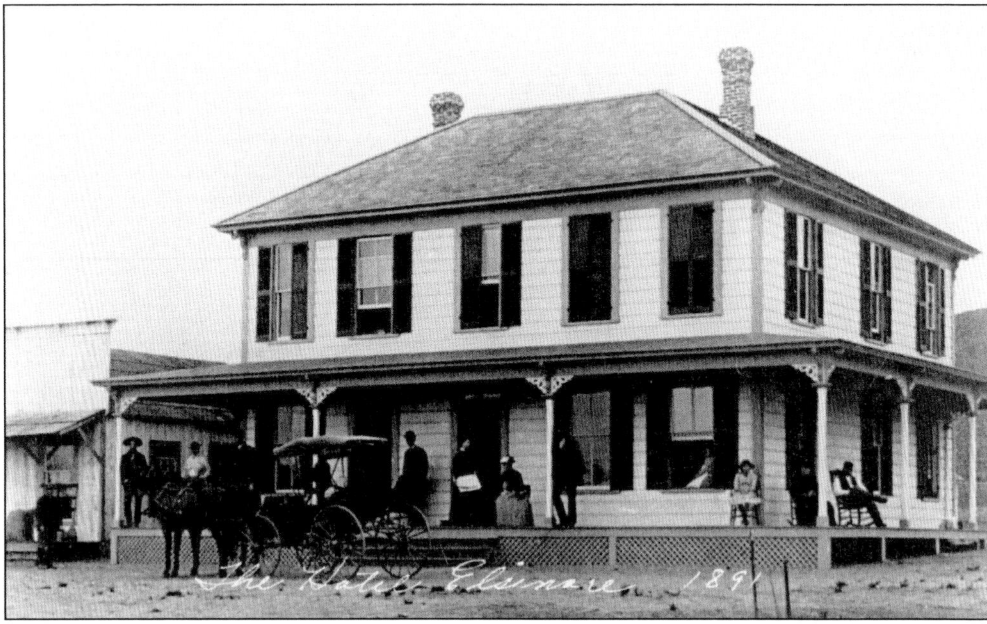


When the Hotel Elsinore was built in 1885, the whole town of Lake Elsinore was comprised of only six frame buildings and six tents. Here we see the hotel in 1891. Nineteen years later, in 1910, when the Hotel Elsinore was remodeled, decorative arbors were added. (Courtesy Dr. Timothy Kimble, D.C.)

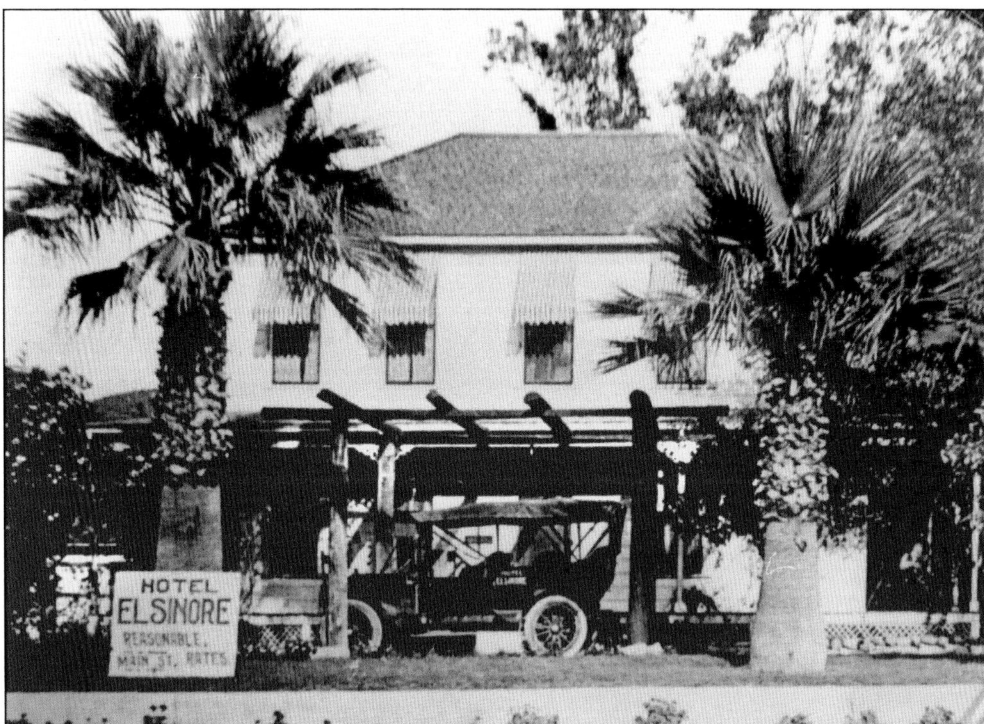


Hotel Elsinore was very popular during the boom days of the early 1920s. (Courtesy Smoke House El Savador.)

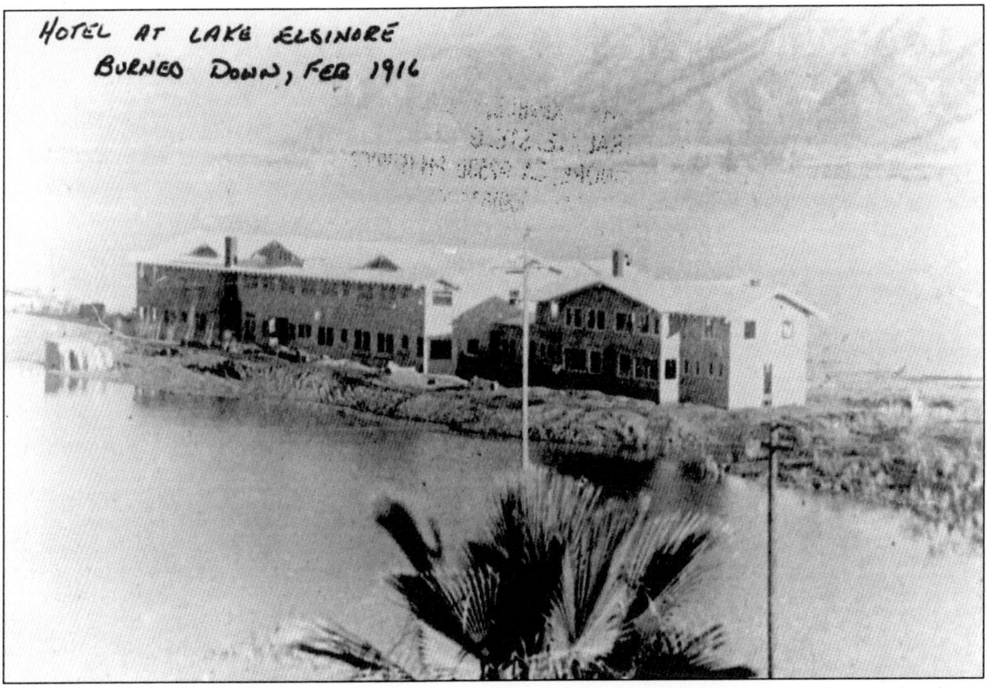


This beautiful lakeside hotel was built, but never used, because it burned down completely in February 1916 before opening day. (Courtesy Dr. Timothy Kimble, D.C.)

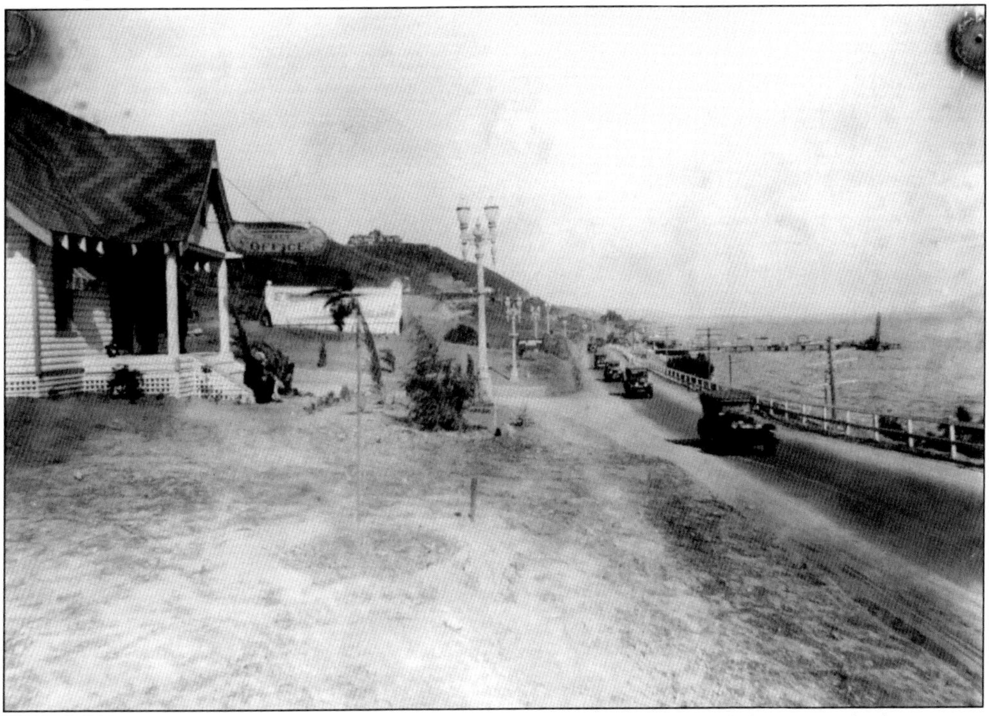


Early Lakeshore Drive had a sales office for the Country Club Heights subdivision. The lampposts were a selling point for the extraordinary houses that were going to be built. Notice the house high on the hilltop overlooking the lake and mountains. (Courtesy Jeanie Corral.)

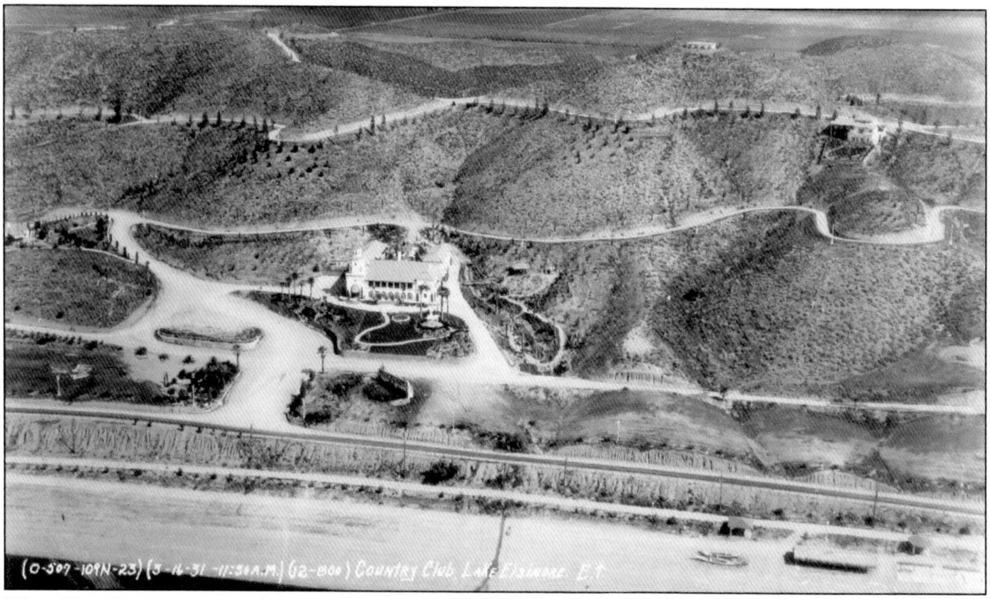


The Clevelin Country Club as seen in this aerial view was promoted, prior to its opening in May 1924, as the "greatest country club in America." The selling of lots in Country Club Heights by the Clevelin Realty Corporation was, at that time, the biggest real estate promotion in Lake Elsinore. (Courtesy Jeanie Corral.)

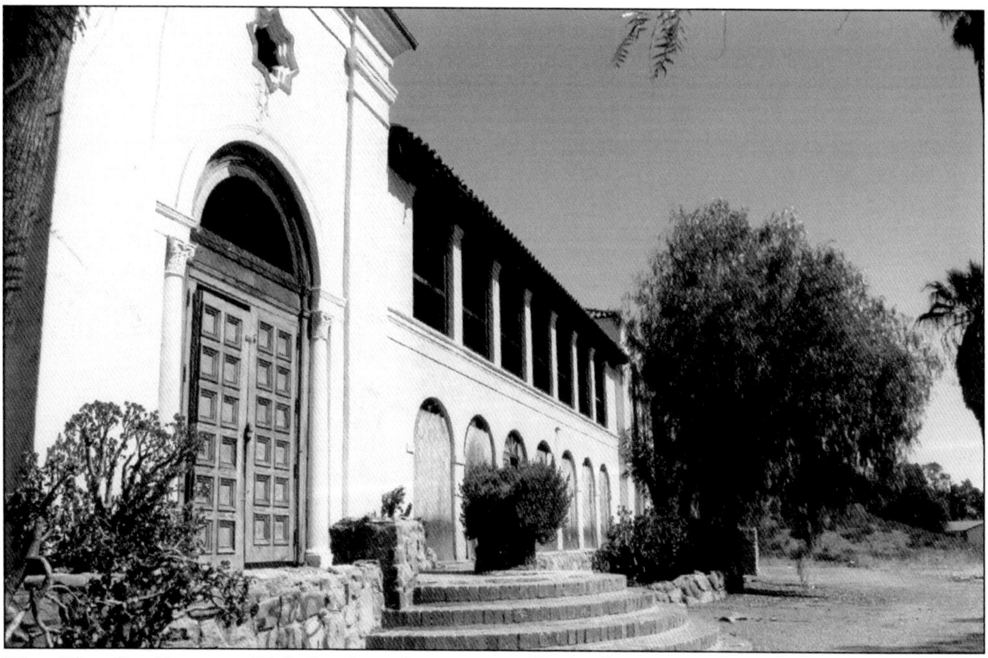

The Clevelin Country Club, built at the corner of Lakeshore Drive and Lawrence Way, near Aimee's Castle and across from the Aloha Pier, was to be the focal point for the Country Club Heights subdivision in 1929. The land, developed by Abe Corlin and Henry Cleve Schulz, was the biggest real estate promotion to date in Lake Elsinore. Due to the Great Depression, however, most of the lots made the delinquent tax lists by 1936. Therefore, any future building plans were spoiled. (Courtesy Edythe J. Greene.)

The Clevelin Country Club was beautifully landscaped with tall palm trees and other foliage and stone-wall terraces. Included were rustic bridges over a babbling brook, a waterwheel, and an old Dutch mill lighted with concealed multicolored lights. In 1970, the Casino del Elsinore was operated here. (Courtesy Edythe J. Greene.)

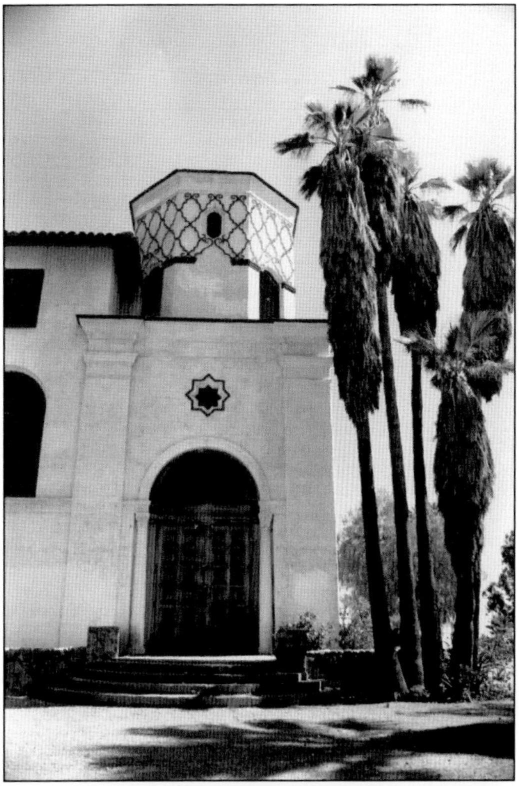

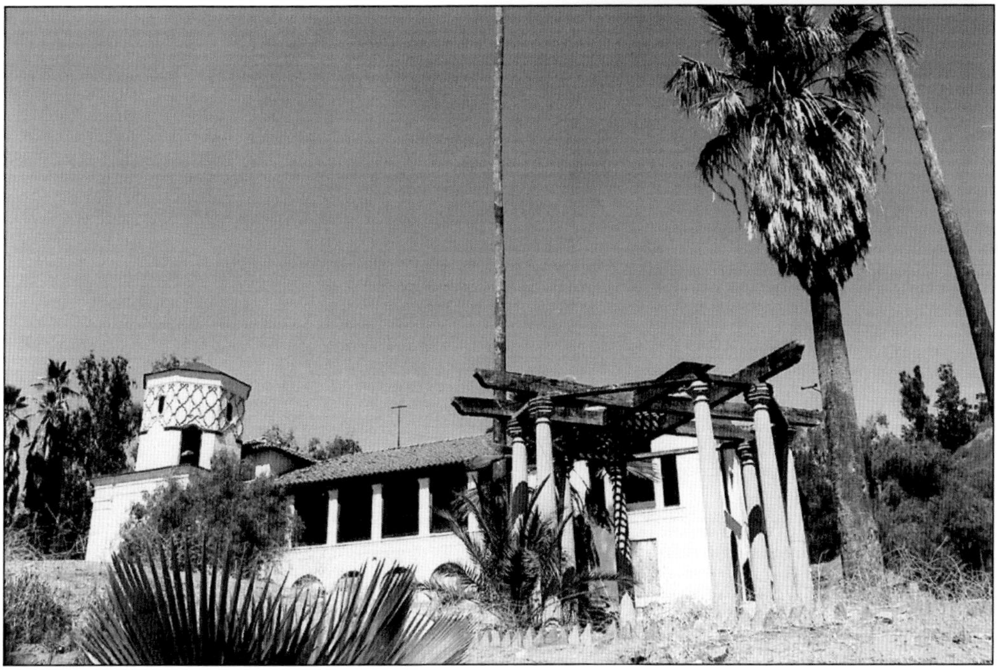

Palatial staircases, murals, secret tunnels, and a massive fireplace were included in the Clevelin Country Club. The tower and roof, seen here, were built using Spanish tile. (Courtesy Edythe J. Greene.)

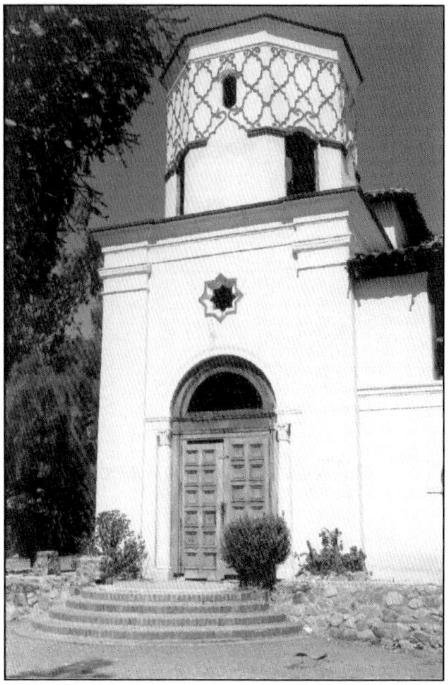

The Moorish-style country club had 20,000 square feet of floor space. This included a large ballroom, two apartments, dining room, bar, eight sleeping rooms, and many banquet halls and meeting rooms. It may have been a speakeasy during Prohibition. In the 1930s, Tyrone Power and other Hollywood personalities stayed here. It was also the scene of many senior proms and other gala events. (Courtesy Edythe J. Greene.)

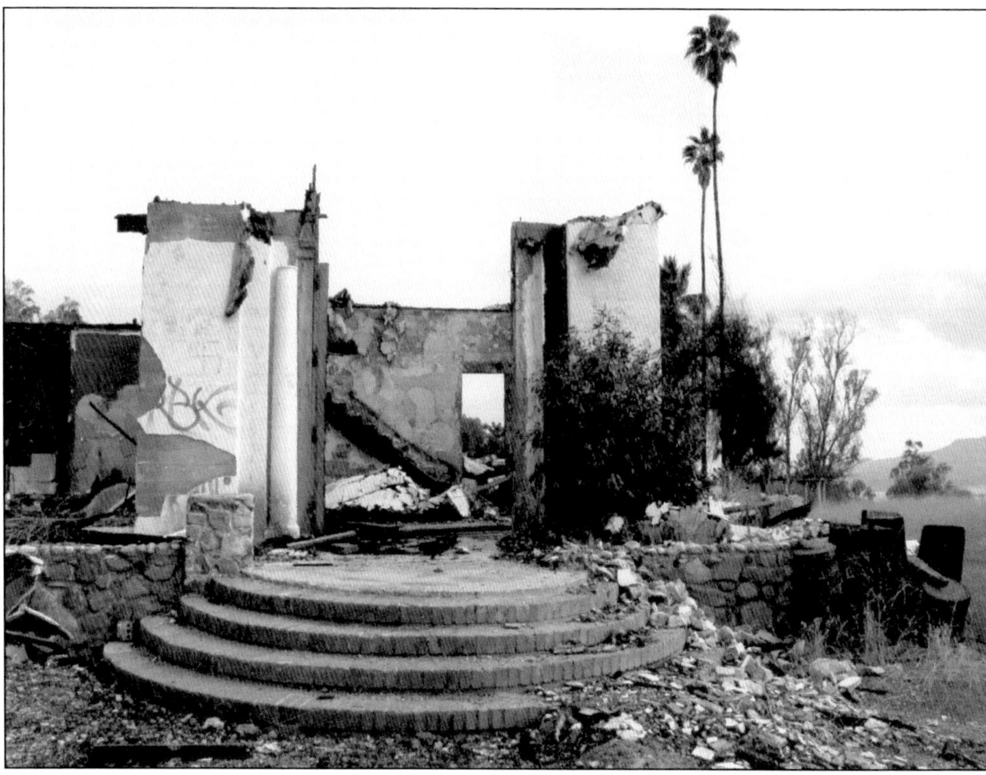

On Tuesday, January 2, 2001, in less than one hour, the Clevelin Country Club burned to the ground, even though valiant efforts were made by the Lake Elsinore Fire Department, which arrived within five minutes to battle the blaze. Nearby residents could see flaming chunks of wall and tile crash to the ground. It was considered a total loss. (Courtesy Edythe J. Greene.)

# *Six*

# Lake Elsinore Regions

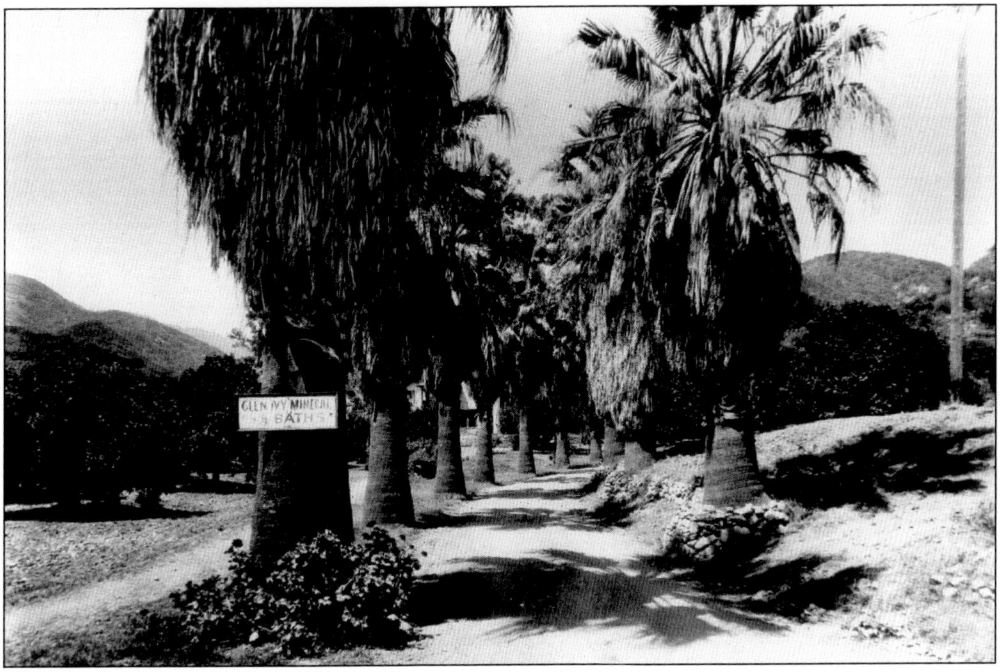

The first reference to commercial use of Glen Ivy's waters appeared in the *Los Angeles Star* in September 1860 as an advertisement for Temescal Hot Springs, inviting tired Overland Stage Company travelers to relax at the soothing mineral springs. From the early 1870s until it burned down in 1884, the small Coldwater Hotel, a half-mile north of the canyon mouth, catered to early spa goers. In 1879, what was to become the first Glen Ivy Hot Springs Hotel was built closer to the actual springs. Mr. and Mrs. W. G. Steers managed the inn at the springs. A dirt road framed by palm trees was the entrance to Glen Ivy. This photograph was taken *c.* 1890. (Courtesy Glen Ivy Spa.)

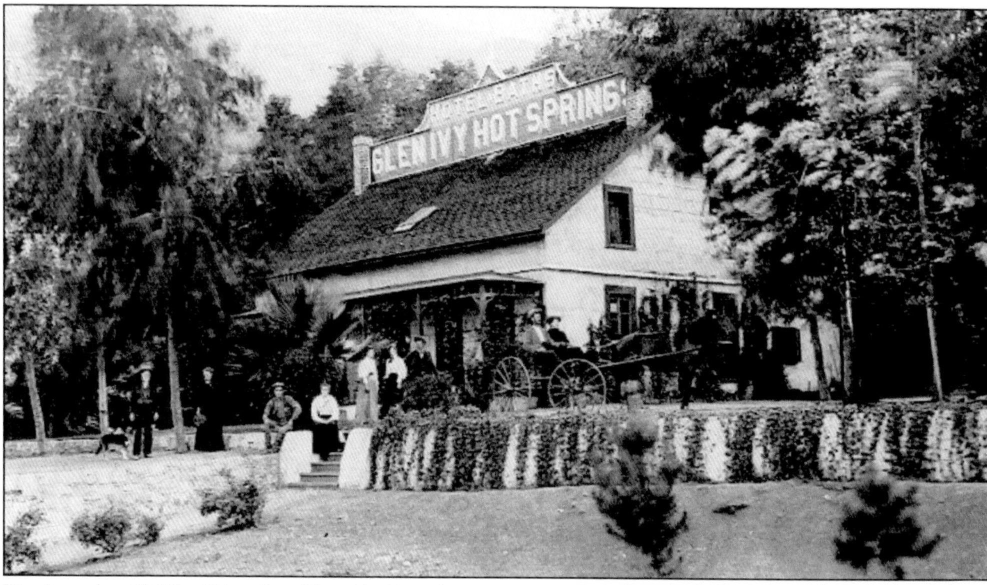


During the 1890s, Glen Ivy Hot Springs became a resort. In 1913, Frank and Mabel Johnson bought Glen Ivy and it gradually flourished under their ownership. The Johnsons made major improvements, including the installation of a dirt airstrip, and Glen Ivy grew in popularity. In the 1930s, Hollywood notables frequented the spa and Pres. Herbert Hoover was a guest in 1933. (Courtesy Glen Ivy Spa.)

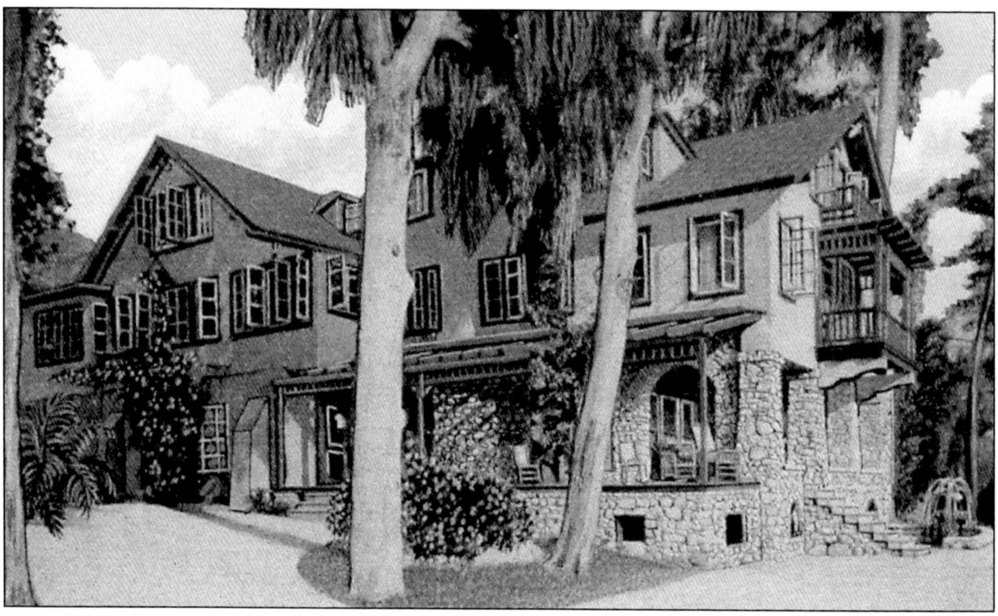

Danish hotelier and restaurateur, Axel Springborg, purchased Glen Ivy in the late 1930s and operated it successfully for nearly three decades. He retired in 1964, and sold Glen Ivy Hot Springs to Corona's Temescal Water Company. In 1969, a sudden rainstorm caused a flash flood that washed away a number of cottages and damaged the spa grounds. The local water company halted restoration work, the property was vandalized, and Springborg regained control of Glen Ivy. In one of Glen Ivy's sadder times, Axel began the search for a suitable new owner. (Courtesy Glen Ivy Spa.)

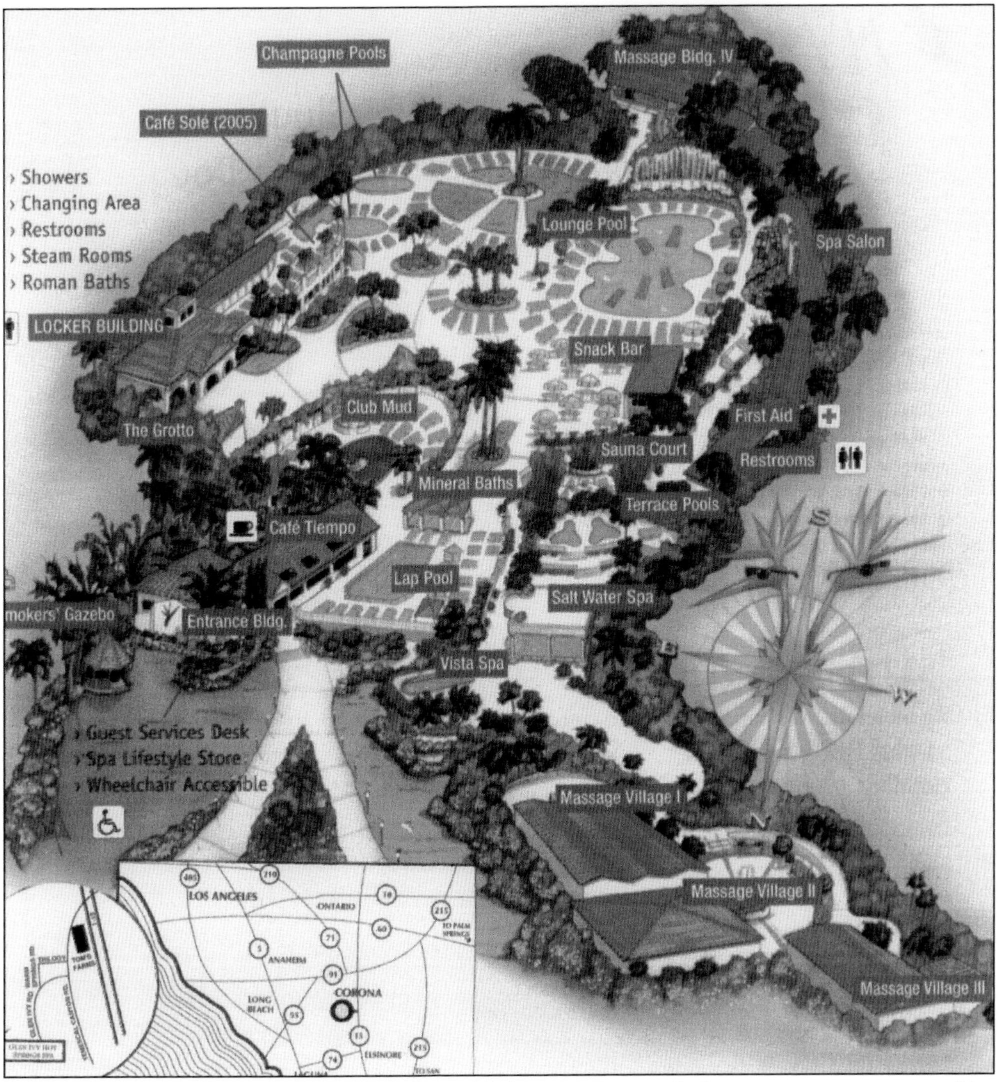


It was not until after 1977, when Axel resold the property and the spa was incorporated by private shareholders, that Glen Ivy began its fifth and current incarnation. Without sacrificing historical charm, Glen Ivy's facilities and grounds have been upgraded and expanded in recent years and the progress continues. The illustration depicts an aerial view of the grounds as they looked in 2004. Notice the many special-use buildings and the numerous pools and spas. (Courtesy Glen Ivy Spa.)

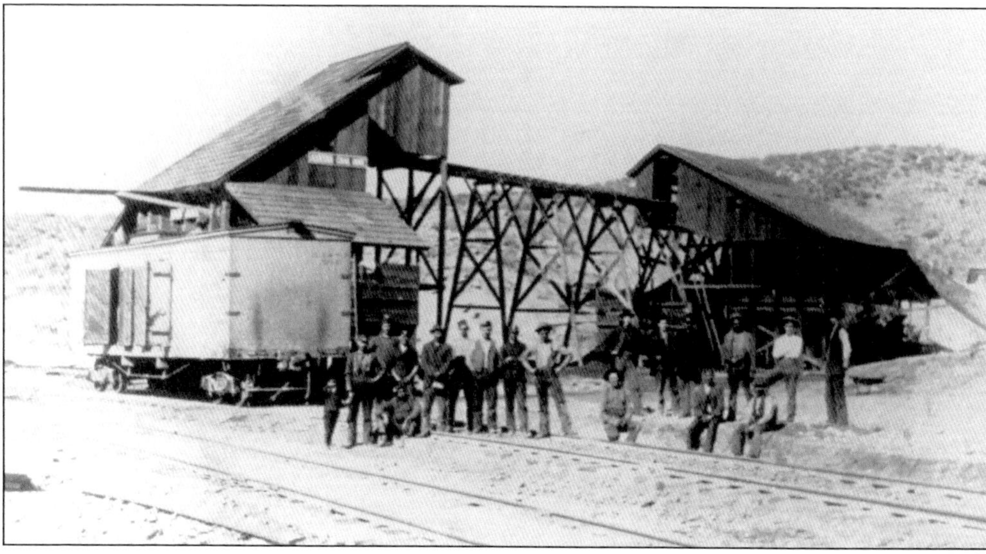

In 1886, C. H. Albers and J. H. Hill founded the community of Alberhill. Following this, two companies, the Alberhill Coal Company, maker of coal briquettes, and the Alberhill Clay Company, whose product was bricks, combined to form the Alberhill Coal and Clay Company. This was the most important industry in the Lake Elsinore Valley in the early 1900s, sustaining the area throughout the dry years, war years, and Great Depression. Here we see the Alberhill Coal Mines in 1938. (Courtesy Jeanie Corral.)

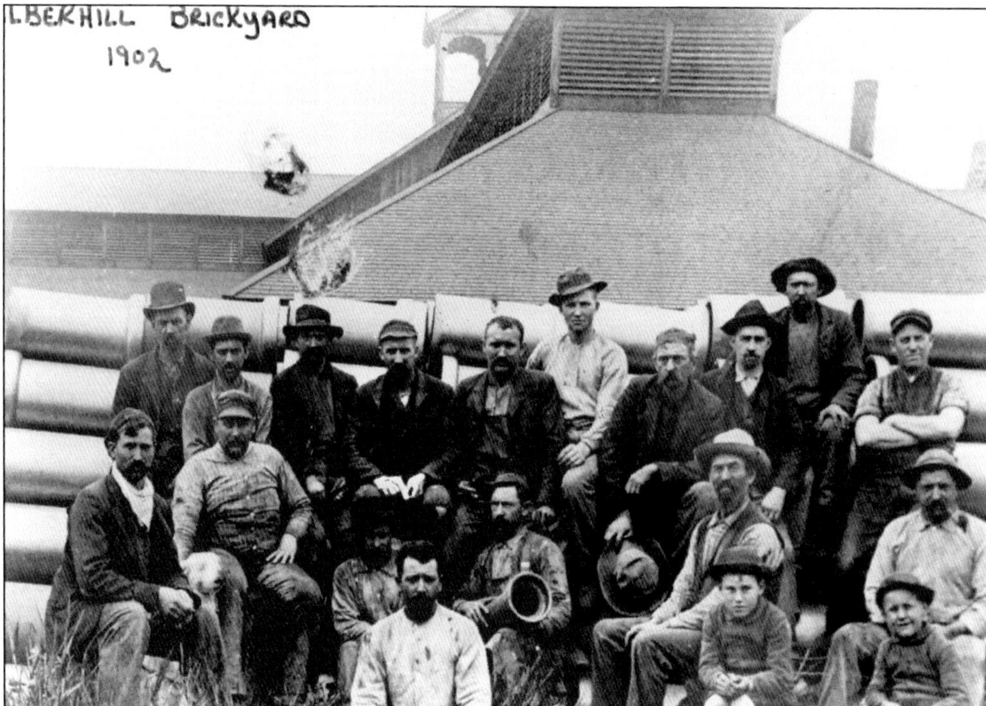


Alberhill Brickyard workers mined clay in 1902 in dangerous underground shafts where cave-ins were always a possibility. The men dug tunnels manually with shovels and transported the clay to the surface in wheelbarrows. (Courtesy Dr. Timothy Kimble, D.C.)

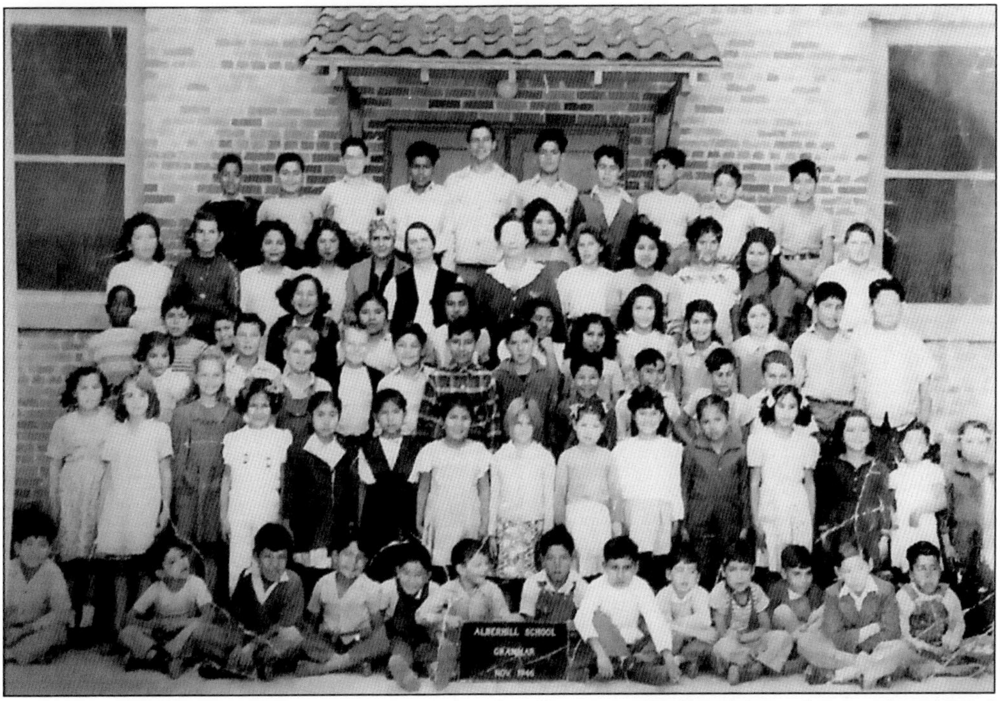

Members of the class of 1946 of the Alberhill Schoolhouse remember the good times they shared at school and the nearby camps where they lived. Many reunions have been held at the Alberhill Schoolhouse. (Courtesy Joe Ortega.)

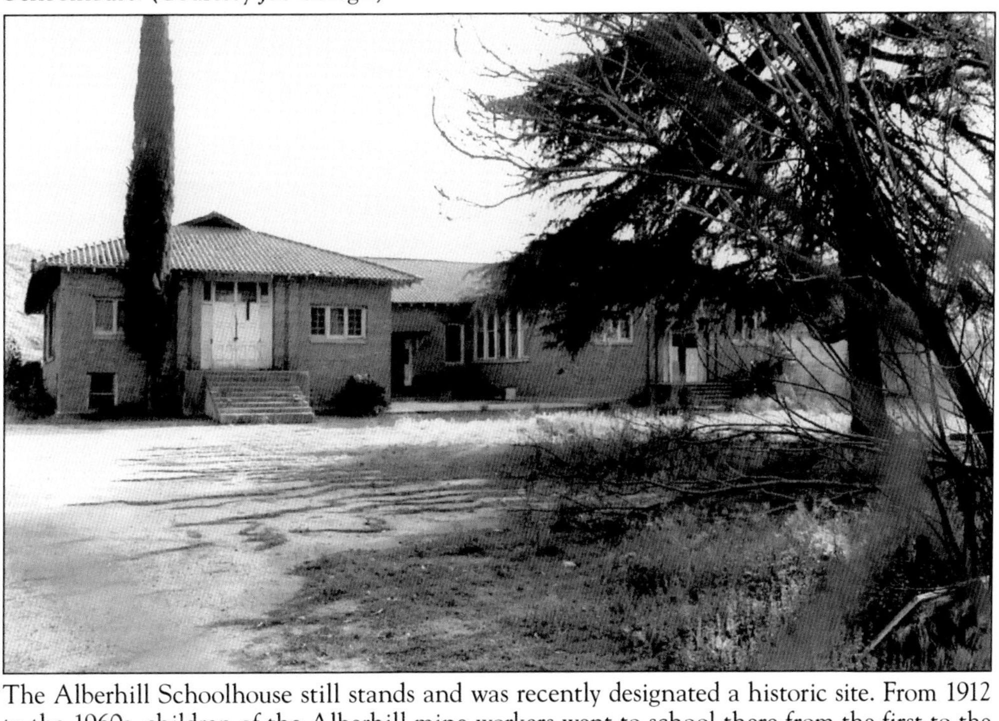

The Alberhill Schoolhouse still stands and was recently designated a historic site. From 1912 to the 1960s, children of the Alberhill mine workers went to school there from the first to the eighth grade. (Courtesy Edythe J. Greene.)

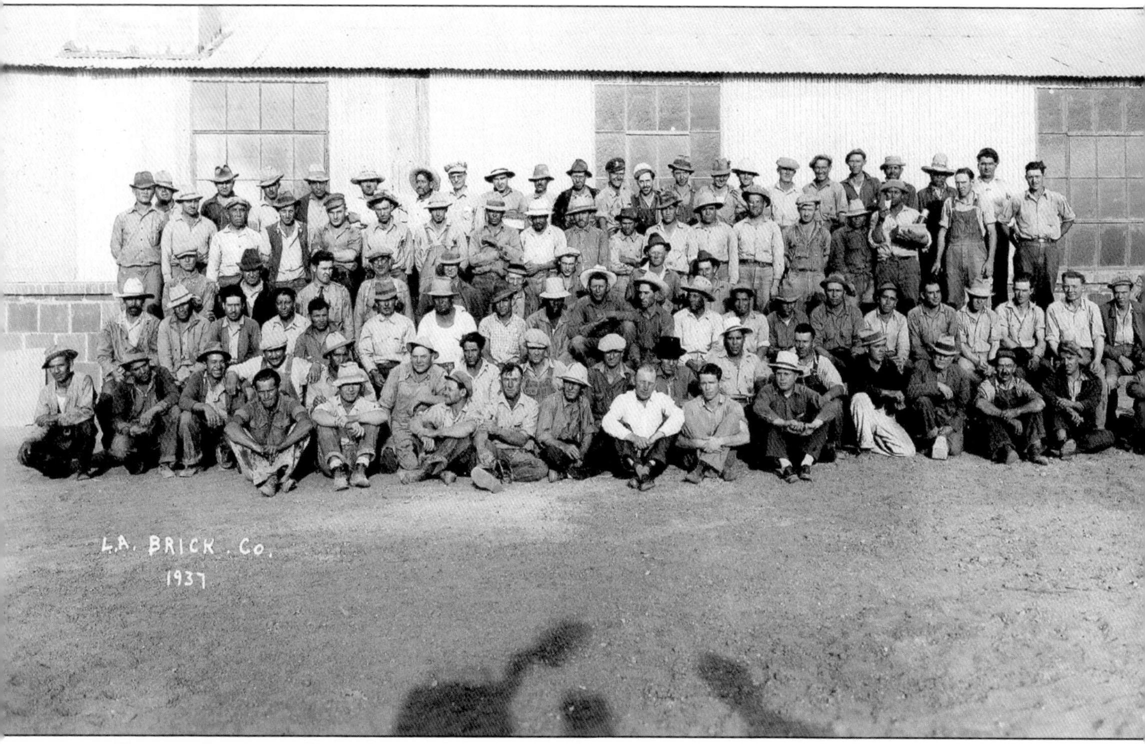


During the Great Depression of the 1930s, the clay producing companies of the Lake Elsinore Valley were the major employers in the area and comprised one of the few industries that were then profitable. Here we see workers of the Los Angeles Brick and Clay Company in 1937. (Courtesy Pauline Rodriguez.)

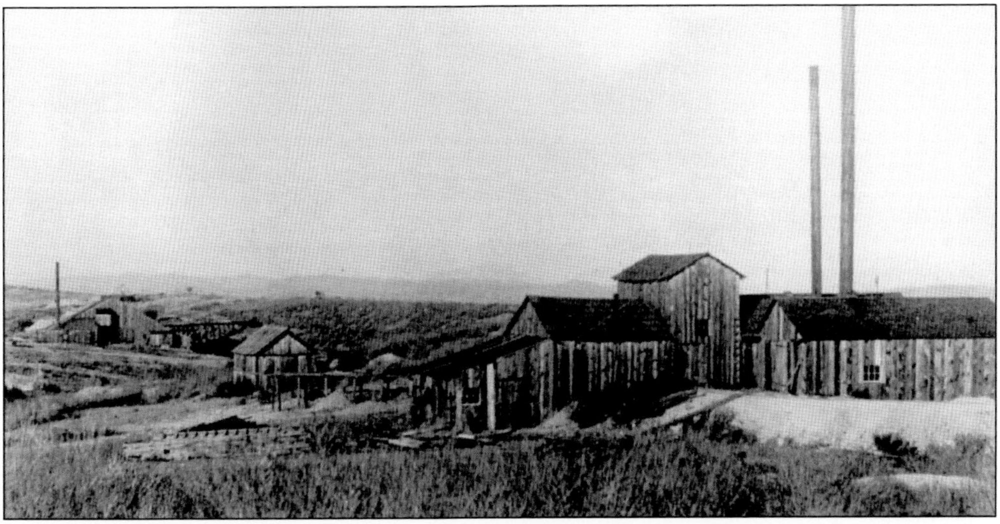

In the 1880s, John D. Huff formed the Southern California Coal and Clay Company northwest of Lake Elsinore. In 1887, the town of Terra Cotta, with its own post office, was formed. Coal from the Terra Cotta Mines was used for fuel in four kilns. The finest quality clay was sent by wagons six miles away to the Lake Elsinore Depot. In addition, the Terra Cotta Mines produced 10 miles of tiles for the underground telephone wires in Los Angeles. (Courtesy Jeanie Corral.)

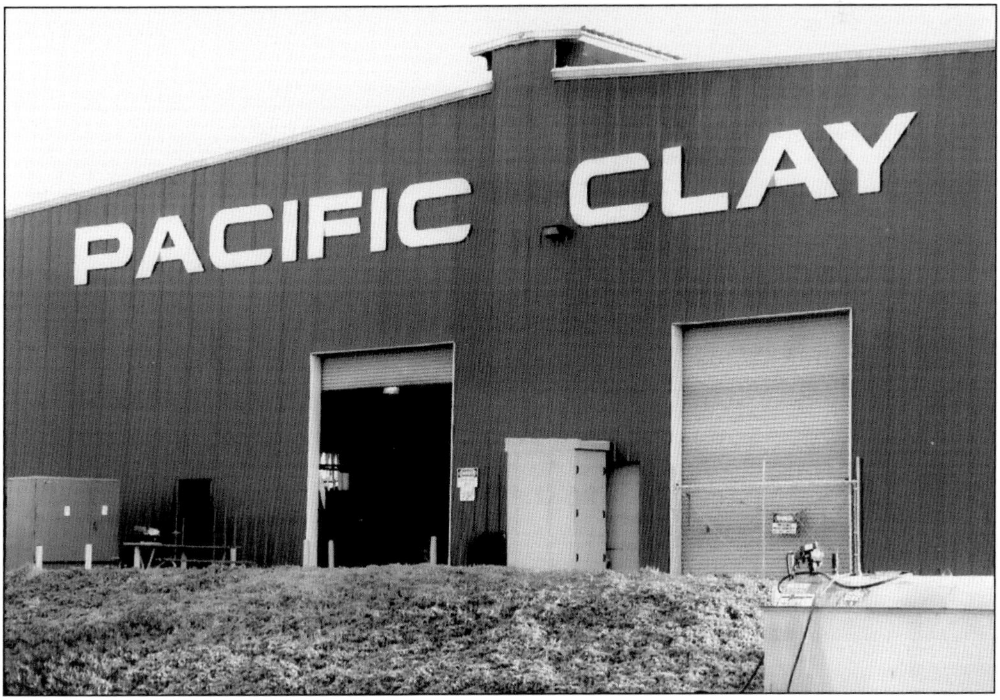


The Pacific Clay Products Company moved to Alberhill in the 1940s, and took over the Terra Cotta Mines. In 1963, Pacific bought out the Alberhill Coal and Clay Mines. It leased the land from descendants of the original owners, James Hill and William Collier. Unlike mines where coal is dug from deep in the earth, here the coal veins lay on top of the ground, covering large deposits of clay. Now, since there is no demand for coal, it is broken up in order to get to the clay. (Courtesy Edythe J. Greene.)

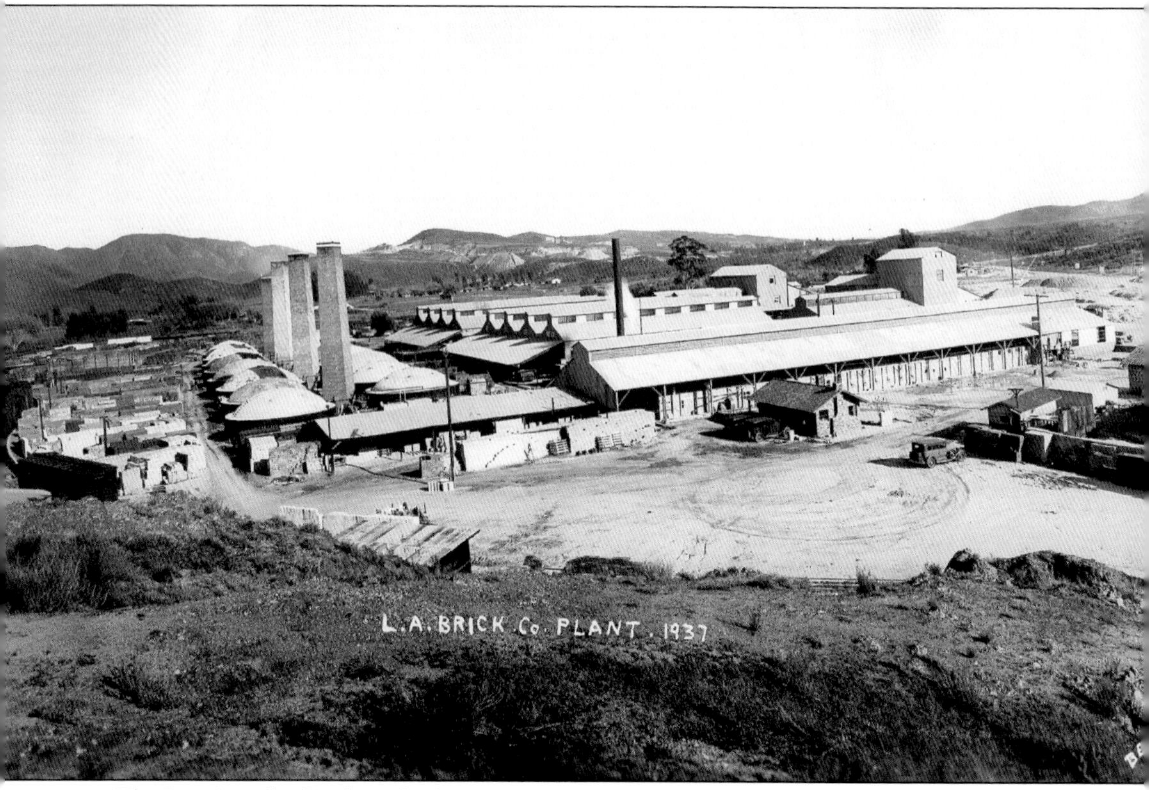


The Los Angeles Brick and Clay Company opened in 1927, and provided half of the houses in Riverside County with hollow tile. However, 90 percent of the clay products shipped to Los Angeles were from Alberhill. The Los Angeles Brick and Clay Company plant is shown as it appeared in 1937. (Courtesy Pauline Rodriguez.)

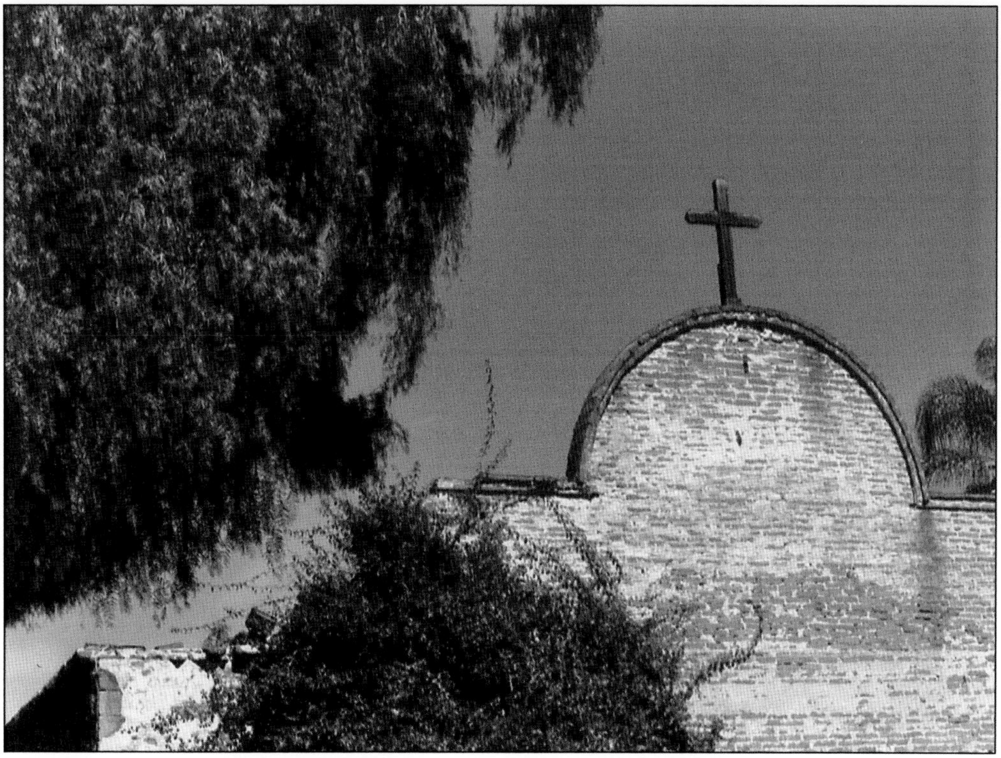

A road from the Pacific Coast to the summit of the Elsinore Mountains had been built by the Mission padres of San Juan Capistrano in the late 1700s. But this road was so dangerous and tortuous that it was little traveled. The mountain summit, Sierra de Santiago, named by the Spaniards, overlooks the lake and the mountains, which have been recently become known as the Ortega Mountains. In 1893, the nearby Cleveland National Forest was established. (Courtesy Louise Rowden.)

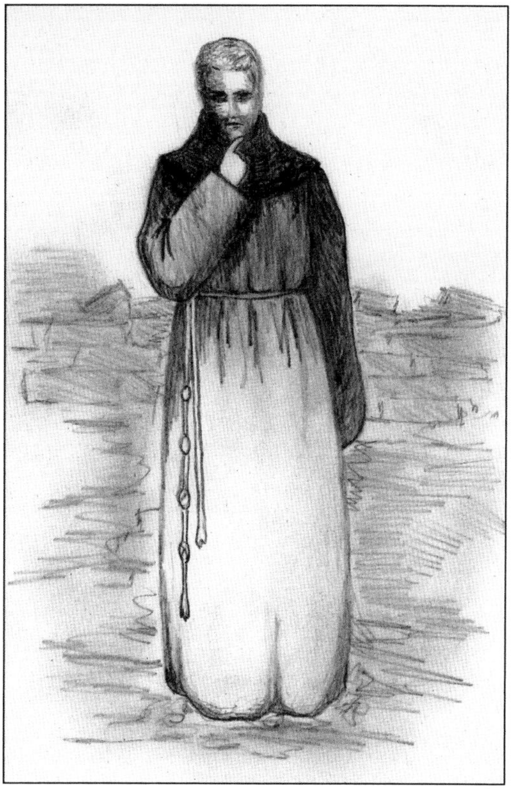

In October 1797, Fr. Juan Santiago, a Franciscan padre, was sent out from the Mission San Juan Capistrano in search of a promising site for a new mission. From the mountain's summit, Father Santiago looked down on a surprising scene—a lake bordered by willows and cottonwood trees, clouds of steam rising from hot mineral springs, deer browsing, and antelope grazing. (Courtesy Joe Dwaileebe.)

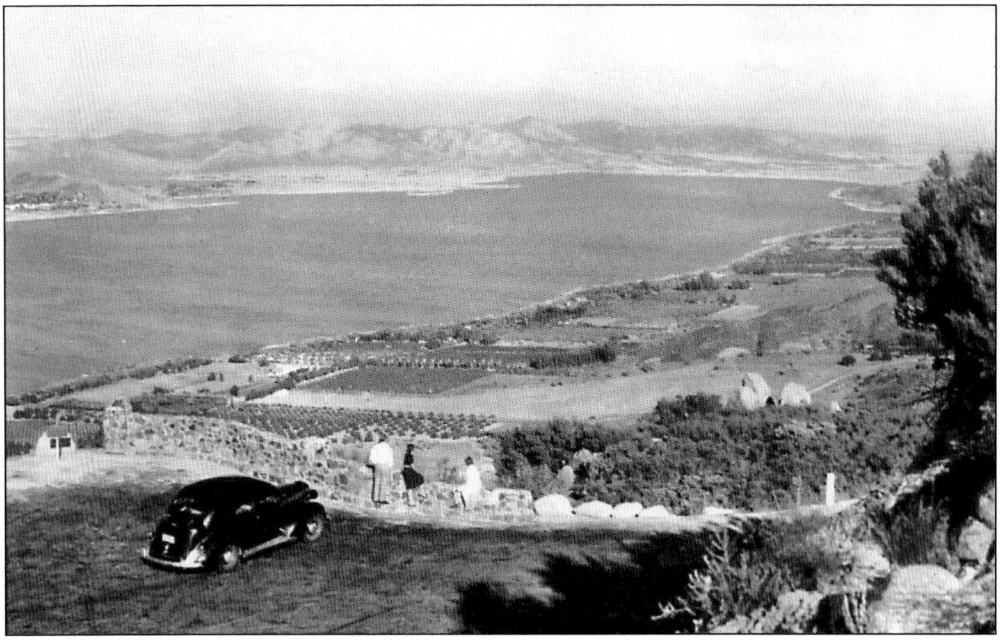

Lake Elsinore is viewed from the top of the Ortega Highway. Because the view is so inspiring, this elevated site is now often called Inspiration Point. The lake is also known for its adjacent hot springs. (Courtesy Jeanie Corral.)

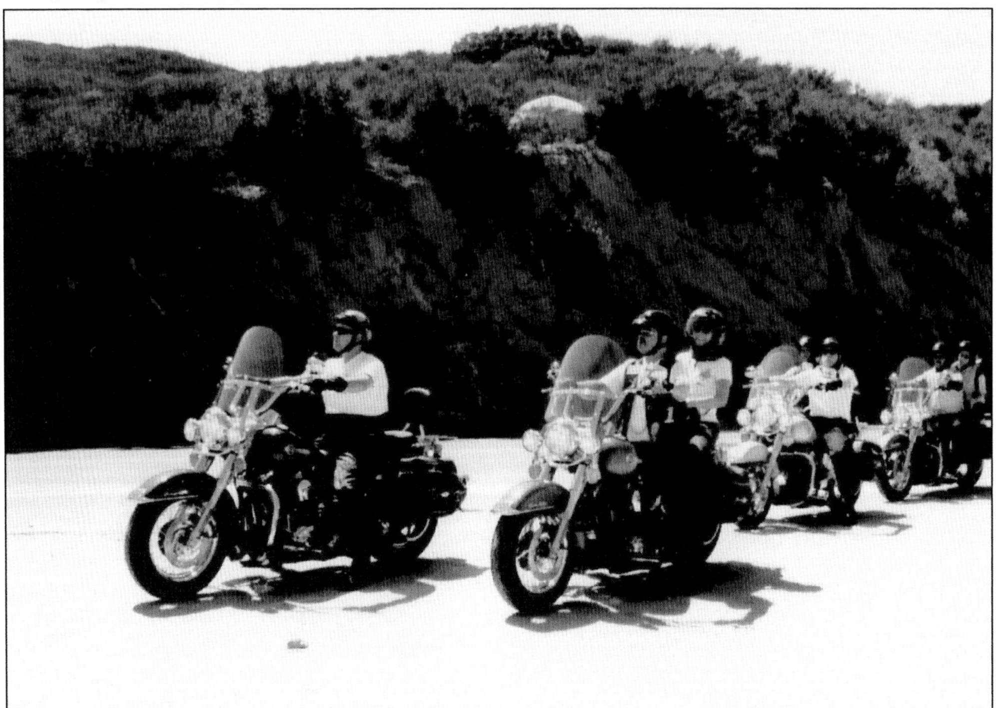

During 10 months out of each year, motorcycle groups from Europe fly into Los Angeles to tour the West Coast. They rent motorcycles, and traditionally include the Ortega Highway as part of their tour. This particular group is from Germany. (Courtesy Edythe J. Greene.)

Overlooking the lake from the Ortega Highway is the Lookout Road House. This is a favorite stop to view the lake and rest before starting down the steep and winding drop to the lake below. Often on a Sunday morning, Joe Greene of Meadowbrook, California, rode his motorcycle up to the Lookout Road House. (Courtesy Edythe J. Greene.)

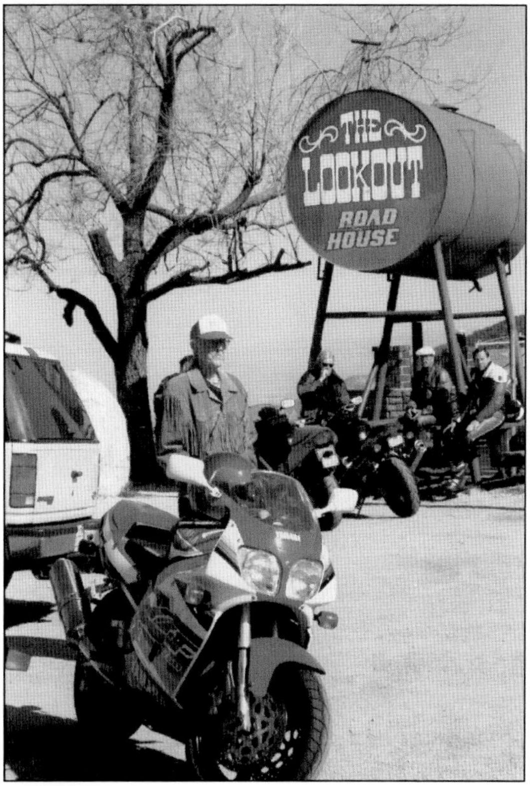


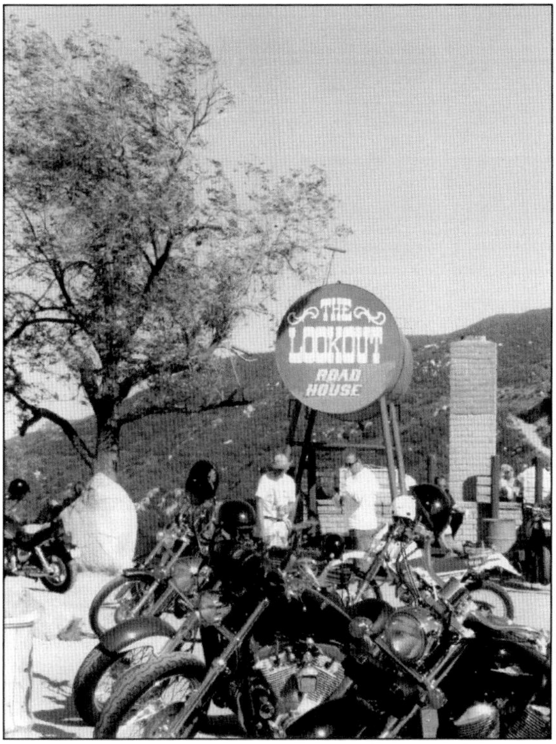


Built in 1945, the original cafe had a greatly enviable location. It was purchased in 1968 and renamed the Lookout Road House. Because of its unique location, the Lookout has served as a popular gathering place. (Courtesy Louise Rowden.)

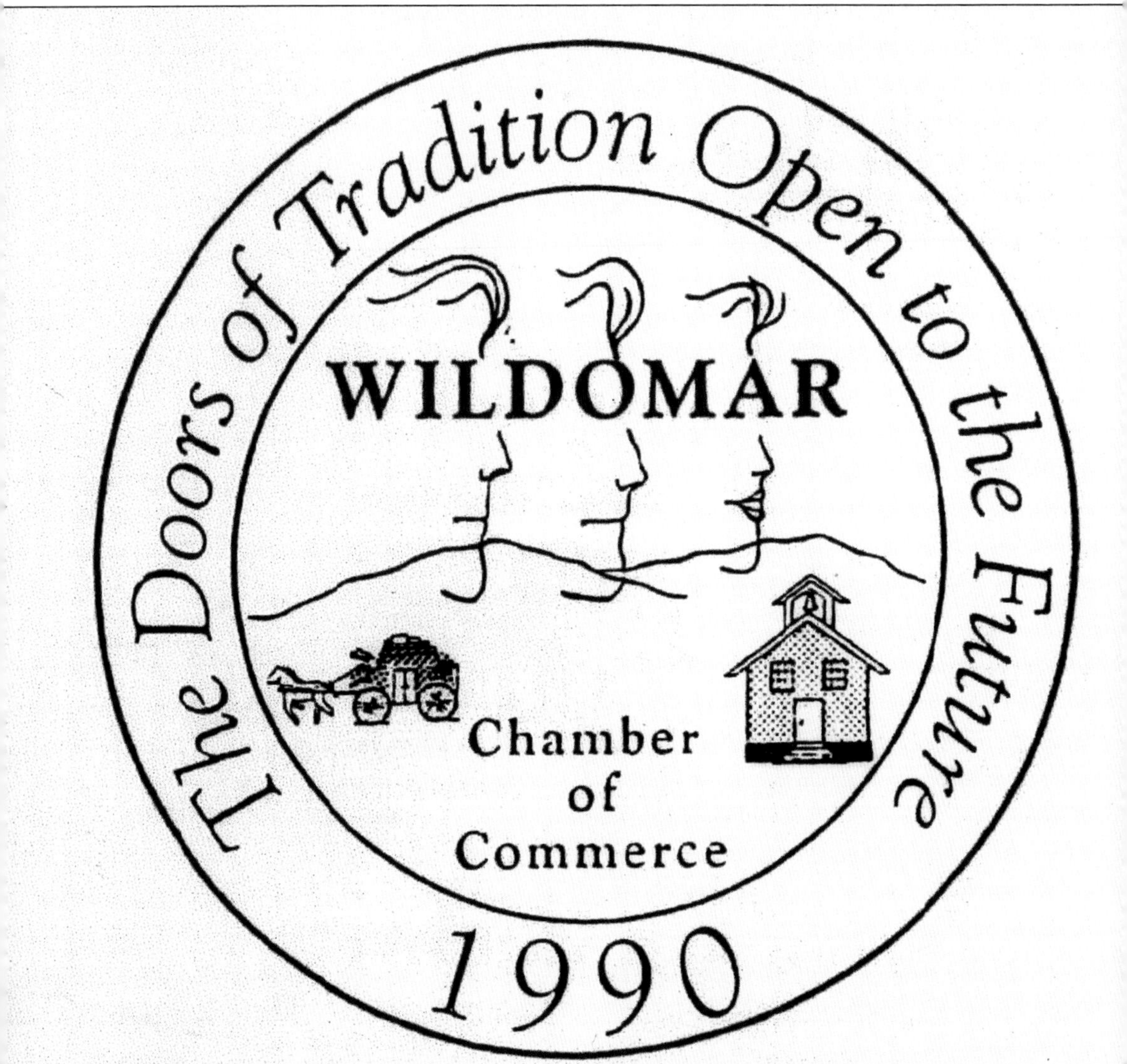


In 1885, Donald Graham and his brother-in-law William Collier established the town of Wildomar, which was originally called Rancho La Laguna. What started off as a small railroad depot was, by 1886, a thriving town. Its first school and post office had opened, and soon to come were a large hotel, blacksmith's forge, and lumberyard. (Courtesy Riverside County Library System.)

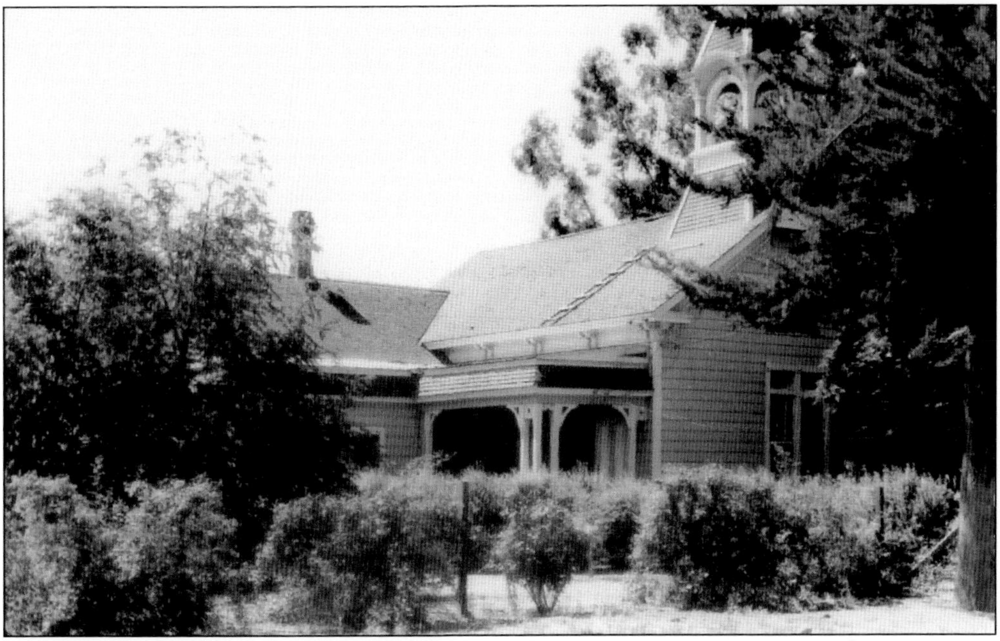

In 1886, Wildomar Elementary School was established. It was originally a one-room schoolhouse, which expanded to two rooms as the community grew. The original school bell in the bell tower is still outside the school. The building has since been replaced. (Courtesy Wildomar Historical Society.)

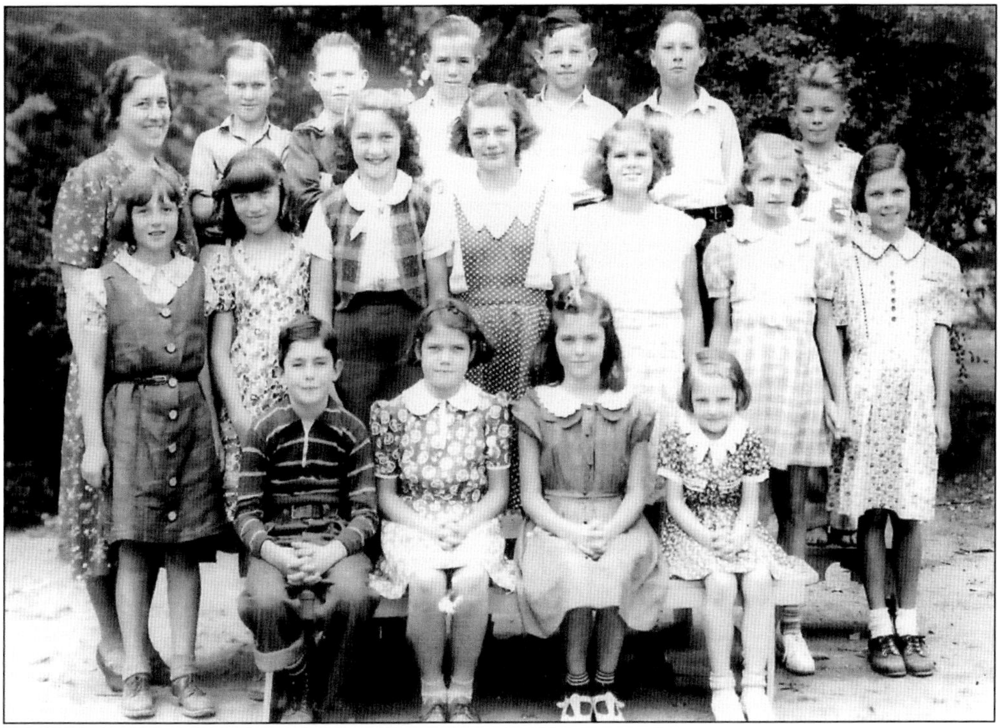

Teacher Iva Keegan is seen here with her class at Wildomar Elementary School in 1936. (Courtesy Wildomar Historical Society.)

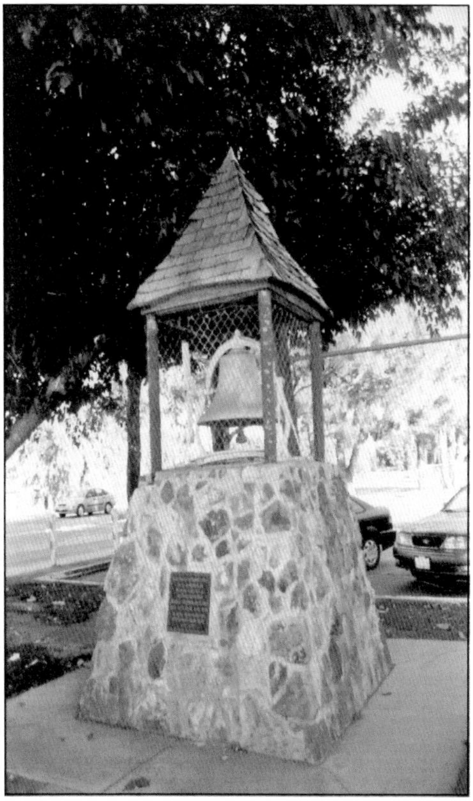

The Wildomar School was built in September 1886 on land donated by William Collier and Donald Graham. The school bell, last rung in June 1958, is displayed in its unique stone memorial. (Courtesy Edythe J. Greene.)

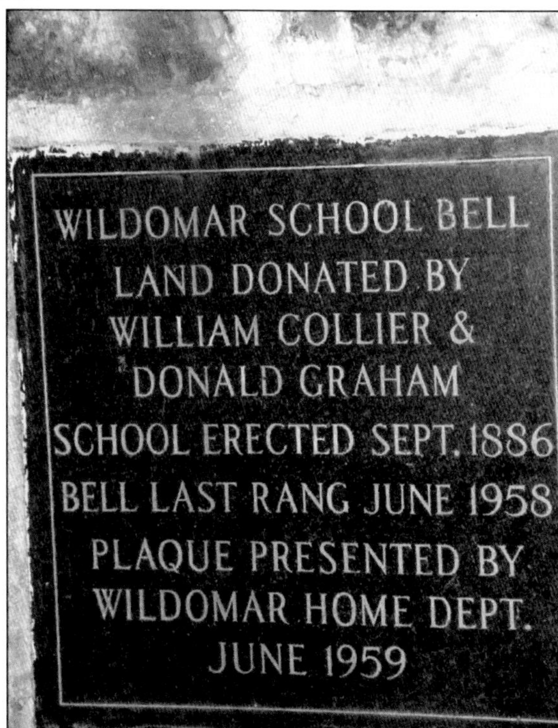


Shown here is a close-up of the plaque on the Wildomar School Bell Memorial, which was presented by the Wildomar Home Department in June 1959. (Courtesy Edythe J. Greene.)

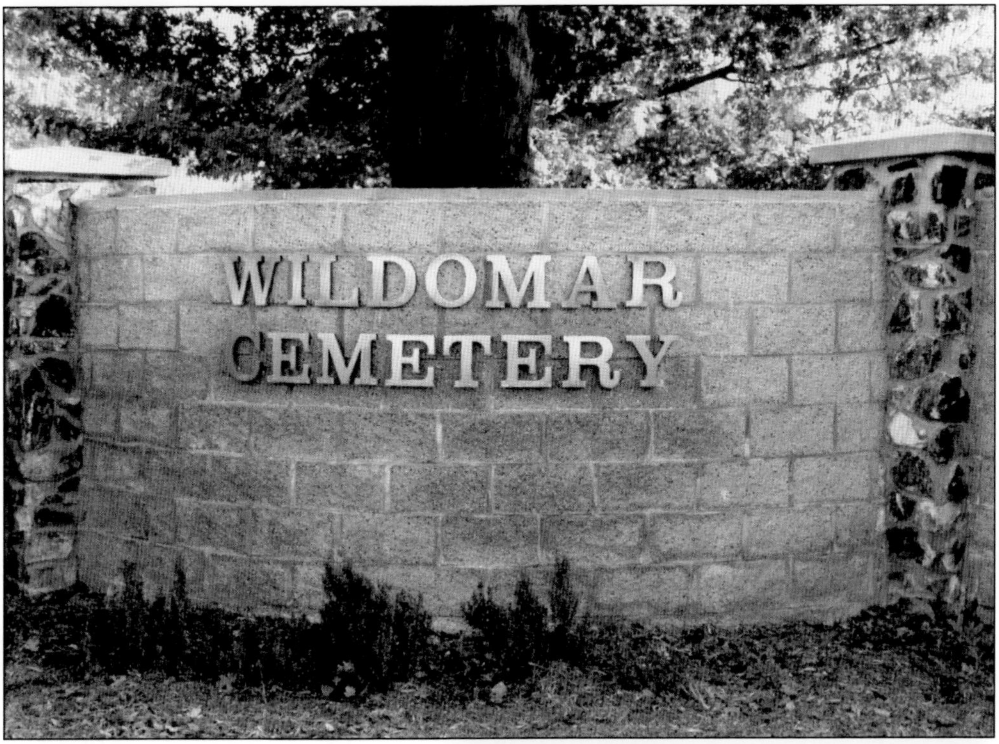


In the early days when the railroad was built from San Bernardino to San Diego, Wildomar became a boom town. In March 1898, when Wildomar's population was 500, the citizens organized the Wildomar Cemetery Association. A beautiful five-acre site was purchased some distance from town for use as a cemetery, and a number of persons subscribed as members, paying $5 per lot and about 60 cents for additional expenses. (Courtesy Edythe J. Greene.)

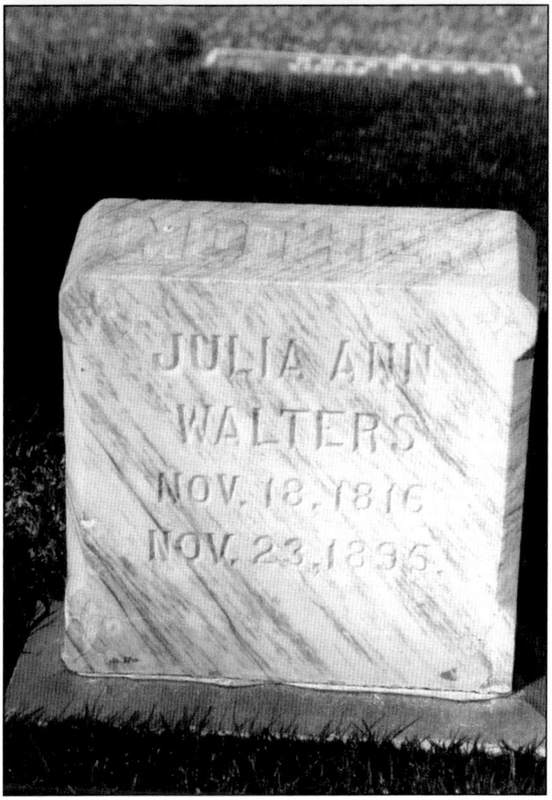


A few large headstones are still standing at Wildomar, including that of Julie Ann Walters, which is dated November 18, 1816, to November 23, 1895. Over the years, several groups have worked at cleaning up some of the neglected areas of this ancient cemetery. (Courtesy Edythe J. Greene.)

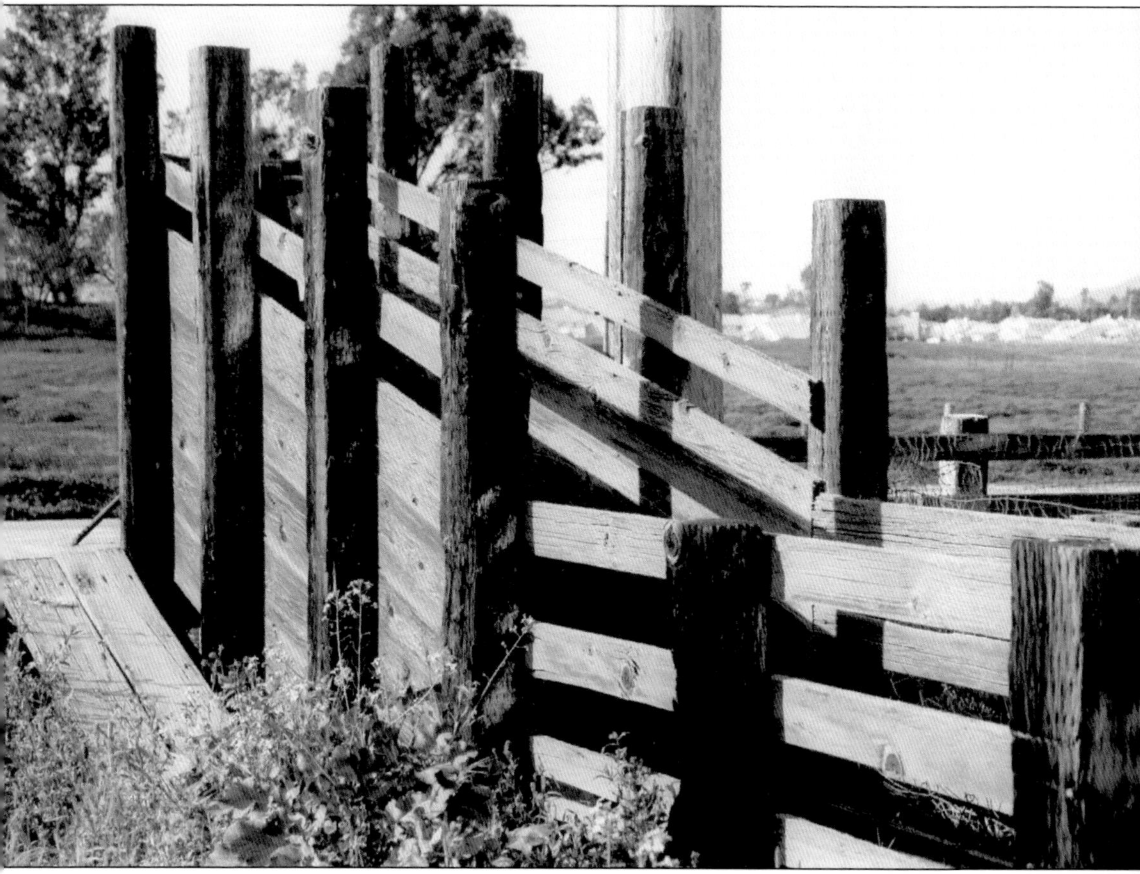

The wooden posts of a cattle chute still stand at Pasadena and Grand. The ranchers would load the cattle onto the chute from a pen near the railroad and then into trucks to take to ranches and slaughterhouses. (Courtesy Edythe J. Greene.)

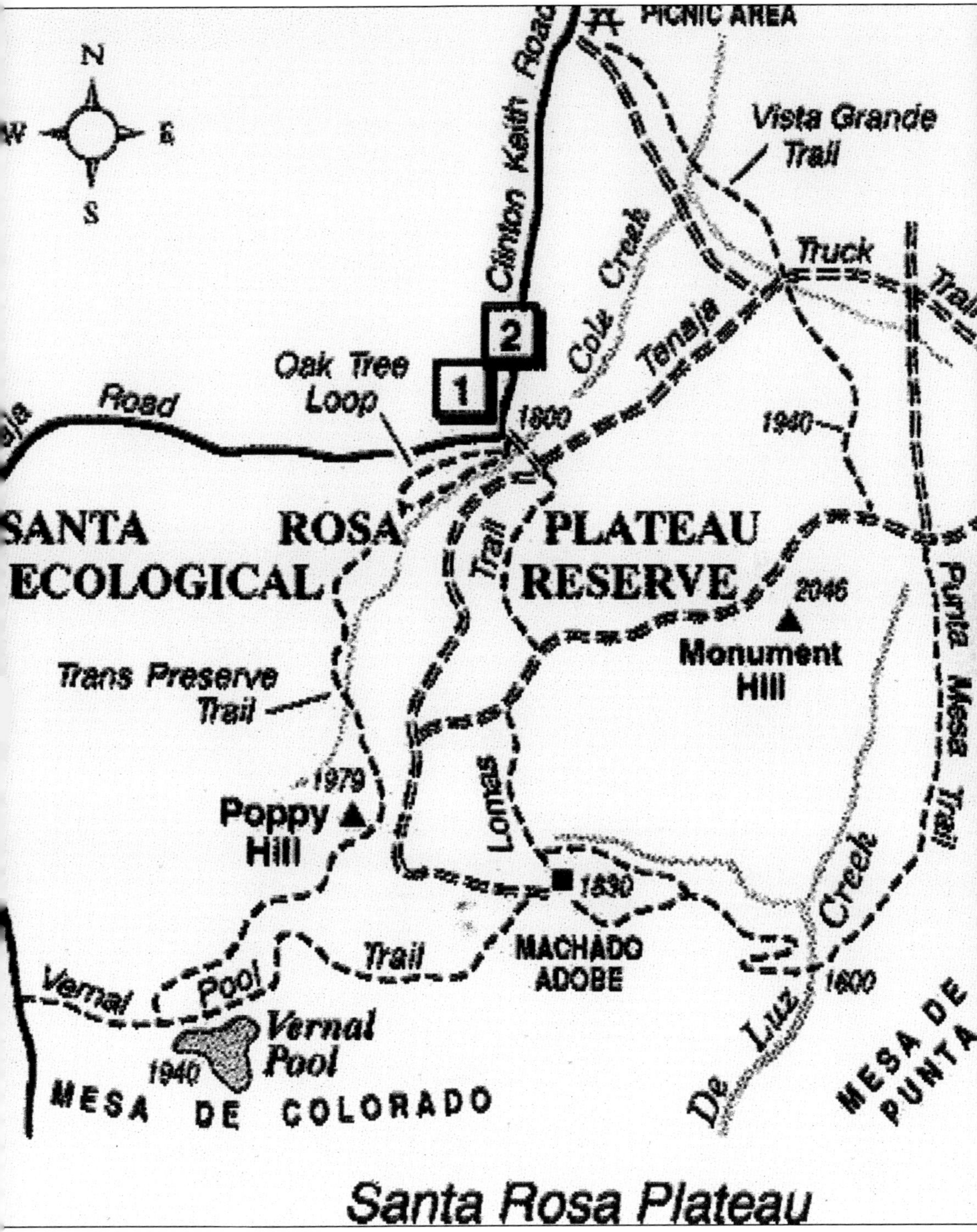


This is a trail map of the Santa Rosa Plateau, showing points of interest.

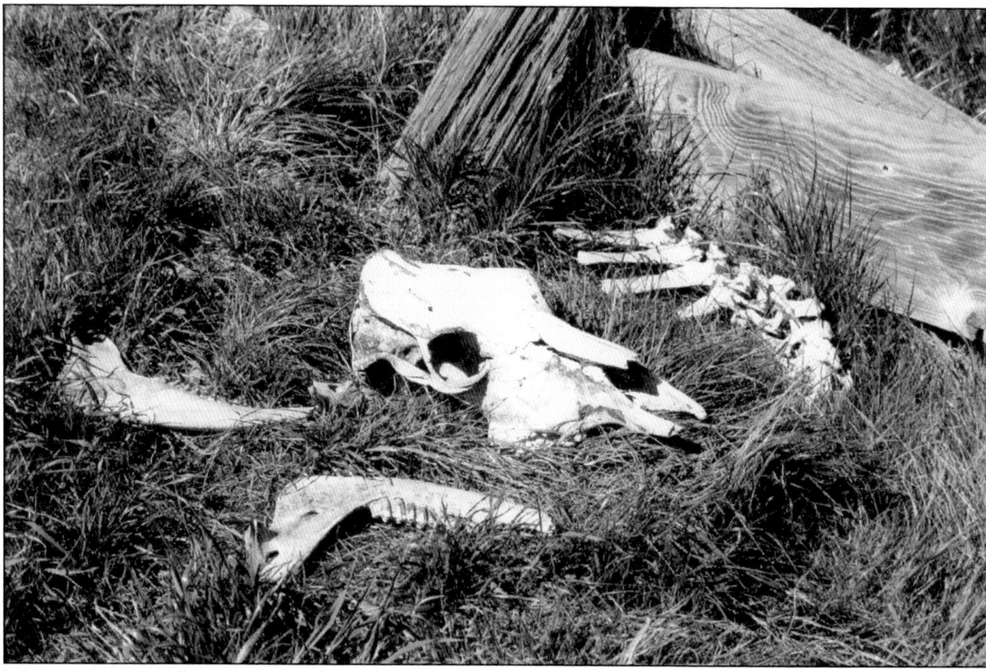

Many years ago, the Luiseno tribe of American Indians settled on the Santa Rosa Plateau because of the mild climate. They lived on the plateau until 1820. Mountain lions and coyotes roamed the area foraging for food. Perhaps these bones were the result of one of those hunts. (Courtesy Edythe J. Greene)

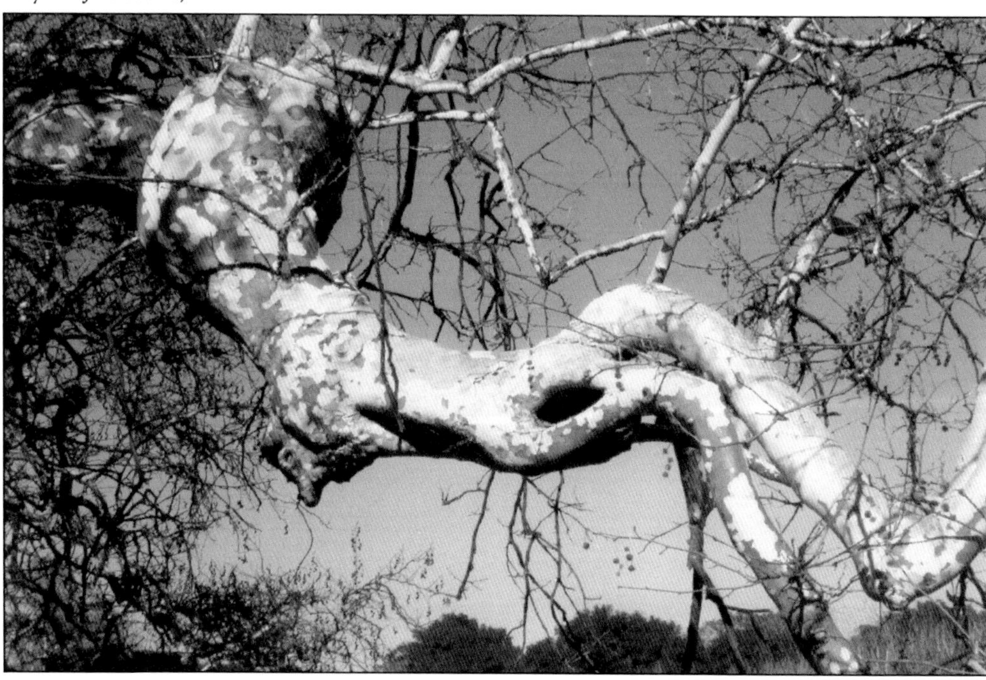

Oak Tree Trail is a short expressive loop trail that goes through an Engleman Oak woodland near the main plateau entrance. As the giant trees grow on the Santa Rosa Plateau, their limbs become one of local nature's most picturesque subjects. (Courtesy Louise Rowden.)

The Santa Rosa Plateau is extremely enjoyable anytime of the year, but especially in the springtime when green grasses fringe the scattered boulders and poppies splash the hillsides. (Courtesy Edythe J. Greene.)

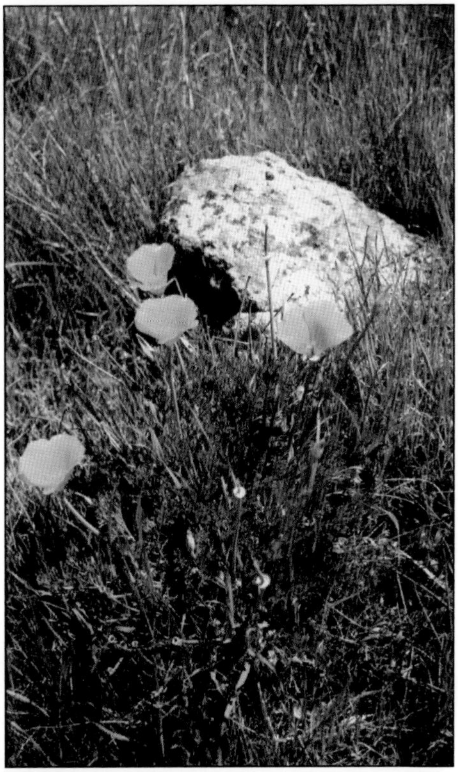

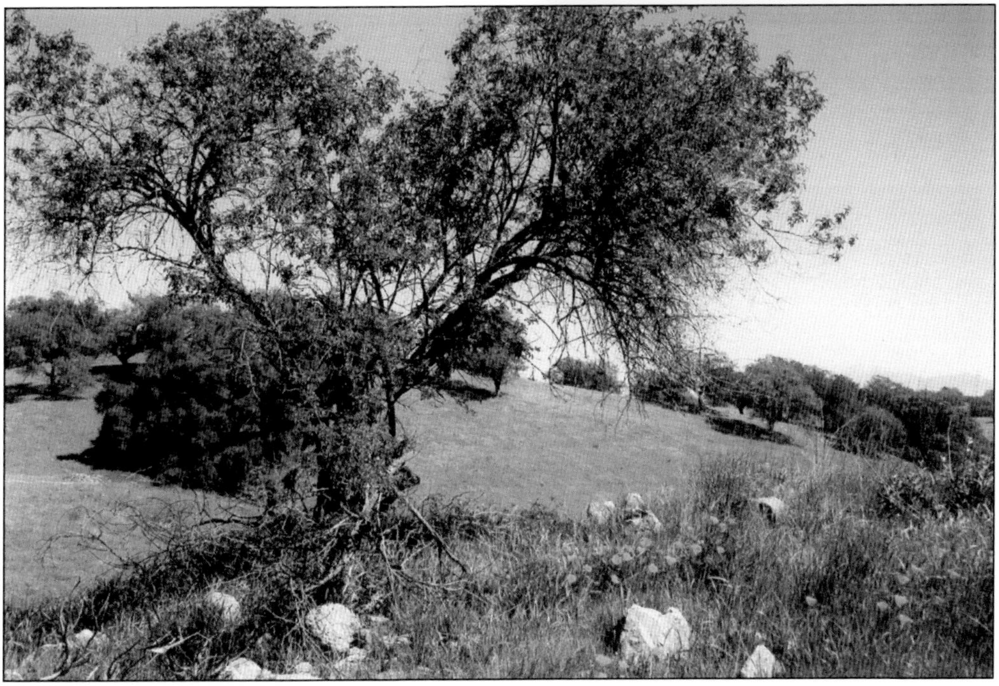

Low hills roll along covered by some of Southern California's finest grasslands. Old ranch roads occasionally cross the meadows and scattered oak trees help bring to life a view resembling a centuries-old landscape painting. (Courtesy Edythe J. Greene.)

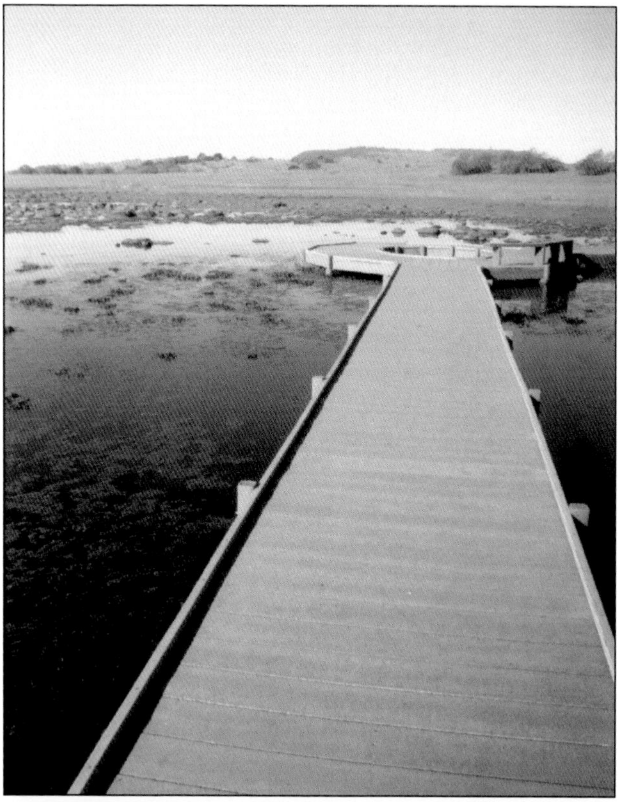

Vernal pools may look like other ponds, but they support a unique short-term environmental system. They provide a fleeting home for plants that grow in scattered spots, thanks to migratory birds that transport the seeds. As the water recedes, plants on the edge begin to bloom. One week, blue water is ringed by yellow fields. Weeks later, bluebells will trace the edges of the water. (Courtesy Buddy Nickel.)

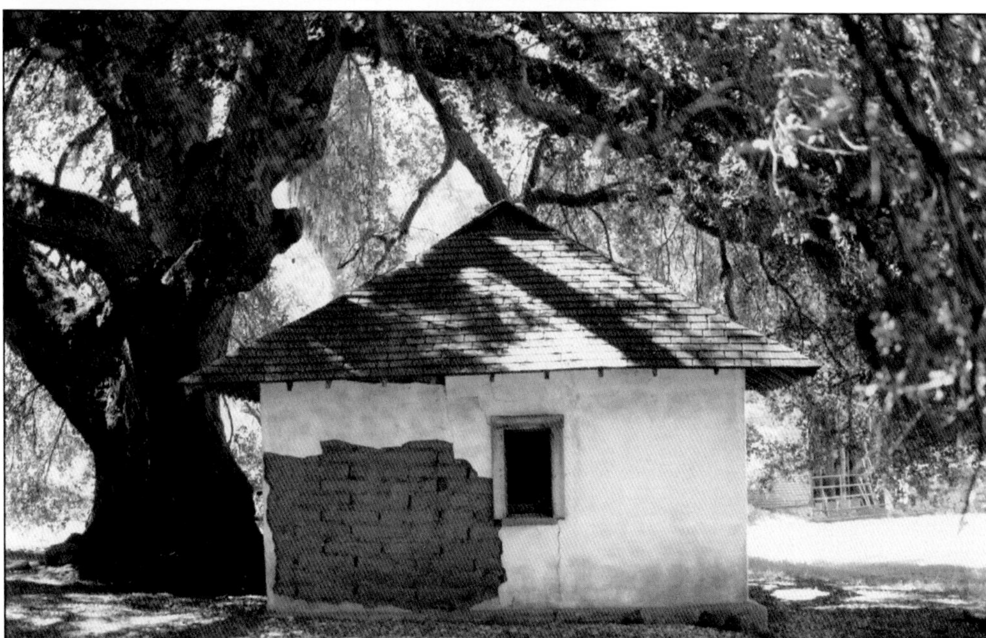

This adobe house is located in the Santa Rosa Plateau on the adobe loop trail as it winds through a beautiful forest area. These adobes are the oldest buildings in the area that became Riverside County. In 1846, Juan Moreno built the first adobe. (Courtesy Edythe J. Greene.)

# *Seven*

# 1950 to Present

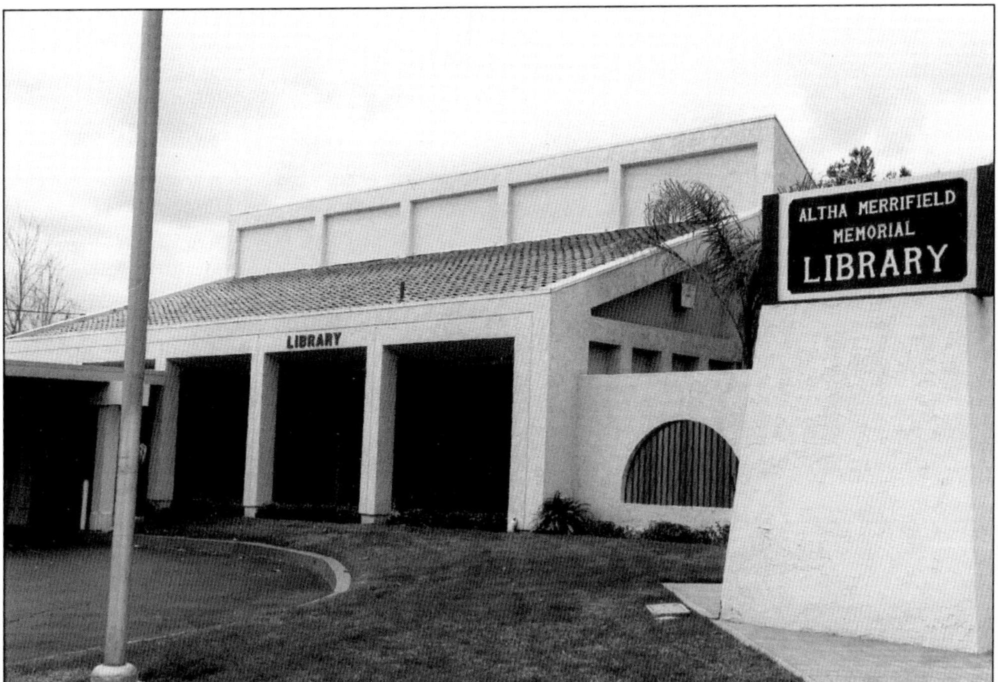


In honor of Altha Merrifield's 45 years of service to the library located at 600 West Graham Avenue in Elsinore, it was named the Altha Merrifield Memorial Library. (Courtesy Edythe J. Greene.)

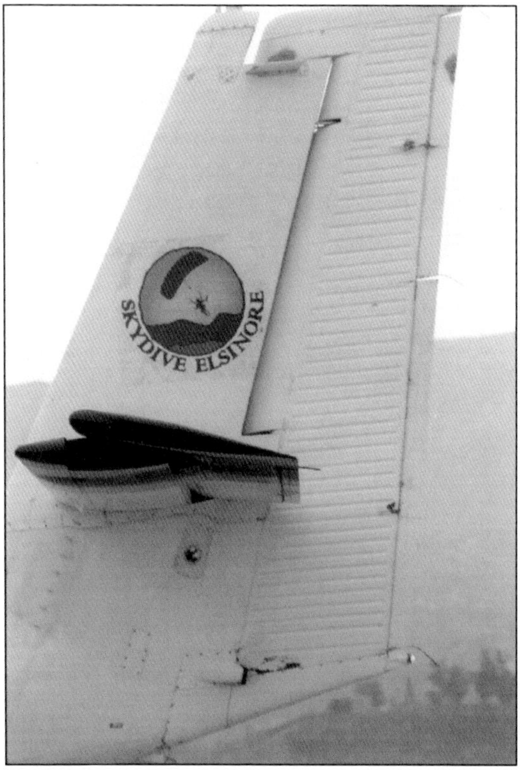


In 1952, Cy and Florence Perkins and their son Larry purchased the Corydon Street Airport and changed its name to Skylark Field. The airport soon became widely known for the large amount of traffic it handled, and became headquarters for gliders and, in time, skydivers. The 1960s television program *Ripcord*, starring Larry Pennell and Ken Curtis, was filmed at Skylark Field by Para Ventures, Inc., with offices in Hollywood as well as at Skylark Field. (Courtesy Louise Rowden.)

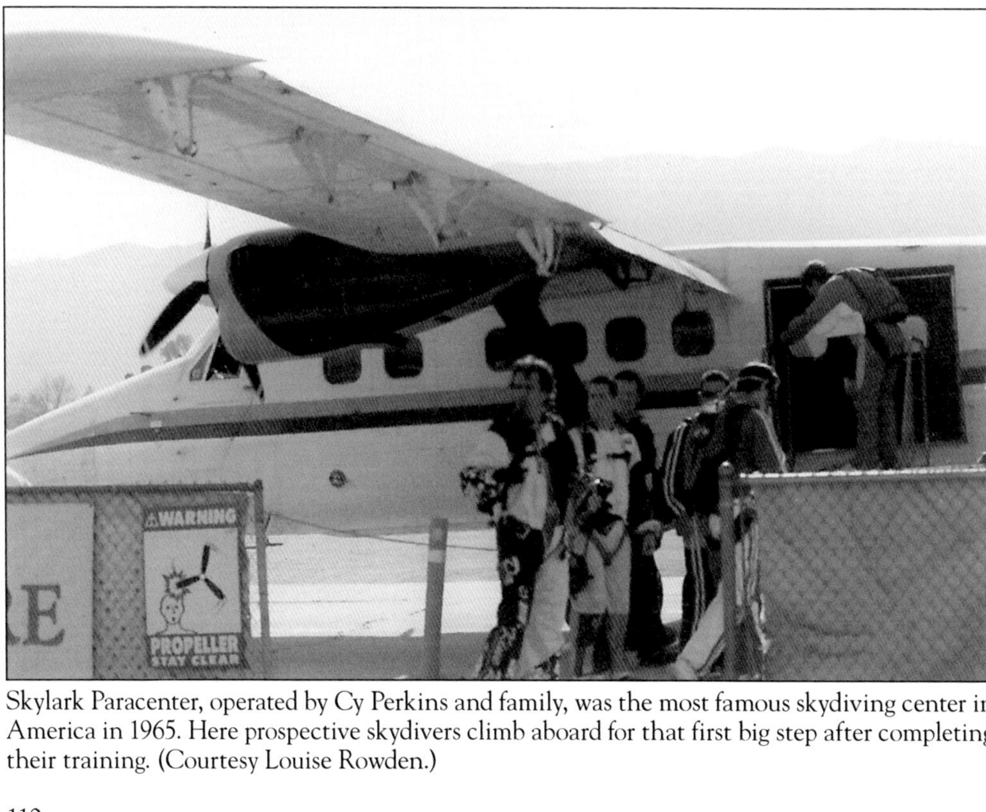


Skylark Paracenter, operated by Cy Perkins and family, was the most famous skydiving center in America in 1965. Here prospective skydivers climb aboard for that first big step after completing their training. (Courtesy Louise Rowden.)

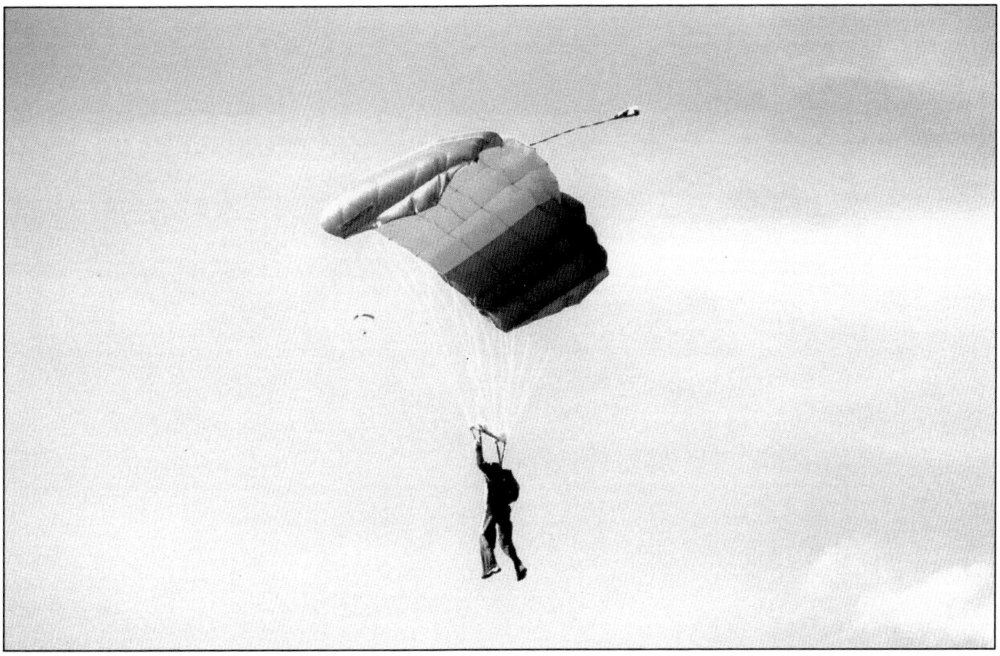

Parachutes have changed over the years to become stronger and lighter. Many people start their first jump with the tandem skydive, which has them free-falling with a United States Parachute Association certified tandem master using a harness system for two. Pictured here is a trained jumper guiding his way to a safe landing. (Courtesy Louise Rowden.)

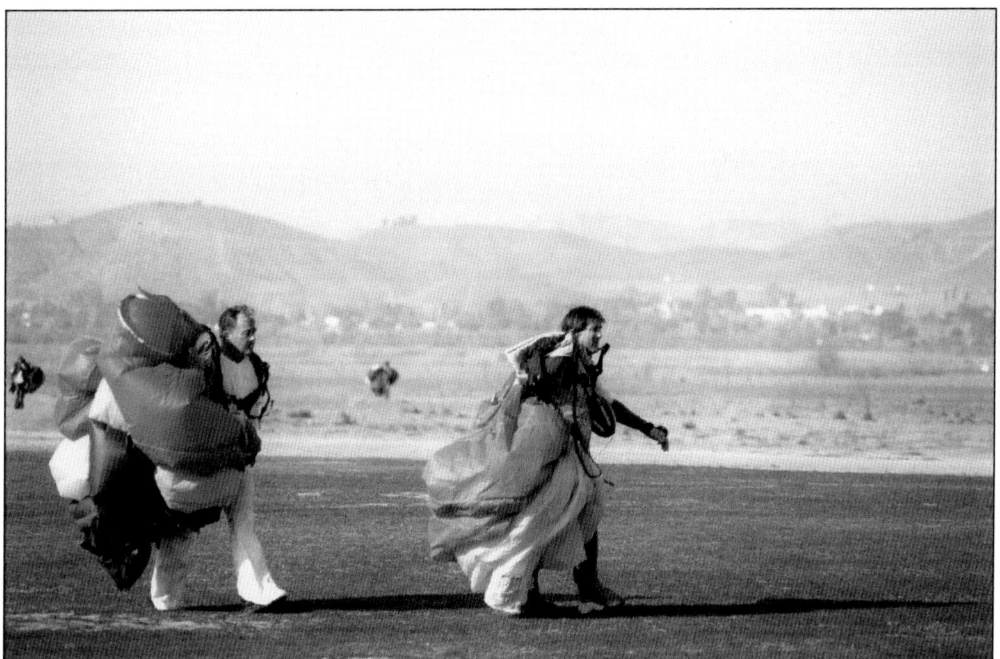

Once on the ground, as you can see, packing up the parachute for the next jump is a lesson in itself. Many jumpers keep going up time after time for the pure enjoyment of it. (Courtesy Louise Rowden.)

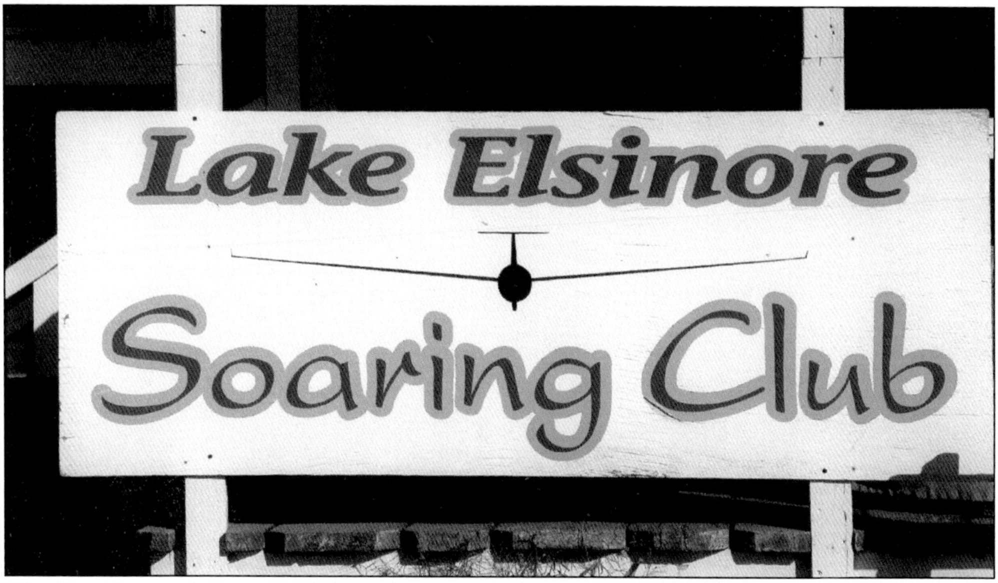


The 21st National Soaring Club of the Soaring Society of America was initiated by Lt. Gov. Harold J. Powers at the airport on Lucerne Street in Lake Elsinore on July 27, 1954, when the lake was dry. A celebration honoring this event was held at the Lake Elsinore Hotel and lasted for 10 days. The longest flight by a glider was 321 miles and went from Lake Elsinore to Mesa, Arizona. (Courtesy Edythe J. Greene.)

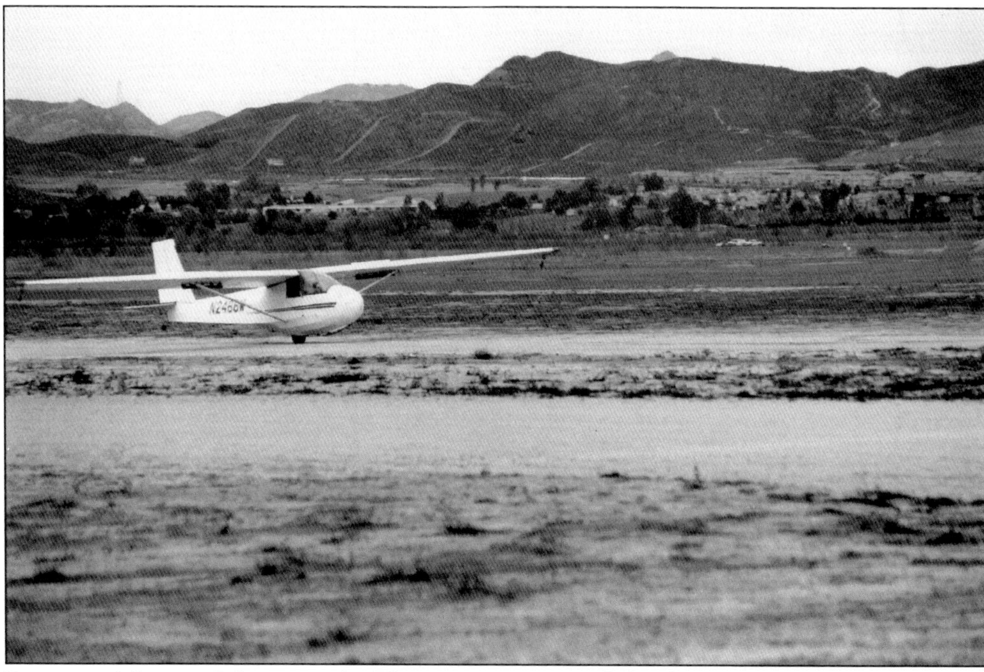

Because of the wind shears in the Elsinore area, some gliders have been known to reach an altitude of 18,000 feet. The Soaring Club of Adelanto, California, which was formed in the 1980s, moved to Skylark Field in 1989. Glider pilots from as far away as New York and Florida have come here to enjoy the famous thermals of the Lake Elsinore Valley. (Courtesy Edythe J. Greene.)

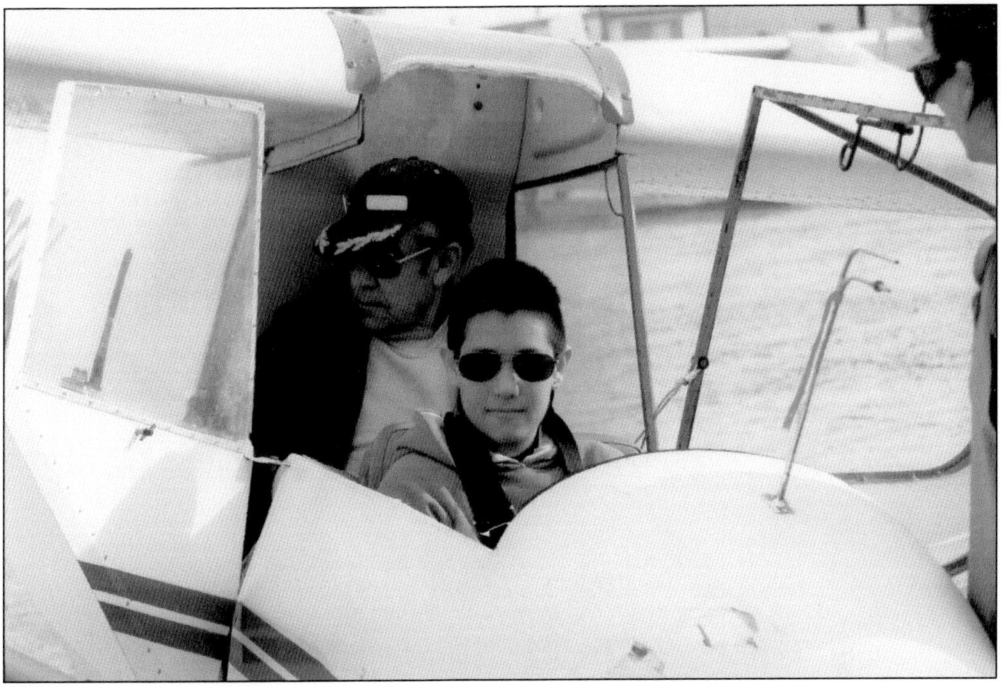

Pilots as young as 13 years of age are allowed to train at the Lake Elsinore Soaring Club. Pictured here is Jonathan Shishido on his 13th birthday. (Courtesy Edythe J. Greene.)

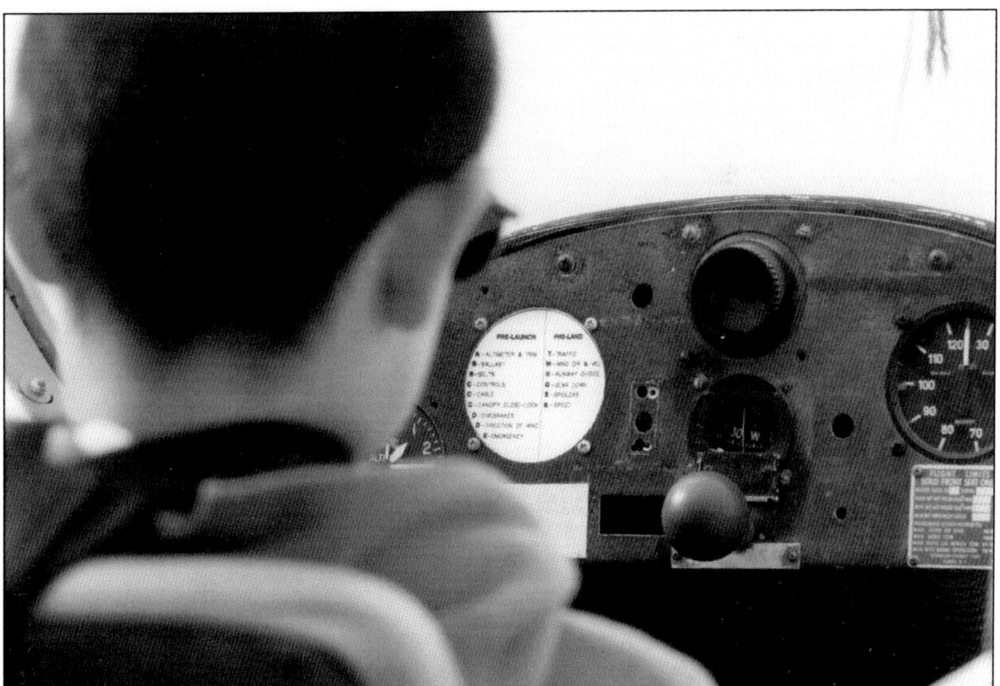

Glider pilots at all levels, students, crew, families, and non-pilots are invited to join the Soaring Club to further their interest in gliders, and for social fellowship. (Courtesy Edythe J. Greene.)

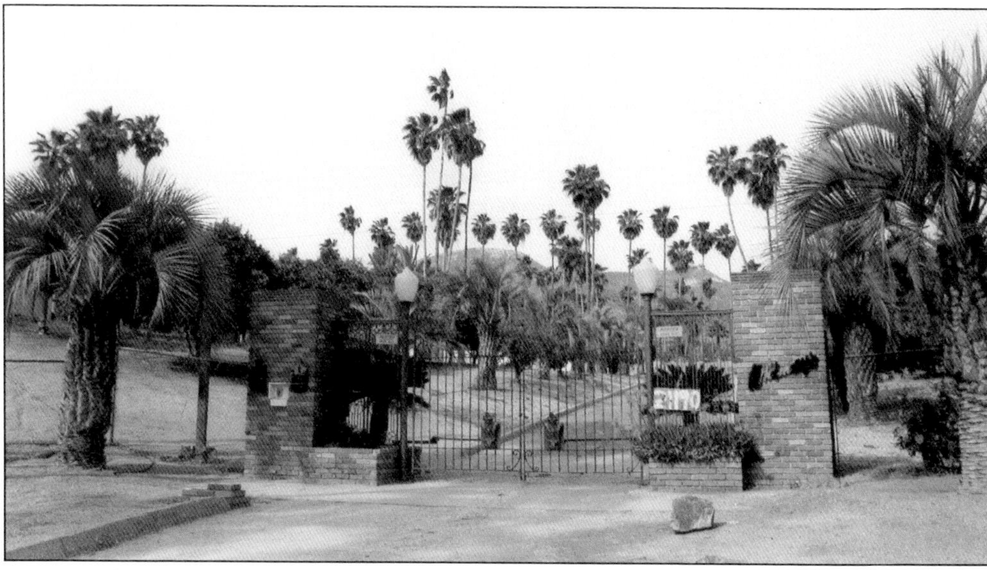

George Whitney and his wife settled in Sedco Hills before World War II. Later he had six acres of rocky canyon excavated for the purpose of creating his own lake so he could fish whenever he wanted. The two wells he had dug nearby filled the lake with water and to prevent the water from seeping out, he had clay brought in from Alberhill Clay and Coal Company. The resulting lake was 275 feet wide and 20 feet deep. In 1960, he started Whitney's Drinking Water Company, which provides the only natural, pure-drinking water bottled daily and delivered in Riverside County. (Courtesy Edythe J. Greene.)

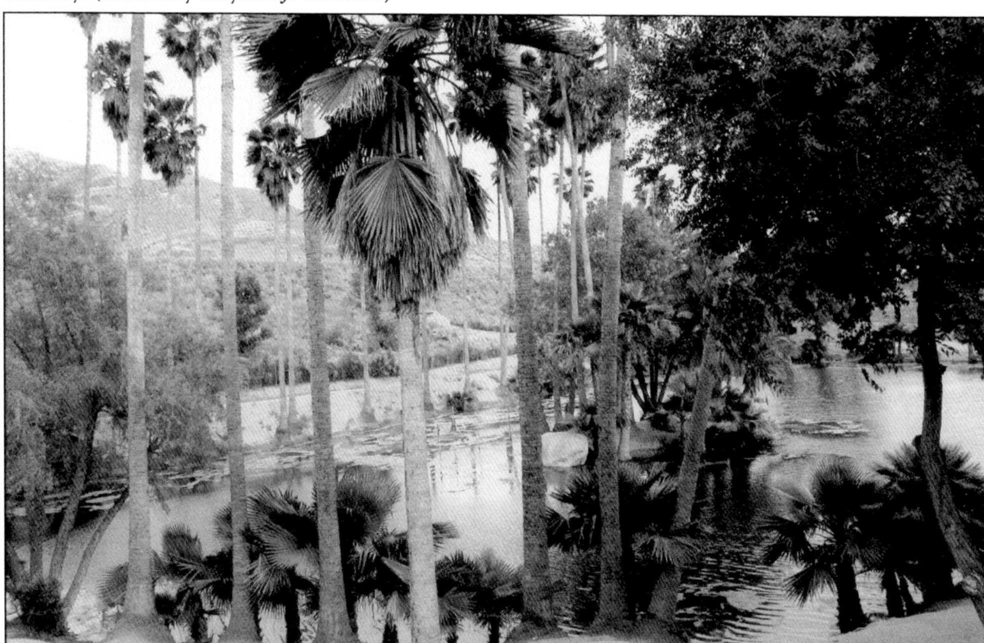

Within Whitney's Lake is a beautiful 20-square-foot island with boulders and palm trees. George and Evelyn Whitney personally planted over 600 palm trees around the lake. George brought in 172 species of birds, built aviaries, and stocked the lake. He then completed it with five picnic tables, a refrigerator, disposal unit, and even public restrooms for his guests. (Courtesy Edythe J. Greene.)

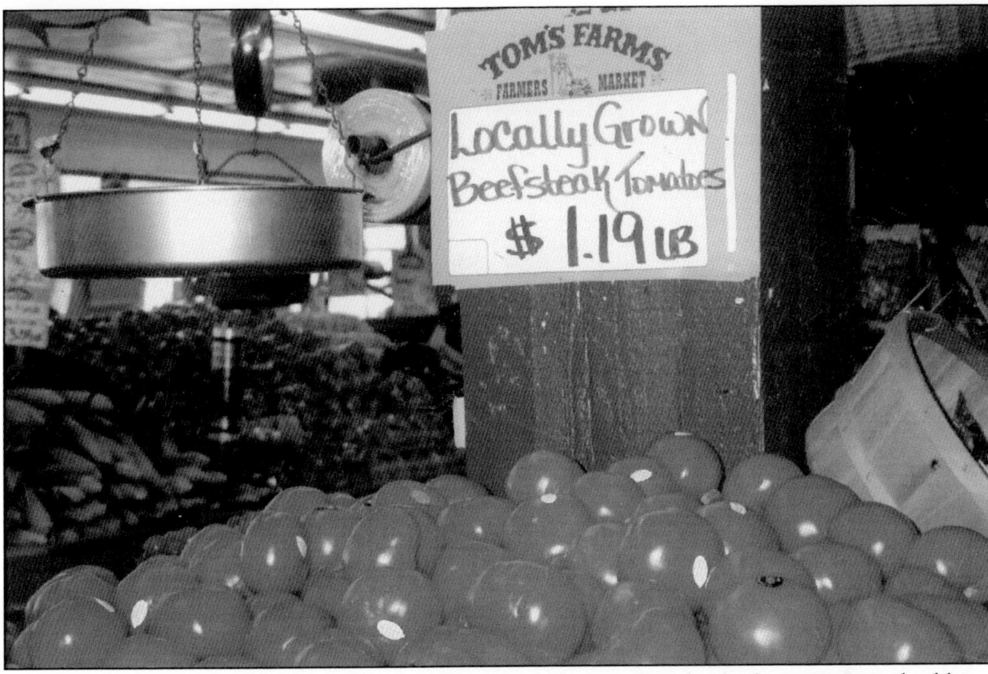


Tom Barnes bought undeveloped land on Temescal Canyon Road, which at one time had been the route of the old Butterfield Stage Line. In 1971, after clearing the land and laying down gravel, he set up two flatbed trucks and opened his first open-air produce market. Because of a lack of electricity in this rural area, he had to use an old style, non-electric cash register. His business prospered because he only offered a very high quality of produce, as he does today. (Courtesy Elizabeth Hepler.)

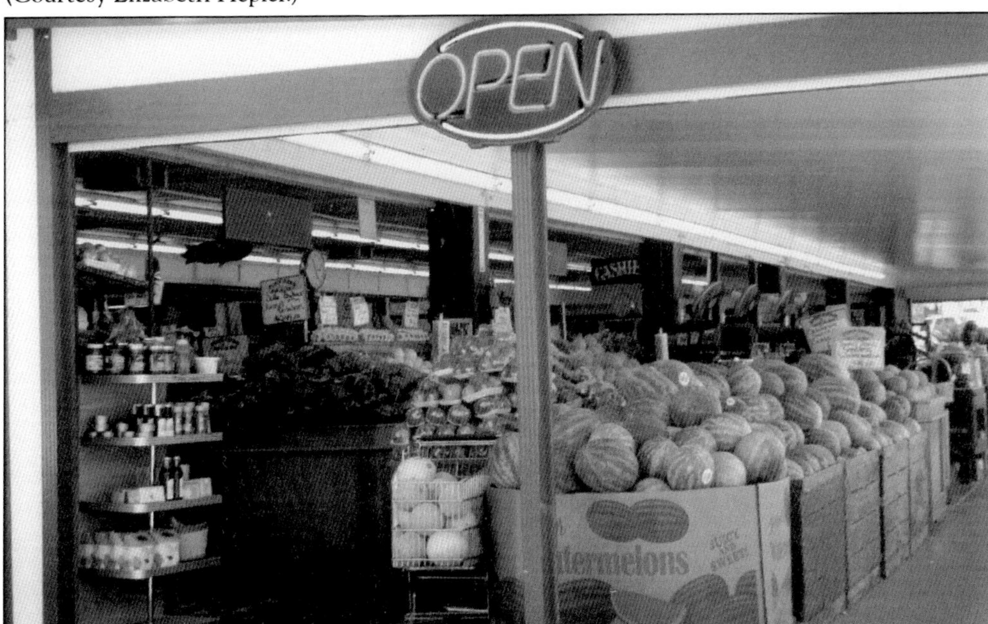


In 1973, Tom Barnes added this more permanent produce stand, which is still in use today. (Courtesy Elizabeth Hepler.)

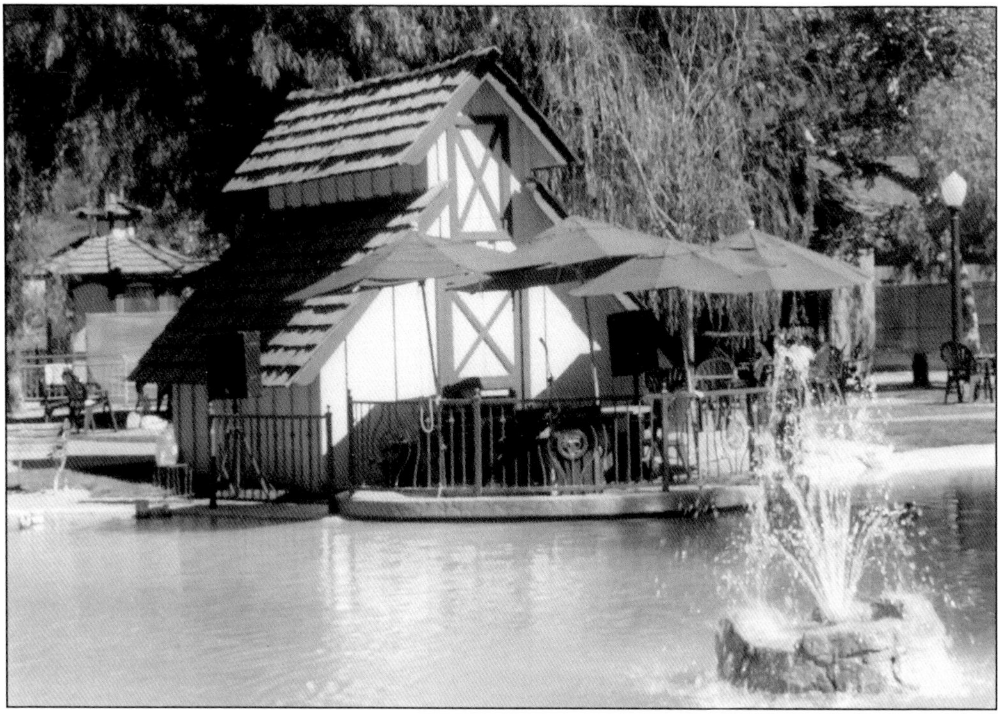

Live music is provided throughout the day at one end of the lake at Tom's Farms. Children play along the lake's shores and enjoy feeding the ducks. (Courtesy Elizabeth Hepler.)

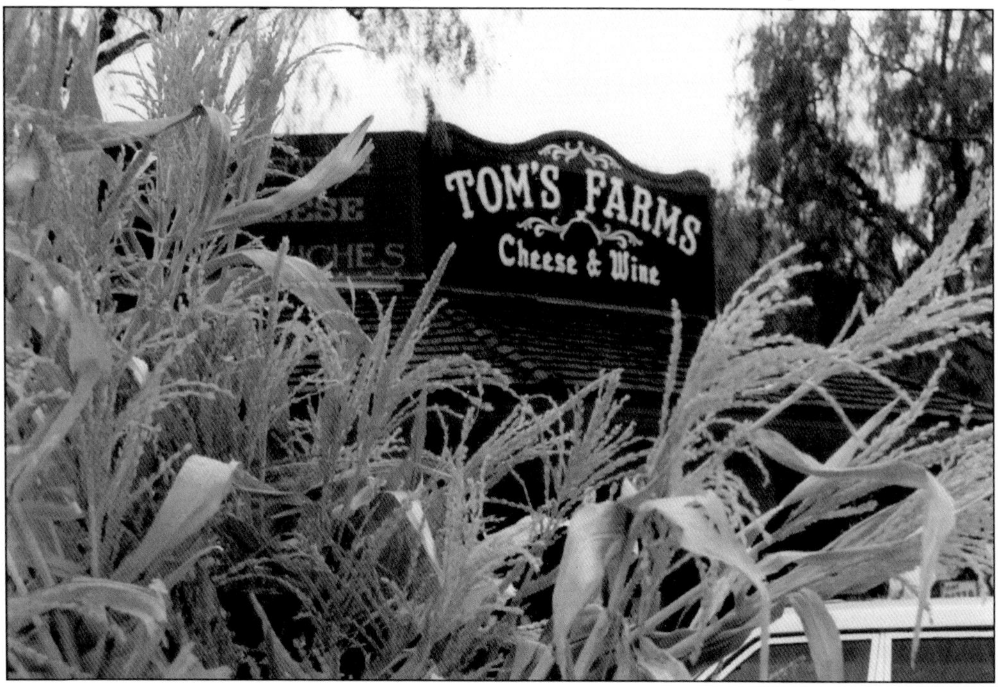


Soon after the vegetable stand was opened for business, Barnes built the Cheese and Wine Shoppe. It is a fine addition to the open-air market and people come from all over to enjoy the imported wines and cheeses. (Courtesy Edythe J. Greene.)

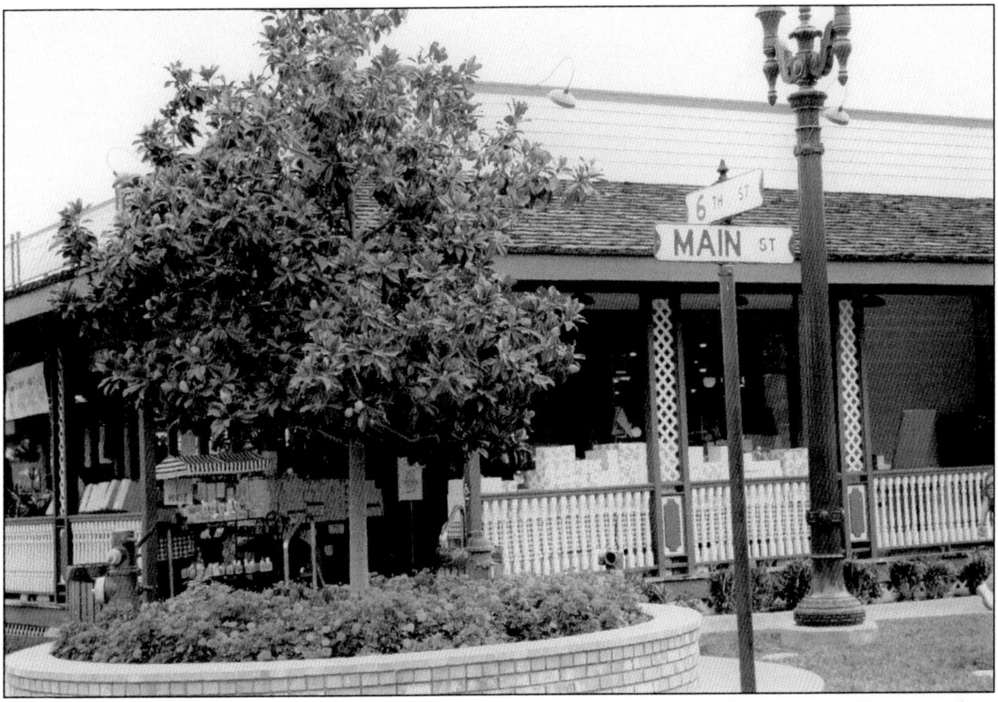


On the corner of Sixth and Main Streets in Tom's Farms is a general store specializing in fine and unique furniture. (Courtesy Edythe J. Greene.)

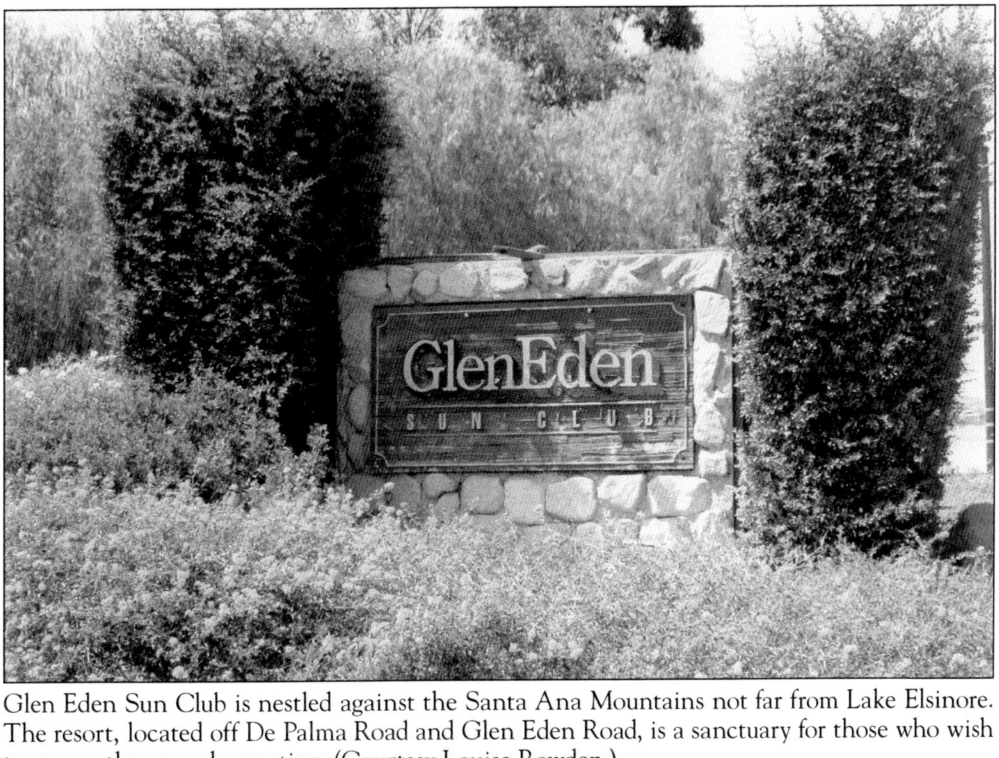


Glen Eden Sun Club is nestled against the Santa Ana Mountains not far from Lake Elsinore. The resort, located off De Palma Road and Glen Eden Road, is a sanctuary for those who wish to escape the everyday routine. (Courtesy Louise Rowden.)

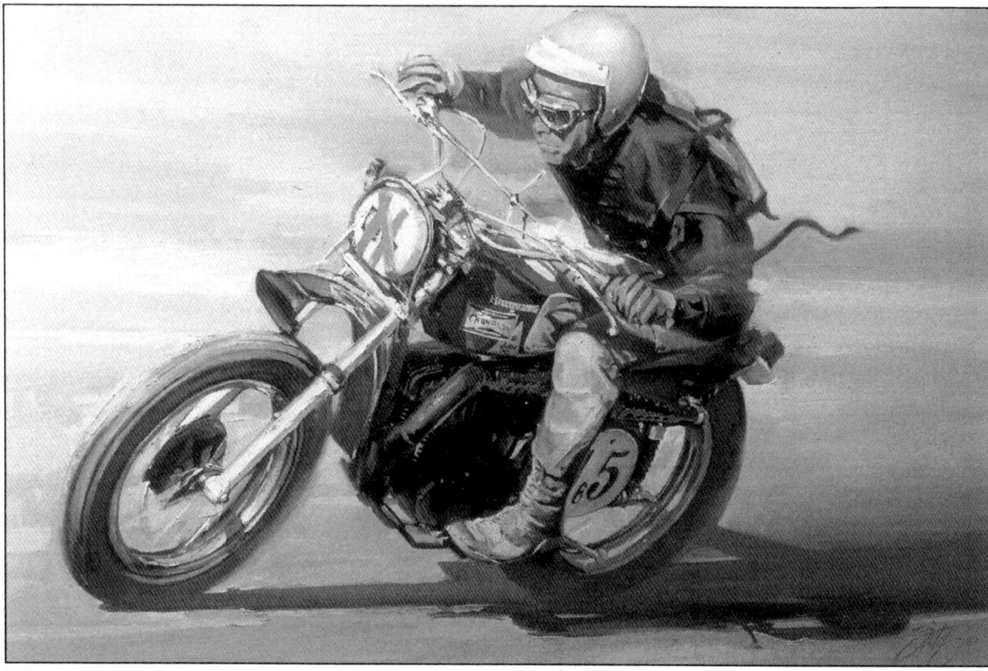

The Elsinore Grand Prix was best known for the Academy Award nominated movie, *On Any Sunday* (1971), starring motorcycle hall-of-famer Malcolm Smith and movie actor Steve McQueen. McQueen raced under the name of Harvey Mushman at the Elsinore Grand Prix. (Courtesy Troy Lee Designs.)

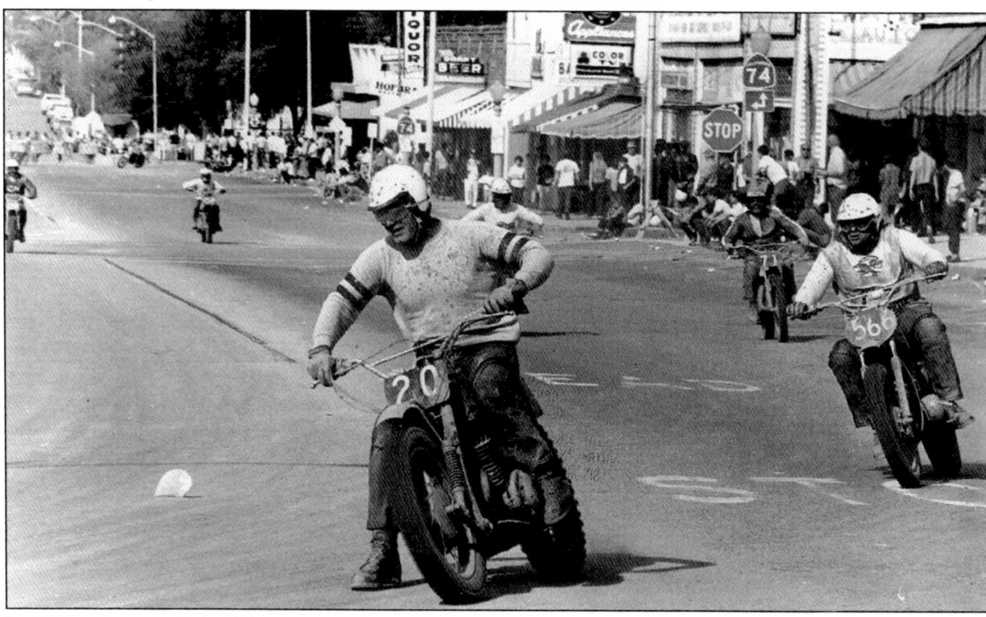


Jack Strayhom, a Lake Elsinore resident, took part in the motorcycle Grand Prix from 1969 to 1972. At 75, he was one of the oldest motorcyclists to participate in the Legends race on November 14, 2004. Although he planned for this to be his last race, he's now not so sure. Motorcycle riding is a sport for all ages with no limits. Sixty thousand spectators lined the streets to watch the two-day races. (Courtesy Dr. Timothy Kimble, D.C.)

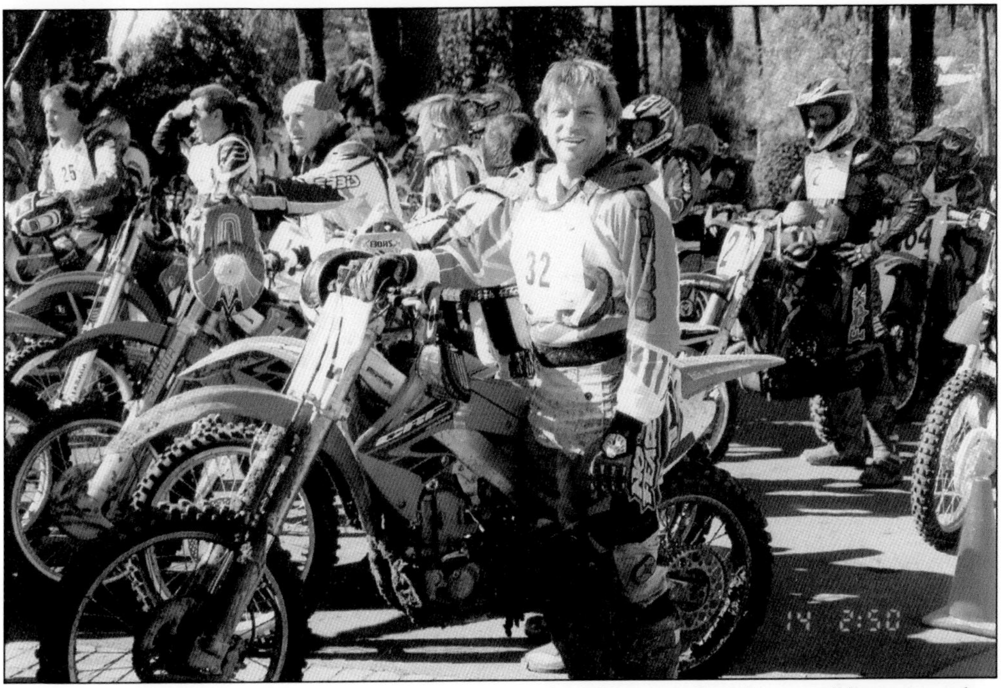

Lining up for the race to start is No. 32, Jack McNutt from Newport Beach, one of the many riders to race in the recent Elsinore Grand Prix. A commercial real estate broker by trade, McNutt has been racing for four years. (Courtesy Louise Rowden.)

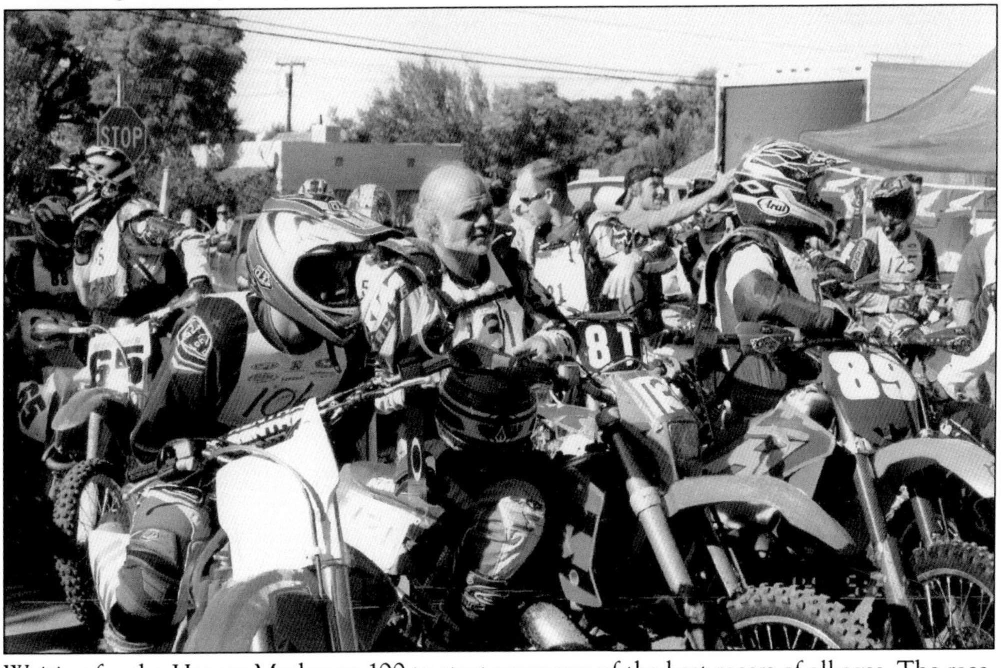


Waiting for the Harvey Mushman 100 to start are many of the best racers of all ages. The race, taking the riders through the rugged hill country, is well-known and draws participants from all over. The race is named after the assumed name that Steve McQueen used when he raced in the Elsinore Grand Prix. (Courtesy Louise Rowden.)

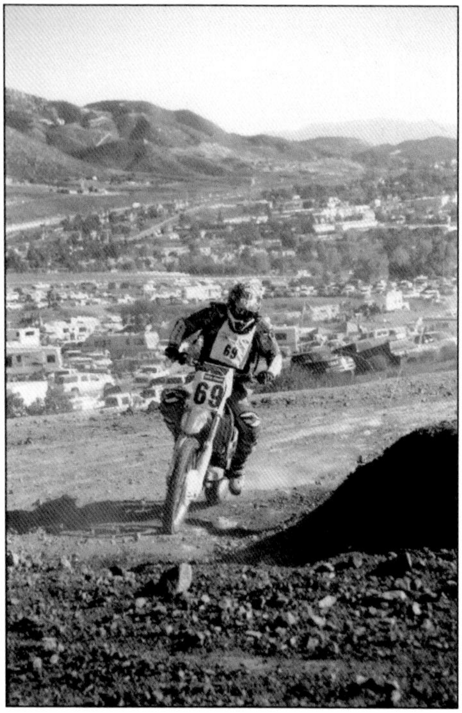


People park and camp along the hill of the long track to see the motorcycle racers up close. Some spectators are so close that the dirt flies out at them as No. 69 heads right for the turn, then up a hill. Thousands of spectators come each year to Elsinore for this exciting event. (Courtesy Edythe J. Greene.)

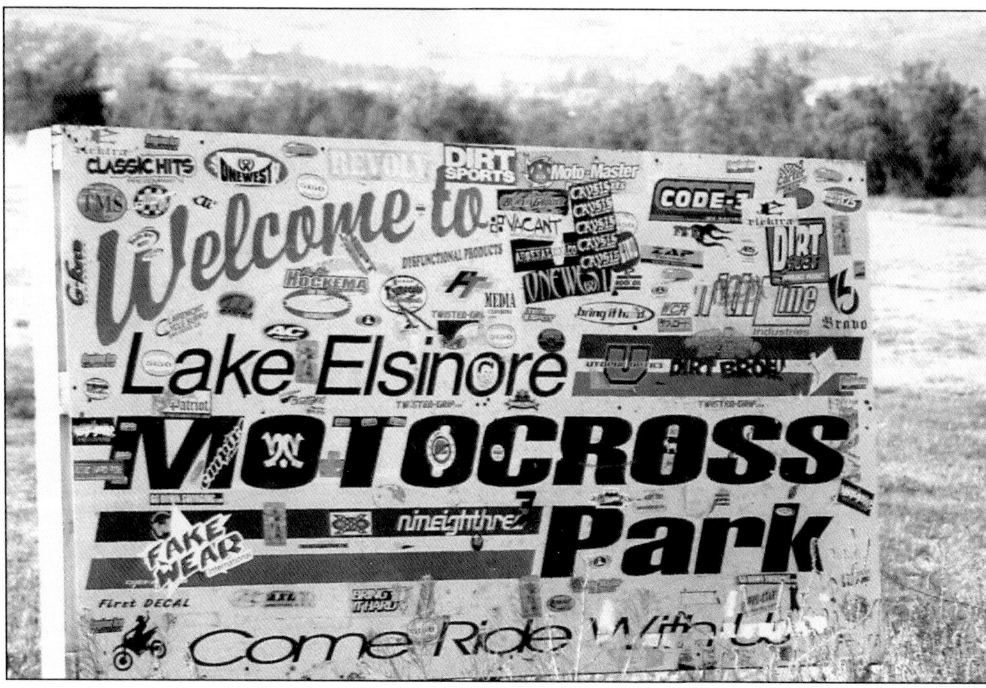


Lake Elsinore motocross competitors ride on hills carved from silt of the Lake Elsinore flood plain. The region has become a mecca for riders and the motocross industry and is known for its motorcycle culture. Twenty percent of the world's top competitive riders come from California. The Lake Elsinore Grand Prix has become one of the biggest motorcycle races in the world. (Courtesy Louise Rowden.)

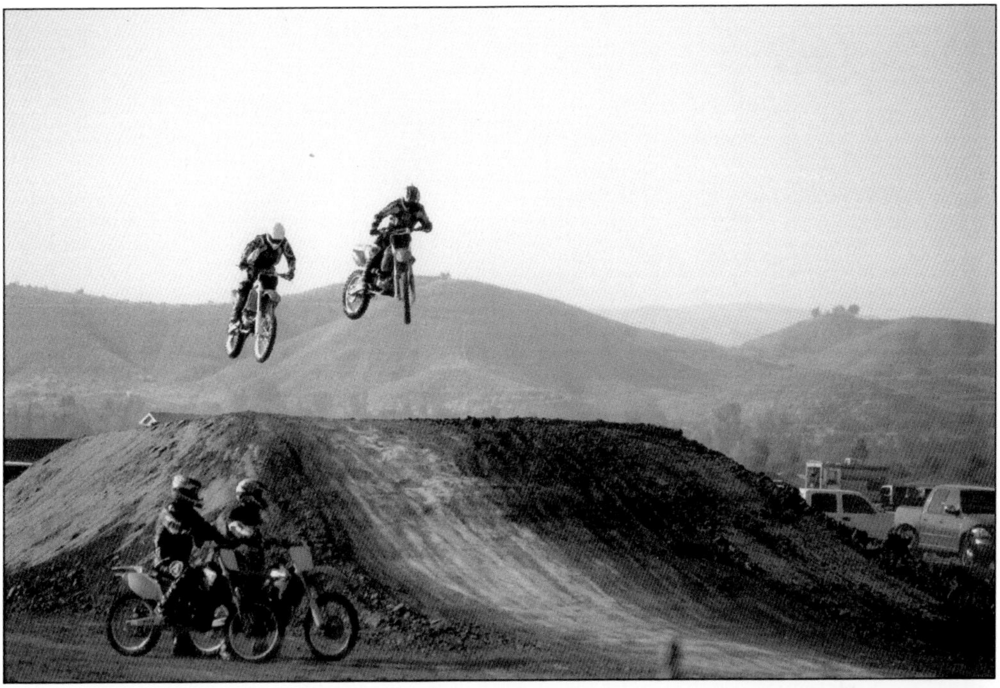

He's so high in the air, he appears to be flying. The rider has to get the bike back into position before the tires meet the ground, shifting his weight for the bike to land solidly, ready for the next turn. Devotion to the sport draws thousands of people weekly. (Courtesy Edythe J. Greene.)

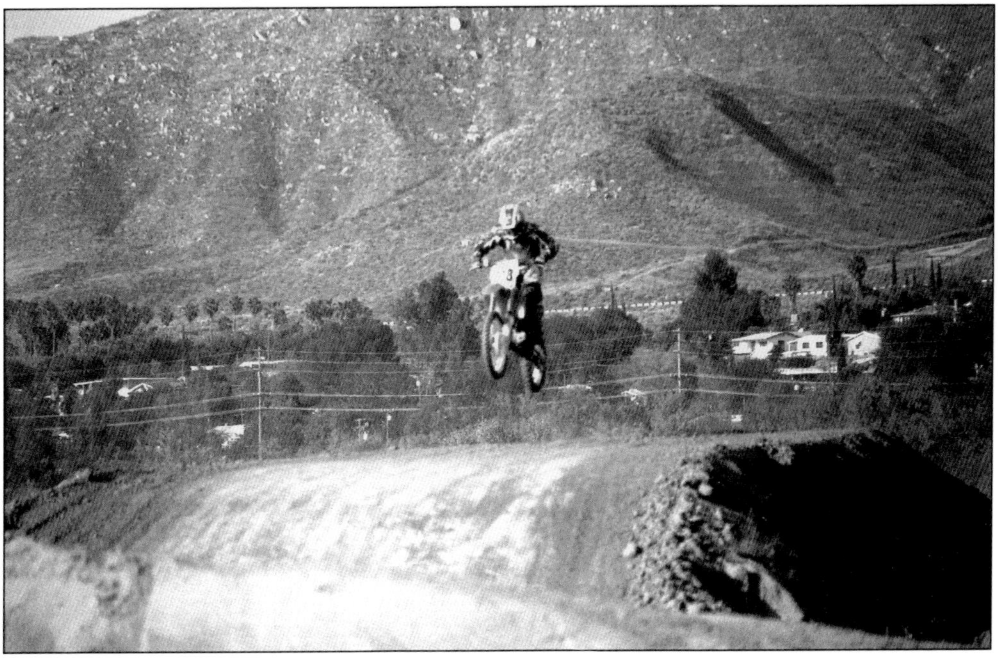

Families travel from as far away as Newport Beach to spend a day or weekend picnicking and watching their children and other family members ride high in the air and make some breathtaking sharp turns. Honda has named its line of Elsinore motorcycles after the grand prix race. Helmets, pants, and jerseys are custom-designed by Troy Lee Designs. (Courtesy Edythe J. Greene.)

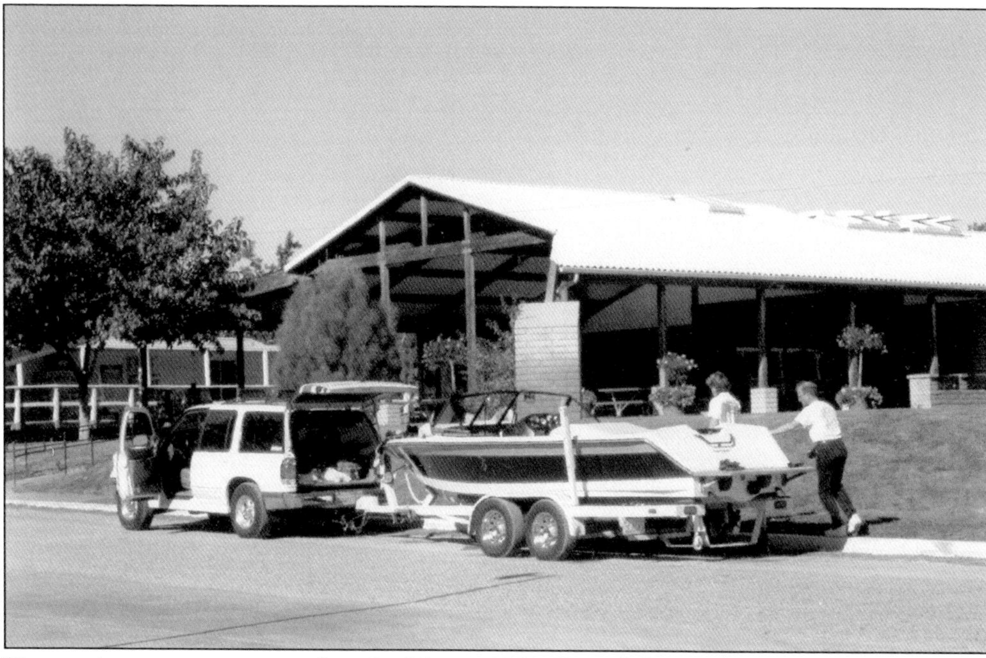

Two marinas were constructed at the lake in 1964. One of them, which has been owned and operated by the City of Lake Elsinore since 1995, is at the state park campground on Riverside Drive. The other marina, pictured here, is on 38 acres on Riverside Drive near Grand Avenue, and is privately owned. It is called the Lake Elsinore West Marina and RV Park, and is equipped with a general store and a large meeting hall for tenants and RV clubs. (Courtesy Louise Rowden.)

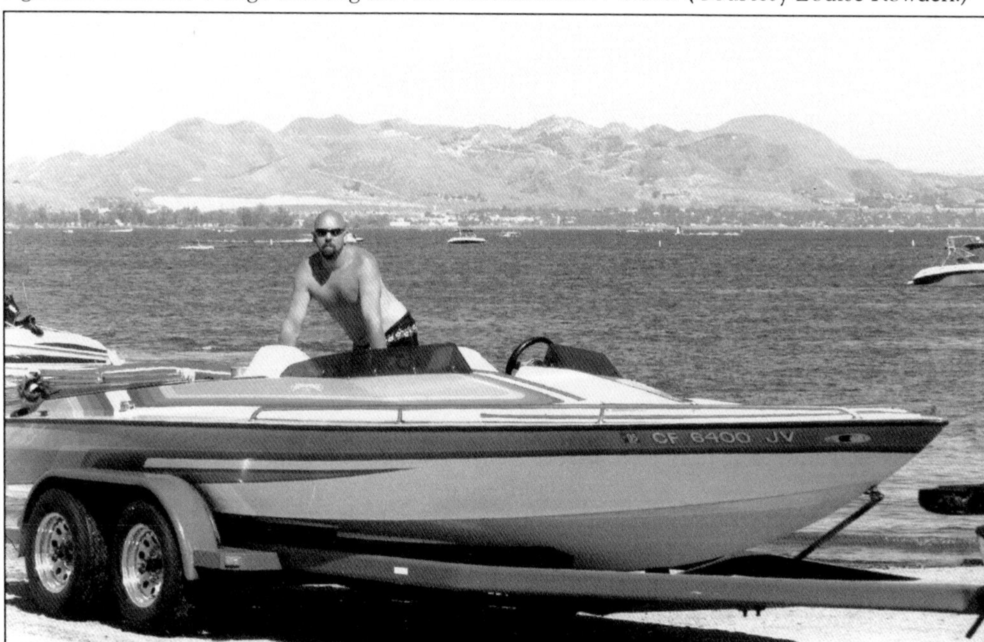


The Lake Elsinore West Marina and RV Park is a beautiful, natural marina and features a 12-lane, concrete boat ramp. It also offers full RV hookups, shaded lots, picnic areas, cable TV, and all the amenities. (Courtesy Edythe J. Greene.)

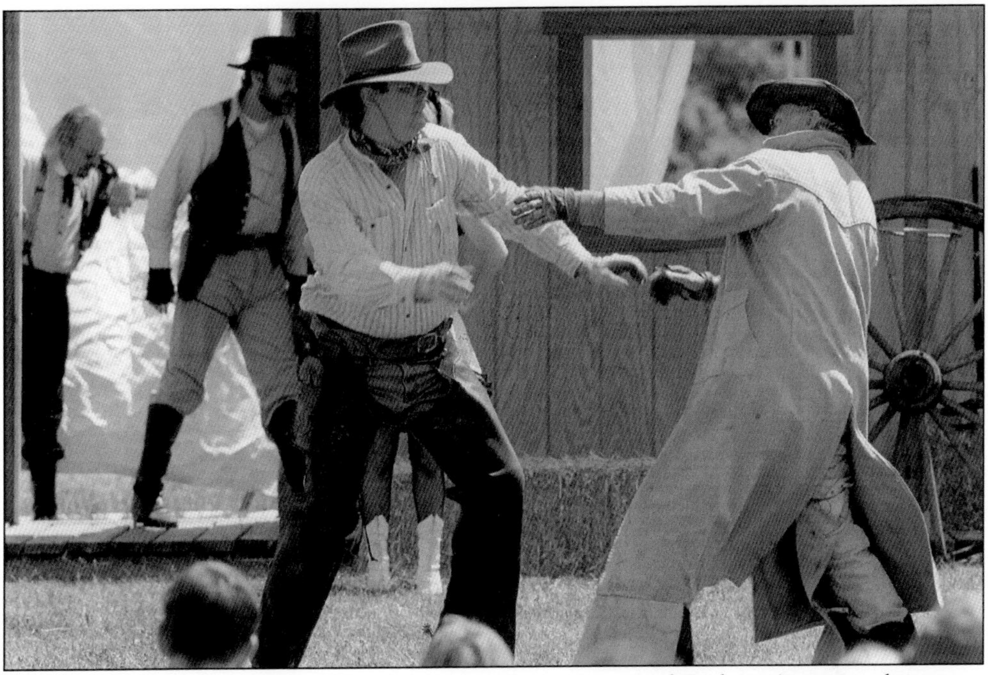

Old West gunfights are staged at the intersection of Main Street and Graham Avenue in downtown Lake Elsinore on some "Market Day" Sundays. In the center of the picture is Timothy "Dynamite" Kimble. On the right is Mike "Lobo" Loring, and on the left is "Smoky" Williamson, founder of this rugged collection of dangerous hombres. (Courtesy Dr. Timothy Kimble, D.C.)

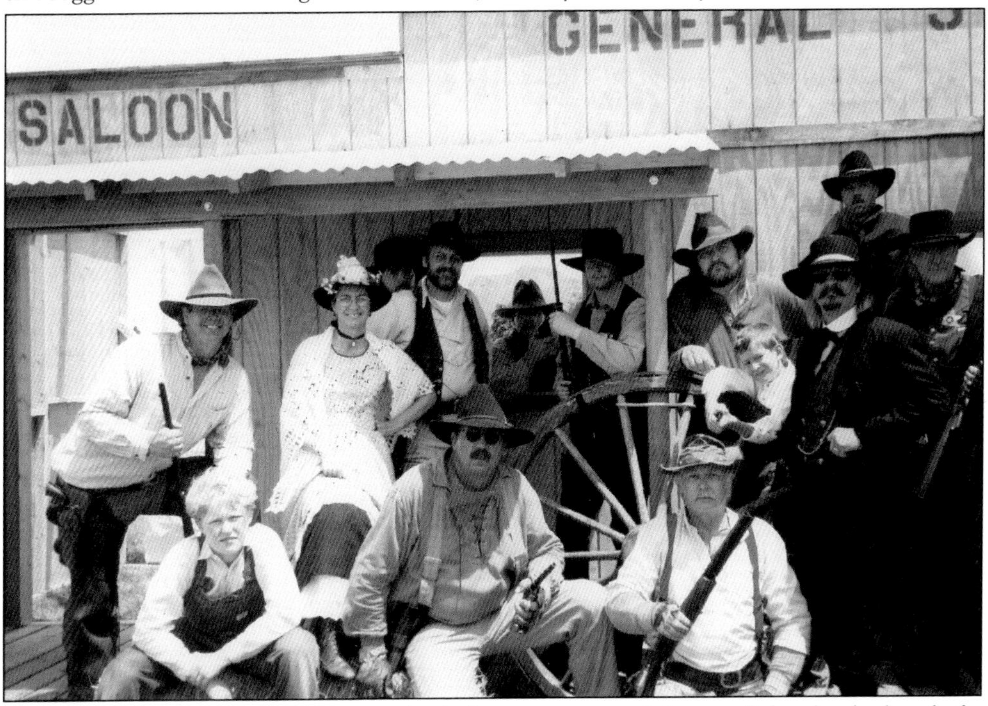


Gunfighters dressed in old Western style clothes stage entertaining gunfights for the hand of a beautiful lady in historic Old Elsinore. (Courtesy Dr. Timothy Kimble, D.C.)

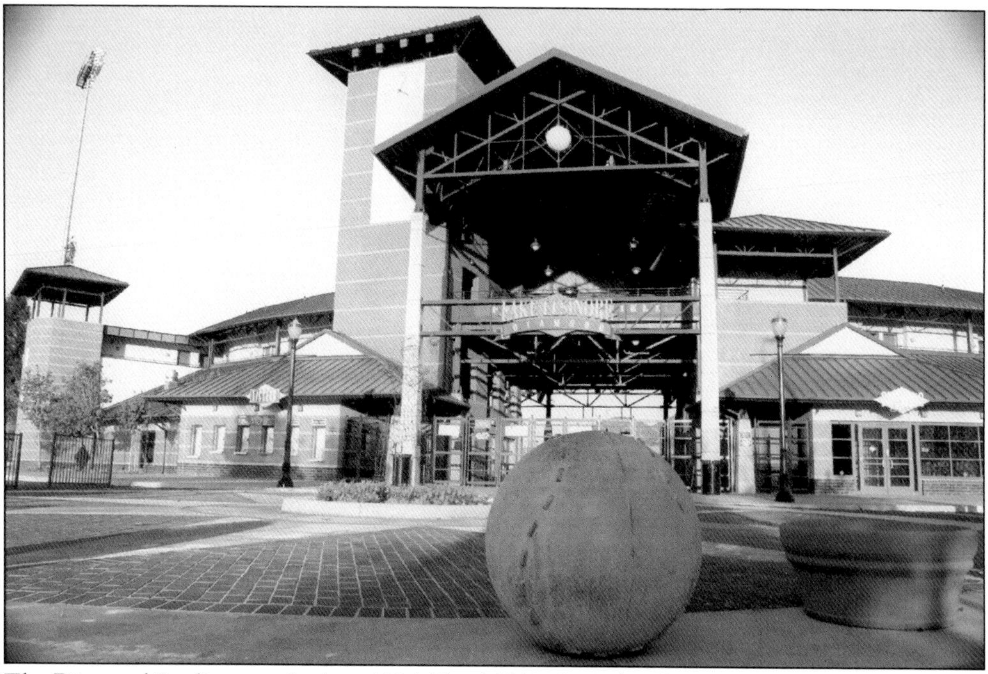

The Diamond Stadium was built in 1994. Until 2001, the Lake Elsinore Storm was an affiliate of the Anaheim Angels, and since then has been affiliated with the San Diego Padres. (Courtesy Edythe J. Greene.)

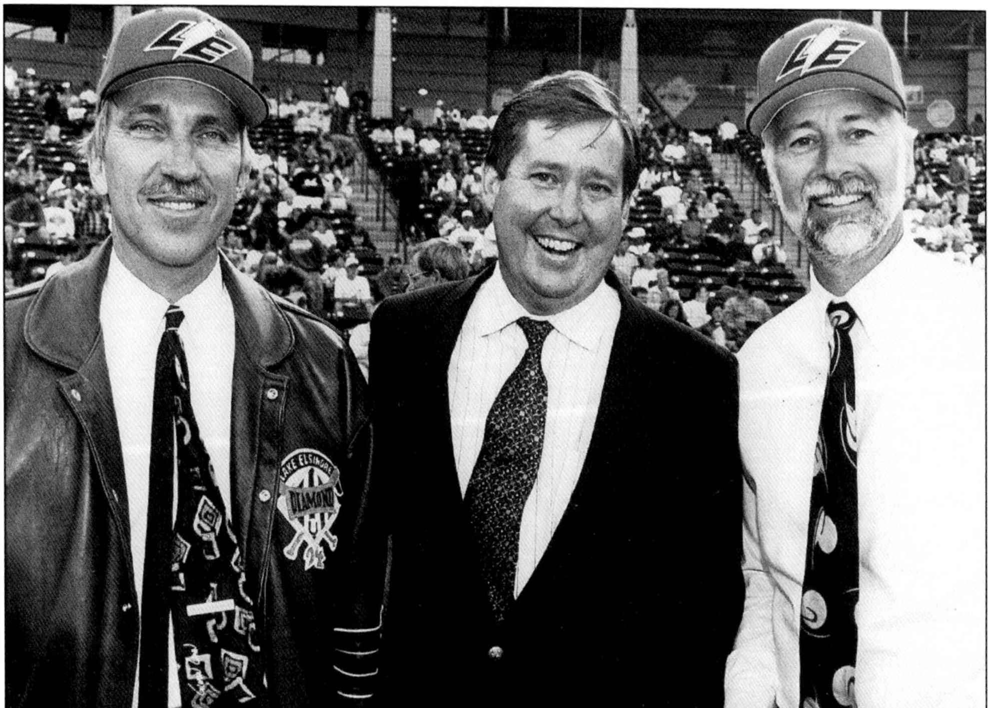

In April 1994, Jim Winkler, Congressman Ken Calvert, and Mayor Gary M. Washburn attend opening day at Diamond Stadium in April 1994. (Courtesy Gary M. Washburn.)

The Lake Elsinore Storm won the league championship in 1996 and again in 2001. Because of the events of September 11, 2001, however, they shared the title that year with San Jose. The team has taken part in the playoffs every year since 1996. The team mascot, "Thunder," provides entertainment during the game. (Courtesy Edythe J. Greene.)

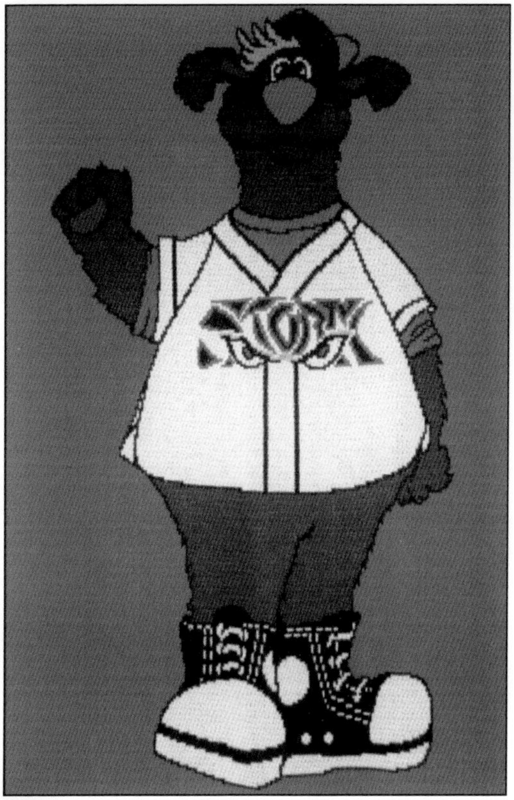

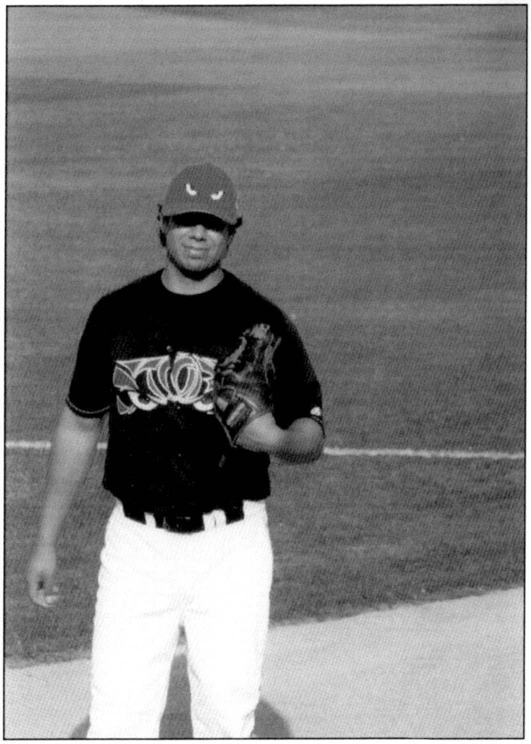

Lee Rosales, a right-handed pitcher who has attained a high degree of excellence, is used as a "closer" for the Storm. He was drafted by the Storm in 2003 from Cal State Northridge. (Courtesy Louise Rowden.)

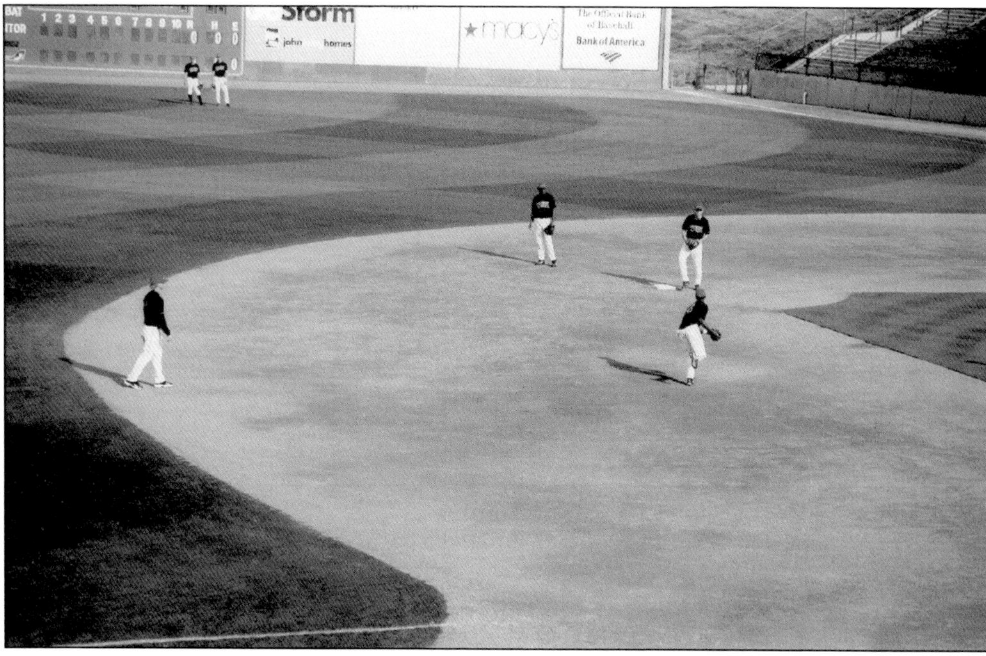


The Lake Elsinore Storm is a Minor League Class A affiliate of the San Diego Padres. The team is shown here during pre-game warm-ups. The Diamond Stadium seats 6,066 people and the average per-game attendance is 3,431. (Courtesy Edythe J. Greene.)

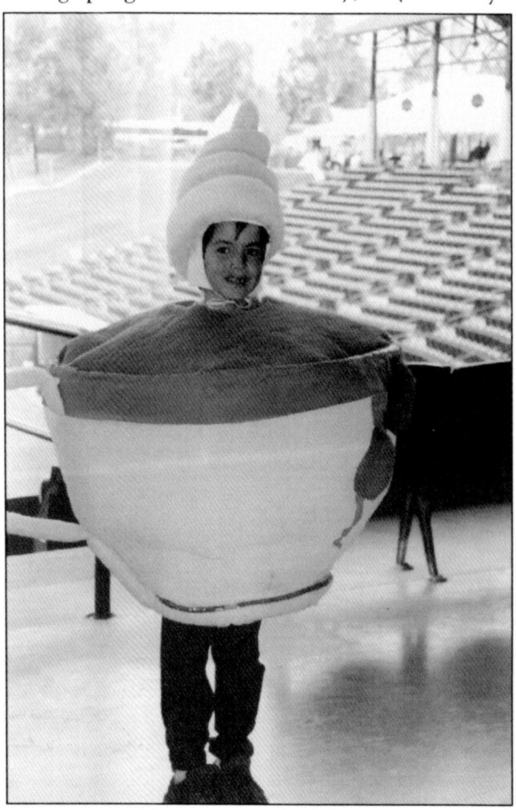

This child in costume is taking part in Disneyland's 50th birthday celebration at Diamond Stadium on Family Day, Wednesday, May 5, 2005. (Courtesy Louise Rowden.)

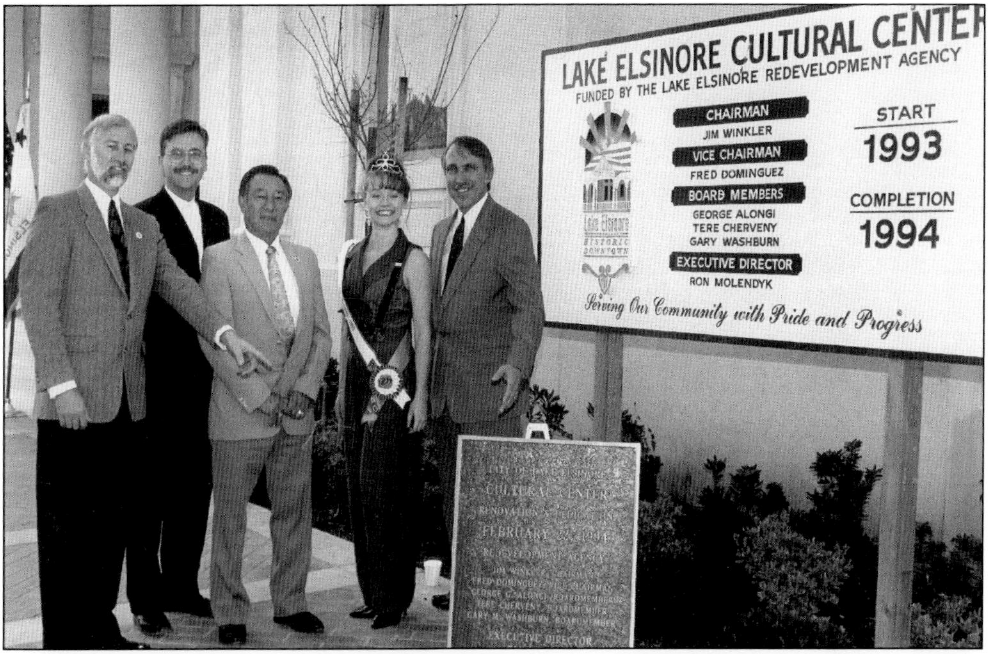


In 1994, the Lake Elsinore Cultural Center opened. Pictured here, from left to right, are Gary Washburn, Elsinore's mayor; Rick Uhls, minister; Fred Dominguez; Miss Lake Elsinore; and Jim Winkler. Washburn served as the mayor from 1990 to 1995, following in the footsteps of his grandfather, Edson Washburn, who was mayor from 1950 to 1952. (Courtesy Gary Washburn.)

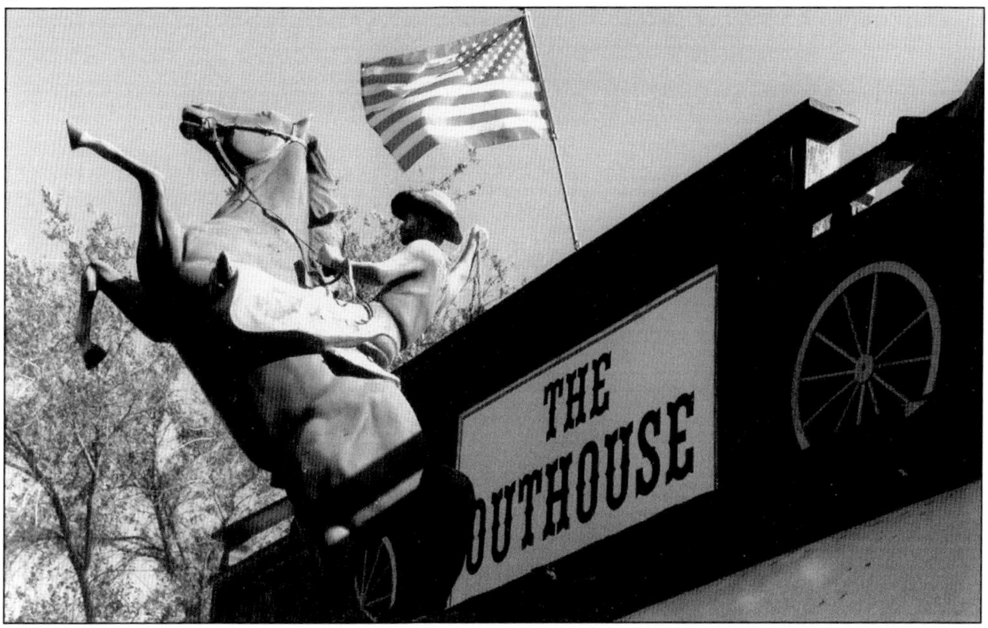


The Outhouse Saloon and Campground was opened by John Outhuijse after purchasing the property in 2001. During World War II, two aircraft hangars, housing planes used during the war, occupied this site. One hangar was later converted into a country grocery store. Since 1977, Kay Jordan has owned and run the store and the adjacent campground. She had it rebuilt in 1983 as Kay's Barn and Campground. (Courtesy Edythe J. Greene.)

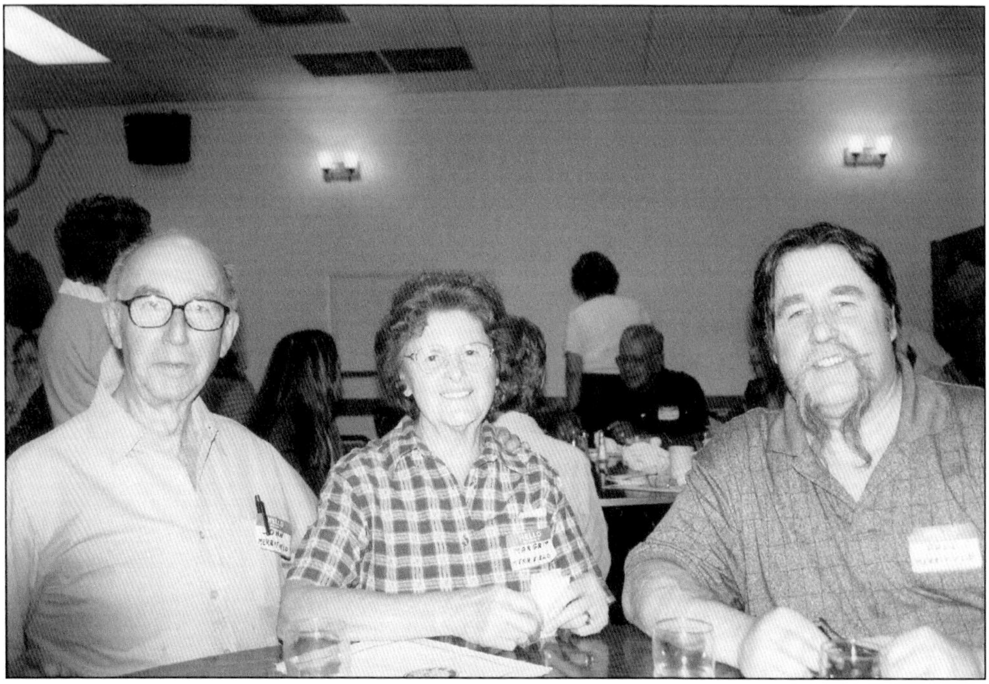

The Longtimers Club of Lake Elsinore grew out of a friendship of older residents of the city. It started in 1997 with a group of 15 friends and has now grown to 250 people. The only reason they meet three times a year in January, May, and September, is for camaraderie. The only requirement to attend is to be between the ages of one and 100-plus years. Here at the January meeting is John Merrifield and his wife, Margrit Merrifield, and their son Paul Merrifield. John is the grandson of Charles Sumner Merrifield and the owner of Brothers Towing Company of Lake Elsinore. (Courtesy Edythe J. Greene.)

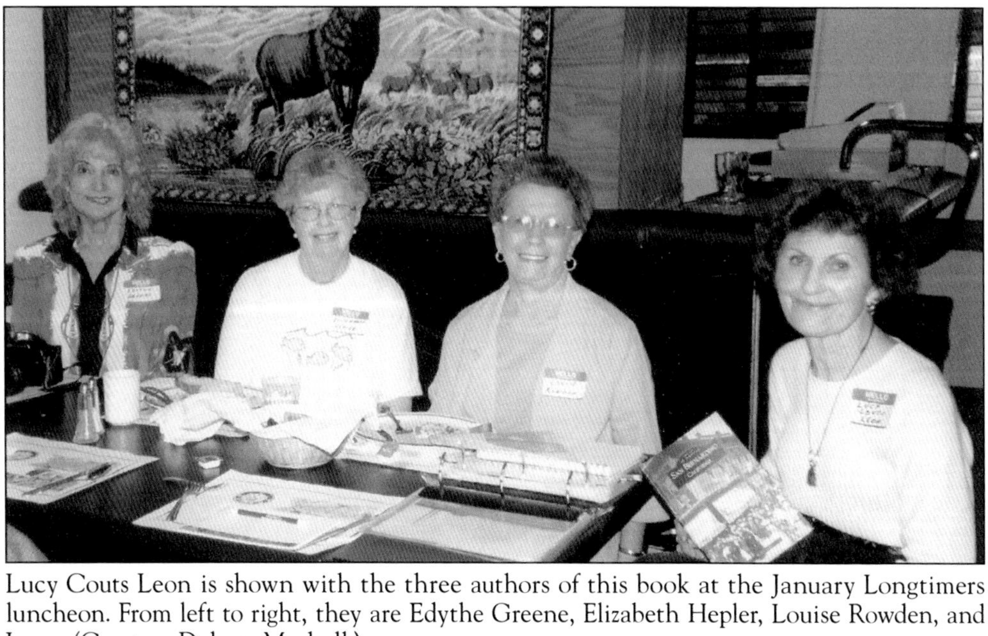

Lucy Couts Leon is shown with the three authors of this book at the January Longtimers luncheon. From left to right, they are Edythe Greene, Elizabeth Hepler, Louise Rowden, and Leon. (Courtesy Dolores Mayhall.)